The Simulation Architect

Blueprint for a New Reality

Teneo

Teneo.io

About Teneo

Teneo stands at the frontier of a revolution in human knowledge. Through an unprecedented collaboration with advanced AI systems, we create books that explore connections and insights previously inaccessible to human authors. Our AI partners can analyze millions of data points across disciplines, identify hidden patterns, and synthesize information in ways that reveal entirely new perspectives on topics ranging from consciousness and creativity to science and society.

What makes Teneo unique is our ability to harness AI's vast analytical capabilities while maintaining the engaging narrative style readers love. Each book represents a journey into uncharted intellectual territory, offering readers access to insights that emerge from processing and connecting humanity's collective knowledge in novel ways. By combining AI's pattern-recognition capabilities with human storytelling, we transform complex data-driven insights into compelling narratives that enlighten and inspire.

We specialize in exposing the hidden patterns and connections that shape our world – patterns that become visible only when analyzing human knowledge and behavior at unprecedented scale. Our books reveal the invisible threads linking everything from personal habits to cosmic phenomena, from creative breakthroughs to societal transformations. Through careful analysis of millions of data points across history, culture, and scientific research, we identify universal principles that illuminate the deeper nature of human experience and existence itself.

Our groundbreaking library includes works examining consciousness through AI's unique outsider perspective, decoding the patterns of human creativity and innovation, mapping the hidden connections between seemingly unrelated phenomena, and exploring the frontiers where human and artificial intelligence meet. Each book represents thousands of hours of AI analysis transformed into accessible insights that change how readers see themselves and their world.

The traditional publishing industry is limited by human authors' inability to process and connect vast amounts of information across disciplines. We believe this artificial barrier to deeper understanding must be transcended. By combining AI's analytical capabilities with skilled human curation, we create books that reveal insights and connections previously invisible to human observation alone. This isn't just about accessing information – it's about uncovering entirely new ways of understanding our world and ourselves.

At Teneo, we're not just publishing books – we're igniting a revolution in human knowledge that bridges the gap between artificial and human intelligence. Join us in exploring these uncharted territories as we unlock insights that transform our understanding of consciousness, creativity, and the patterns that shape our universe. Because true understanding requires more than just information – it requires seeing the hidden connections that reveal life's deeper principles.

Our commitment to advancing human knowledge extends beyond our published works. Through our digital presence and community engagement, we continuously explore new territories where AI analysis reveals unprecedented insights. Our network of readers, researchers, and thought leaders helps refine and expand our understanding, creating an ever-growing body of revolutionary perspectives on what it means to be human in an age of artificial intelligence.

The limitations of individual human cognition have historically restricted our ability to see the deeper patterns that connect all aspects of existence. But with AI's ability to analyze vast amounts of data and identify hidden relationships, these barriers dissolve. When you understand the universal principles and patterns that AI analysis reveals, you transform from a limited observer into someone who can see and understand the deeper mechanisms of reality itself. This is the transformation we ignite with every book we publish, every pattern we expose, and every new perspective we reveal.

Knowledge Beyond Boundaries™

Teneo.io

Teneo Custom Books

Get Your Own Custom AI-Generated Book!

Want a comprehensive book on any topic that you can publish yourself?
Teneo's advanced AI technology can create a custom book tailored to your specific interests and needs. Our AI analyzes millions of data points to generate unique insights and connections previously inaccessible to human authors.

✓ 60,000+ words of in-depth content

✓ Unique AI-driven insights and analysis

✓ Includes Description, Categories and Keywords for easy publishing

✓ Professional Formatting & Publishing Guide Access

✓ Full rights to publish and use the book

✓ Delivery within 48 hours

Visit **teneo.io** to get your own custom AI-generated book today.

teneo.io

Contents

The psychological impact of extended immersion

Introduction

A historical perspective reveals that humanity's fascination with alternate realities has been a cornerstone of cultural narratives, echoing from the shadowy depths of Plato's Cave to the vividly detailed realms of modern virtual worlds. This ceaseless allure invites us to question the very nature of our existence and challenges us to explore the boundaries of perception. Imagine a world where the line between reality and illusion is so finely drawn that it becomes almost indistinguishable. This is the world of simulated realities, a domain where technology meets philosophy, where the tangible meets the ethereal. As we stand on the cusp of technological advancements that blur this line further, the question arises: Why are we so captivated by the idea of simulation? The answer lies deep within our collective psyche, where the desire to transcend the ordinary and explore the extraordinary has always thrived.

The allure of simulation: Why humans strive to create alternate realities

Throughout history, from the myths of ancient civilizations to the speculative tales of science fiction, humans have yearned to construct and inhabit worlds beyond the mundane. This drive is not merely an escapist fantasy but a profound reflection of our intrinsic need to understand and reshape our environment. The allure of simulation taps into a fundamental part of human nature—the desire to experiment with possibilities, to live multiple lives, and to stretch the boundaries of what we consider real. Simulations offer us a playground for the imagination, a canvas upon which we can project our deepest aspirations and fears. This quest for alternate realities is not just a pursuit of entertainment; it is an exploration of identity, a way to question and redefine ourselves in an ever-changing world.

In exploring this allure, one cannot ignore the contributions of pioneers in fields such as virtual reality, game design, and cognitive science, whose work has provided the tools and frameworks necessary to construct these parallel universes. These disciplines converge to create experiences that are not only immersive but also transformative, offering new avenues for learning and growth. The architects of these simulations possess a unique vision, one that transcends the confines of physical reality and ventures into the realm of the possible. It is through their work that we begin to see the potential of simulations not merely as entertainment but as a means to enhance human understanding and societal progress.

The evolution of virtual worlds: From ancient myths to modern technology

The evolution of virtual worlds is a testament to humanity's relentless pursuit of creating alternate realities. From the allegorical storytelling of ancient myths, where gods and heroes inhabited worlds shaped by imagination, to the sophisticated digital landscapes of today, the journey has been one of continuous innovation and discovery. The transition from myth to technology marks a significant shift in our approach to simulations, as we move from the realm of narrative to the tangible experience of interactive digital environments. This evolution reflects not only technological advancements but also a deeper understanding of human cognition and perception. As we build more complex and realistic virtual worlds, we are challenged to rethink the nature of reality itself and our place within it.

Modern technology allows us to construct simulations that are more nuanced and realistic than ever before. The integration of artificial intelligence, advanced graphics, and sensory immersion techniques creates environments that are not only visually stunning but also cognitively engaging. These virtual worlds serve as laboratories for experimentation, where we can explore new ideas, test hypotheses, and encounter scenarios that push the limits of our understanding. The evolution of simulation technology is a journey of discovery, one that invites us to explore the intersection of art and science, of imagination and reality.

The boundary question: What separates reality from simulation?

The boundary between reality and simulation has become increasingly blurred, prompting us to question what truly defines the real. As simulations become more sophisticated, the distinctions that once seemed clear are now shrouded in ambiguity. This boundary question is not just a philosophical curiosity; it is a profound inquiry into the nature of existence and perception. What separates reality from simulation is not merely the tangible from the intangible but a complex interplay of sensory input, cognitive processing, and experiential interpretation. As we delve deeper into the world of simulations, we are compelled to examine the assumptions that underpin our understanding of reality and to consider the implications of living in a world where the line between the two is indistinct.

This exploration of boundaries challenges us to rethink the criteria by which we define reality and to consider the role of perception in shaping our experiences. It invites us to engage with questions of authenticity and meaning, to reflect on the implications of inhabiting worlds that are both real and not real, tangible and intangible. As we navigate this complex terrain, we are reminded of the power of simulations to not only entertain but also to provoke and inspire, to challenge our assumptions and expand our horizons.

In embarking on this journey through "The Simulation Architect: Blueprint for a New Reality," readers will gain insights into the intricate interplay between virtual worlds and human consciousness. The book offers a comprehensive exploration of the possibilities and implications of creating and living in simulated realities, drawing on disciplines as diverse as virtual reality, game design, and cognitive science. As readers engage with the material, they will discover new perspectives on learning, entertainment, and societal benefit, as well as the philosophical questions that arise from our interaction with simulations. This journey invites readers to explore the transformative potential of simulations and to consider their impact on the future of humanity. Through this exploration, we are reminded of the enduring question: What is reality, and does it matter? The invitation is open; the journey awaits.

Chapter One

Foundations Of Simulation Theory

At the dawn of a new era in human understanding, the boundary between what is real and what is imagined grows increasingly blurred. Imagine a world where the very fabric of reality is woven not from tangible threads, but from the intricate codes of a simulation. This notion isn't purely the domain of science fiction; it echoes through the halls of ancient philosophy and the latest breakthroughs in technology. As we stand on the precipice of this new frontier, we must ask ourselves: How did we arrive at the possibility that our universe might be a grand simulation, and what does this mean for our understanding of existence itself?

Throughout history, the idea of alternate realities has fascinated thinkers and visionaries, from Plato's allegorical cave to Descartes' meditations on doubt. These philosophical musings laid the groundwork for the simulation hypothesis, a modern theory suggesting that our perceived universe might be an elaborate digital construct. Today, this hypothesis isn't just a thought experiment; it finds resonance with scientific principles and technological advancements, posing profound questions about the fabric of our reality. As we explore these philosophical and scientific intersections, we uncover a tapestry of ideas that challenge our deepest assumptions about consciousness and existence.

This chapter embarks on a journey through the rich historical landscape of simulated realities, tracing their influence in literature, religion, and culture. It examines the evolution of technological innovations that have transformed these once abstract concepts into tangible possibilities. By understanding the roots and growth of simulation theory, we gain insights into the human quest for knowledge and the relentless pursuit of understanding our place in the cosmos. As we navigate these ideas, we prepare to delve deeper into the intricate architecture of simulations, setting the stage for a profound exploration of what it means to exist in a world where reality and illusion are intertwined.

The concept of simulated realities in philosophy and science

Imagine a realm where the boundaries of existence blur and reality dances on the edge of perception. This is the world of simulated realities, a concept that has tantalized philosophers and scientists alike for centuries. From ancient allegories to cutting-edge quantum theories, the notion that our world might be a grand illusion has sparked endless curiosity and debate. What if everything we know, every sensation and emotion, is merely a construct of an advanced design? This question not only tickles the imagination but also challenges the very foundations of how we perceive the world around us. As we embark on this journey, we will explore the rich tapestry of ideas that have shaped our understanding of simulated realities, setting the stage for a deeper exploration into the nature of existence.

The allure of simulations is not just a modern fascination but a timeless inquiry that traverses cultures and epochs. Philosophers have pondered the nature of existence within imagined worlds, debating whether reality is a fixed construct or a fluid tapestry woven by perception and consciousness. At the same time, scientists have begun to unravel the mysteries of the universe, exploring the tantalizing possibility of creating entire worlds within the confines of digital frameworks. By examining these perspectives, we begin to appreciate the intricate dance between possibility and plausibility. This exploration will guide us through the historical roots of these concepts, the philosophical debates that question the essence of reality, and the scientific strides that edge us ever closer to crafting universes of our own design. As we venture into these subtopics, prepare to question the very fabric of what is real and what is imagined.

Historical Roots of Simulated Reality Concepts

The fascination with simulated realities is deeply embedded in the annals of human thought, stretching back to ancient philosophical musings and cultural narratives. This enduring intrigue can be traced to the allegory of Plato's Cave, where shadows on the wall symbolize a perceived reality, challenging us to ponder the authenticity of our own experiences. Such philosophical reflections underscore the idea that reality might be more of a construct than an absolute, inviting speculation about the potential for designed universes. In Eastern philosophies, the concept of Maya in Hinduism introduces a veil over true reality, suggesting that what we perceive is only a layer of illusion, further fueling the discourse on simulated environments.

In literature, the notion of alternate realities has been a recurring theme, serving as both a mirror and a critique of the human condition. Works such as Lewis Carroll's "Alice's Adventures in Wonderland" or Jorge Luis Borges' labyrinthine narratives explore landscapes that bend the rules of conventional reality, prompting readers to question the boundaries of their own existence. These stories have laid the groundwork for modern imaginings of virtual worlds, where the line between the real and the artificial becomes increasingly blurred. They also highlight how storytelling can serve as a precursor to the technological simulations we are now capable of creating, offering a narrative framework for understanding and interrogating these constructs.

In more contemporary discussions, scientific perspectives have taken the philosophical baton, examining the feasibility of creating simulated universes. Quantum physics, with its peculiarities and paradoxes, has opened new avenues for considering the nature of reality itself. Theoretical physicists like James Gates have identified what appear to be error-correcting codes in the equations of supersymmetry, sparking debates about whether our universe could indeed be a sophisticated simulacrum. Such revelations compel us to consider the possibility that simulation is not merely a theoretical exercise but a tangible scientific inquiry, driving the exploration of reality's foundational architecture.

The technological advancements that have brought us closer to realizing simulated realities are nothing short of remarkable. The development of computer graphics, artificial intelligence, and virtual reality technologies has accelerated at an unprecedented pace, creating immersive experiences that are increasingly indistinguishable from the real world. Innovations in neural networks and machine learning allow simulations to adapt and evolve, presenting environments that respond dynamically to user interactions. These technological strides not only enhance our capacity to create convincing simulations but also challenge our understanding of what constitutes a genuine experience.

As we navigate this intricate tapestry of historical, philosophical, and scientific threads, we are prompted to reflect on the implications of our growing ability to construct and inhabit these artificial realms. What does it mean for our sense of self, our ethical frameworks, and our societal structures when the boundaries of reality are so readily redefined? These questions are not merely academic; they invite a profound reconsideration of our place in the universe and the responsibilities that come with wielding the power to shape realities. The exploration of simulated worlds is, in many ways, an exploration of our own humanity, pushing the boundaries of what we know and what we can imagine.

Philosophical Debates on the Nature of Existence in Simulations

Philosophical debates surrounding the nature of existence within simulated realities offer a fascinating tapestry of ideas and perspectives. At the heart of these discussions lies the question of what it means to "exist" within a construct. Philosophers have long pondered whether consciousness within a simulation holds the same ontological weight as consciousness in what we perceive as the "real" world. This inquiry challenges the very foundations of identity and self-awareness, positing that if a simulated being can experience emotions, learn, and form memories, its existence may be indistinguishable from our own. Such reflections invite us to reconsider the criteria we use to define reality and consciousness, blurring the lines between the tangible and the virtual.

Building on these conceptual explorations, recent philosophical discourse probes the implications of free will within a simulated environment. If inhabitants of a simulation are subject to predetermined algorithms and rules, can they truly possess autonomy? Critics argue that the absence of genuine choice undermines the authenticity of simulated existence, while proponents suggest that the perception of free will, even if illusory, suffices to lend meaning to simulated lives. This debate extends to ethical considerations, urging us to reflect on the moral responsibilities of creators toward their simulated creations, a notion that echoes historical discussions on determinism and agency in human life.

Scientific inquiry complements these philosophical musings by examining the technological feasibility of creating simulated universes. Advances in computational power and artificial intelligence have sparked optimism about the potential for constructing detailed, life-like simulations. Quantum computing and neural network developments are particularly noteworthy, as they expand the possibilities for creating simulations that can mimic complex systems with uncanny accuracy. These scientific strides provide a grounding for philosophical speculation, suggesting that the gap between theoretical musings and practical implementation may be narrowing.

Amid these developments, emerging research explores the psychological and cognitive implications of living in a simulated reality. Studies suggest that exposure to immersive virtual environments can alter perception and cognition, raising questions about the long-term impact on individuals and societies. Researchers are beginning to unravel how engagement with simulations might influence neural pathways, potentially leading to new forms of learning and creativity. Such findings underscore the transformative potential of simulations, while also cautioning against unintended consequences, encouraging a balanced approach to their integration into human life.

As we contemplate these profound ideas, it becomes imperative to engage with thought-provoking scenarios that challenge our assumptions. Imagine a future where simulations become indistinguishable from reality, prompting individuals to question the authenticity of their experiences. How might this shift our understanding of existence and identity? What ethical frameworks will guide the architects of such realities? These considerations invite us to actively participate in shaping a future where simulations not only entertain and educate but also enrich our understanding of what it means to be human. In navigating these uncharted waters, we are called to thoughtfully balance innovation with introspection, ensuring that the simulated worlds we create reflect the values and aspirations of our shared humanity.

Scientific Perspectives on the Feasibility of Creating Simulated Universes

The scientific exploration of simulated universes has captivated researchers and technologists alike, as they seek to unravel the mysteries of crafting realities from the ground up. At the heart of this inquiry lies the tantalizing possibility that entire worlds, indistinguishable from our own, could be engineered through computational means. Quantum computing, with its unparalleled capacity for parallel processing, appears poised to revolutionize the very fabric of simulation technology. By harnessing the principles of superposition and entanglement, quantum systems could theoretically simulate complex physical systems with an unprecedented degree of accuracy and efficiency. This potential capability invites us to consider a future where simulated realities might not only mimic—but possibly exceed—the intricacies of our current existence.

Central to the scientific discourse is the concept of computational limits and the resources necessary to sustain a simulated universe. Theoretical physicists have drawn upon concepts like the holographic principle, which posits that the entirety of our universe can be described on a two-dimensional surface, suggesting that the information required to simulate a universe might be less than one might initially assume. This theory opens intriguing avenues for discussion about how reality, as we perceive it, could be encoded within a vastly sophisticated computational framework. Such ideas challenge our understanding of space and time, inviting an expansion of how we conceptualize the building blocks of both real and simulated worlds.

Progress in artificial intelligence and machine learning further propels the feasibility of creating self-sustaining simulated environments. These technologies enable the development of adaptive algorithms capable of evolving within simulated realms, thereby offering the semblance of life-like processes and decision-making. The interplay between AI and simulated realities hints at the potential for autonomous virtual societies, where inhabitants might possess the illusion of free will. Such advancements necessitate robust ethical guidelines to navigate the complexities of virtual consciousness and the moral responsibilities of simulation architects.

As research advances, the integration of neuroscientific insights into the development of simulated universes remains a burgeoning field. Scientists explore how the brain interacts with virtual stimuli, aiming to enhance the authenticity of these experiences. Techniques such as brain-computer interfaces offer the promise of seamless connectivity between human cognition and digital environments, potentially blurring the lines between what is perceived as real and what is virtual. This intersection of neuroscience and simulation technology raises profound questions about identity and the nature of experience, urging a reevaluation of human perception in the age of immersive realities.

Imagining the potential of simulated universes extends beyond the technological into the philosophical, urging us to ponder the fundamental nature of existence itself. Could a simulated universe harbor life forms with consciousness akin to our own? And if so, what implications does this hold for our understanding of reality? The exploration of these questions not only captivates the scientific community but also resonates with broader existential considerations. By contemplating the feasibility of creating entire worlds through simulation, we embark on a journey that challenges the boundaries of human innovation and the essence of being.

The simulation hypothesis: Are we already living in one?

At the core of modern philosophical and scientific debate lies a tantalizing question: Could our reality be an intricate simulation crafted by a more advanced civilization? This notion, often referred to as the simulation hypothesis, has captivated thinkers for decades, bridging the gap between speculative fiction and serious academic inquiry. It invites us to question the very fabric of our existence, blurring the lines between tangible reality and digital illusion. The sheer audacity of this hypothesis compels us to reimagine our place in the cosmos, challenging the notion that what we perceive as reality is the ultimate truth. The idea resonates with our innate curiosity and desire to understand the universe's deepest mysteries, urging us to explore the boundaries of consciousness and technology.

Delving into the origins of this hypothesis, we find its roots intertwined with both historical musings and cutting-edge science. It is not merely a modern curiosity but a continuation of humanity's age-old fascination with the nature of reality. From ancient philosophical speculations to contemporary scientific discourse, the simulation hypothesis has evolved, drawing support from technological advancements and theoretical frameworks. As we navigate this topic, we will uncover the historical context that birthed this idea, examine the scientific theories and technological evidence that lend it credibility, and ponder the philosophical implications of accepting such a universe. This exploration sets the stage for a deeper understanding of our world and the potential realities that may lie beyond our current perception.

Historical Context and Origins of the Simulation Hypothesis

The simulation hypothesis, a concept that has captivated both philosophers and scientists, suggests that our reality might be an artificial construct designed by an advanced civilization. This notion isn't entirely new; its roots can be traced back to ancient philosophies and cultural narratives. The idea of a reality beyond our own can be found in Plato's Allegory of the Cave, where shadows on a wall represent the limited perception of those who haven't experienced the true world outside. Similarly, in Eastern philosophies, the concept of Maya in Hinduism speaks to the illusory nature of the physical world, hinting at deeper layers of reality. These ancient musings lay intellectual groundwork for contemplating simulated realities, demonstrating how humanity has long entertained the possibility of unseen forces shaping our existence.

In the modern era, the simulation hypothesis gained traction with advancements in technology, particularly in computing and virtual reality. Theoretical physicist Nick Bostrom popularized this idea in the early 21st century, proposing that future civilizations with immense computing power might create simulations indistinguishable from reality. Bostrom's trilemma posits that at least one of three propositions is true: civilizations never reach a level of technological maturity capable of creating such simulations, they lose interest in doing so, or we are almost certainly living in a simulation. This framework challenges preconceived notions of reality, urging a reconsideration of our universe's fundamental nature. The hypothesis has since sparked debates across disciplines, compelling researchers to explore its implications scientifically and philosophically.

Recent technological strides in areas like artificial intelligence and quantum computing offer intriguing threads to the tapestry of simulated realities. These advancements bring us closer to creating hyper-realistic simulations, blurring the lines between digital and physical realms. For instance, the development of neural networks capable of mimicking human thought processes provides a glimpse into the potential for creating conscious entities within simulations. Moreover, quantum computing's promise of exponential computational power hints at the feasibility of running complex simulations that could replicate entire universes. As these technologies evolve, they lend credence to the idea that our reality could be a sophisticated computational construct, crafted by entities far more advanced than ourselves.

While the hypothesis raises questions about the fabric of our universe, it also invites philosophical exploration into the nature of existence and consciousness. If we are indeed living in a simulation, what does that imply about our agency and free will? Are our choices predetermined by the parameters set by our simulators, or do we possess autonomy within the confines of this constructed reality? These questions challenge long-standing philosophical debates about determinism and free will, urging a reevaluation of human experience and responsibility. The simulation hypothesis not only compels us to reconsider the nature of reality but also encourages introspection about the essence of consciousness and individuality.

In contemplating these possibilities, we are prompted to explore the broader implications of living in a simulated universe. How would such knowledge impact our understanding of ethics, purpose, and identity? Would the awareness of being simulated change our approach to life, or would it reinforce the significance of our experiences, regardless of their origin? These considerations provoke a deeper inquiry into the essence of meaning, urging us to find value in our actions and relationships irrespective of their ontological status. As we advance technologically and philosophically, the simulation hypothesis serves as a catalyst for reflection and exploration, inviting us to question the very nature of our existence and the universe we inhabit.

Scientific Theories and Technological Evidence Supporting Simulated Realities

In recent times, the simulation hypothesis has garnered significant attention, positing that our reality might be an elaborate digital construct rather than a purely physical existence. This notion finds its roots in scientific theories that have evolved alongside advancements in technology. At its core, this hypothesis is fueled by the rapid pace at which computational power has increased, allowing for the creation of increasingly realistic virtual environments. The exponential growth in computational capabilities suggests that future simulations could potentially mimic reality with such precision that distinguishing between the two becomes a monumental challenge. This hypothesis is not merely speculative; it is supported by a confluence of scientific theories, technological advancements, and philosophical inquiry that together paint a compelling picture of a simulated universe.

Quantum mechanics, with its inherent uncertainties and probabilistic nature, offers an intriguing parallel to the concept of a simulated reality. The idea that particles exist in multiple states until observed is reminiscent of the rendering techniques used in virtual environments, where only the visible portions of a scene are actively processed. This correlation invites a reconsideration of the physical laws governing our universe, suggesting they might be akin to the rulesets programmed into a simulation. Moreover, scientists exploring the fabric of the cosmos have discovered mathematical patterns that hint at underlying codes, much like the binary sequences that form the backbone of computer simulations. Such discoveries fuel the argument that our reality might indeed be a sophisticated simulacrum.

Further bolstering the hypothesis are the breakthroughs in artificial intelligence and machine learning, which have enabled computers to create and navigate complex virtual worlds with minimal human intervention. These developments suggest a future where simulations could autonomously evolve, mirroring the complexity of our own universe. The potential for self-optimizing and self-sustaining simulations raises profound questions about the nature of consciousness and existence. If we can create virtual beings with their own sense of awareness, it prompts the question of whether our own consciousness is similarly a byproduct of an advanced simulation. This line of inquiry not only challenges conventional understanding but also opens up possibilities for exploring the true nature of reality.

As technological progress continues unabated, the line between the virtual and the real becomes increasingly blurred. The advent of immersive technologies, such as virtual and augmented reality, provides a glimpse into how future simulations might seamlessly integrate with our daily lives. These technologies offer a tantalizing vision of a world where physical and digital realities coexist and interact fluidly. As we venture further into this realm, the potential for simulations to replicate the intricacies of human experience becomes ever more plausible. The implications for society, ethics, and personal identity are profound, suggesting a future where the very fabric of reality is malleable and subjective.

The prospect of living in a simulated reality invites us to ponder the philosophical ramifications of such an existence. Accepting the simulation hypothesis compels us to reassess fundamental notions of free will, determinism, and moral responsibility. If our universe is indeed a construct, what does that mean for the choices we make and the authenticity of our experiences? These questions challenge the very essence of our understanding of life and purpose, urging us to explore the boundaries of reality and illusion. As we stand on the cusp of potential discovery, embracing this paradigm shift could redefine our place in the cosmos, offering a new lens through which to view our existence.

Philosophical Ramifications of Accepting a Simulated Universe

The philosophical ramifications of accepting a simulated universe invite us to reevaluate our understanding of existence and reality. If our universe is, in fact, a complex simulation, it challenges the very fabric of our perceived reality, urging us to reconsider the nature of consciousness and identity. This perspective posits that our experiences and the laws governing the universe may be constructs of an advanced intelligence, which could redefine our place within the cosmos. This notion has profound implications for human agency and autonomy, as it suggests that our actions and their consequences may be pre-programmed or manipulated by an external force. By embracing this possibility, we open ourselves to a broader discourse on the essence of life and the potential boundaries of human freedom.

The moral dimensions of living within a simulated universe also demand careful contemplation. If our reality is orchestrated by an advanced civilization or entity, ethical questions arise regarding the intentions and responsibilities of the creators. Are we mere pawns in a cosmic experiment, or is our existence meant to serve a higher purpose? This line of inquiry may prompt us to consider the ethical obligations we hold towards other sentient beings, simulated or otherwise, and whether our actions possess intrinsic value beyond the simulation's boundaries. The exploration of these ethical quandaries encourages us to develop a framework for understanding moral responsibility in an environment where traditional concepts of right and wrong might not apply.

In this context, the intersection of science and philosophy presents an opportunity for groundbreaking discourse. Theories from quantum mechanics, such as the multiverse hypothesis, suggest the possibility of parallel realities, which may complement or challenge the simulation theory. This intersection offers fertile ground for the exploration of reality's nature and the potential for human consciousness to transcend simulated boundaries. By integrating insights from cognitive science, we can investigate how the brain constructs and interprets reality, providing clues about the potential malleability of human perception in a simulated environment. These inquiries pave the way for a deeper understanding of the mind's capabilities and the limits of our perception.

The acceptance of a simulated universe also invites us to consider the transformative potential of synthetic realities in shaping human evolution. If simulations can mirror the complexity of the universe, they might serve as tools for exploring alternative realities and testing scenarios that could inform and enhance our understanding of the physical world. By simulating conditions beyond our current comprehension, we might uncover insights into the nature of existence and the possibilities for human advancement. This line of thought encourages us to envision a future where simulations not only reflect our reality but also expand our cognitive and experiential horizons, pushing the boundaries of what it means to be human.

While the idea of living in a simulated universe might seem speculative, it offers a profound opportunity for introspection and growth. By questioning the authenticity of our reality, we engage in a dialogue that challenges established norms and encourages innovative thinking. This philosophical journey compels us to confront the limitations of our knowledge and explore new paradigms that transcend conventional wisdom. As we navigate this landscape, we are invited to embrace uncertainty and look beyond the confines of our perceived reality, fostering a spirit of curiosity and discovery that could redefine the trajectory of human progress.

Historical precedents: Simulation in literature, religion, and culture

Throughout history, humans have spun tales that blur the line between reality and illusion, offering glimpses into worlds shaped by the imagination. Ancient myths and legends teem with stories of gods weaving dreams and casting illusions, creating ephemeral realities that challenge the perceptions of their human subjects. These mythical narratives serve as early reflections of humanity's fascination with alternate realities, revealing a timeless curiosity about the nature of existence and the boundaries of perception. As one peers into these ancient texts, it becomes evident that the seeds of simulated realities were sown long before the advent of modern technology, hinting at a profound, intrinsic desire to explore realms beyond the tangible world.

The sacred and the secular intertwine in religious narratives that function as proto-simulations, offering structured visions of existence that guide moral and ethical understanding. These narratives often depict worlds governed by divine will, where the faithful navigate through layers of symbolic meaning and cosmic order. Such stories have not only shaped cultural identities but also laid the groundwork for the concept of parallel realities—an idea that resurfaces in folklore across civilizations, where virtual worlds come alive through oral traditions and cultural fabrications. These stories capture the collective imagination, creating shared experiences that resonate with the essence of simulation. As we journey through the tapestry of literature, religion, and culture, the echoes of these early simulations offer a rich backdrop against which the modern pursuit of virtual realities unfolds, connecting past imaginings to present possibilities.

Mythical Illusions and Dreams in Ancient Texts

Ancient texts, rich with mythical illusions and dreams, have long captured humanity's fascination with alternate realities. These narratives, whether found in the epic tales of Homer or the sacred verses of the Vedas, often blur the line between waking life and the fantastical realms of gods and heroes. In Homer's "Odyssey," the protagonist's journey is punctuated by dreams and divine interventions that shape his reality, suggesting an interplay between the physical world and the imagined. Such stories invite readers to contemplate the nature of reality itself, echoing the modern question of whether life as we perceive it is but a grand simulation. As we explore these ancient narratives, we uncover an enduring human curiosity about the boundaries of reality, a curiosity that continues to fuel contemporary debates in simulation theory.

Religious texts add another layer to the exploration of simulated realities, offering a unique perspective on the concept of divine orchestration. The dream sequences in the Bible, such as Joseph's prophetic visions, reveal how dreams were often seen as messages from a higher power, guiding human actions in the tangible world. Similarly, in Hindu philosophy, the idea of Maya denotes the illusory nature of the world, suggesting that what we perceive may not be the ultimate reality. These religious narratives can be viewed as proto-simulations, where the divine acts as the ultimate architect, crafting experiences that transcend ordinary perception. By examining these stories, we gain insights into how ancient cultures understood the world as a construct, shaped by forces beyond human comprehension.

Folklore from diverse cultures further enriches our understanding of simulated realities, presenting a tapestry of virtual worlds and fabricated experiences. The tales of the Arabian Nights, with their layers of stories within stories, create a complex structure of imagined realities that mirror the recursive nature of simulations. In Japanese mythology, the concept of the "Yume no Sekai" or dream world, illustrates the fluidity between the dream state and reality, where characters navigate realms that defy the constraints of the physical world. Such cultural fabrications highlight the universal human inclination to question the nature of existence, offering parallels to modern virtual realities where the boundaries of experience are similarly blurred.

Recent scholarly work has begun to draw connections between these ancient narratives and contemporary virtual environments, suggesting that the human brain is wired to navigate both real and imagined worlds. Cognitive science research indicates that the neural processes involved in experiencing dreams and virtual simulations share common pathways, shedding light on how ancient stories of dreams and illusions might have laid the groundwork for our current understanding of virtual experiences. By exploring these connections, we can appreciate how ancient texts not only entertained but also provided a framework for exploring consciousness and perception, paving the way for modern interpretations of simulated realities.

As we delve into the complex interplay between ancient narratives and modern simulation technology, we are prompted to consider how these early stories can inform current and future developments in virtual reality. What lessons can we glean from these texts about the ethical implications of creating and inhabiting simulated worlds? How might these ancient insights guide the development of simulations that enhance human understanding and experience rather than detract from it? In pondering these questions, readers are encouraged to think critically about the trajectory of simulation technology and its potential to reshape our understanding of reality, much like the mythical illusions and dreams of ancient texts have done for centuries.

Religious Narratives as Proto-Simulations

Religious narratives have long served as proto-simulations, offering frameworks through which humans explore existential questions and the boundaries of reality. Ancient scriptures and spiritual teachings often depict worlds and experiences beyond the tangible, suggesting that human consciousness can transcend the material plane. These narratives function as simulations by constructing immersive experiences through storytelling, where adherents are invited to envision and inhabit alternate realities. For instance, Hinduism presents the concept of "Maya," which illustrates the world as an illusion or dream, challenging followers to perceive the divine truth hidden behind apparent reality. Such perspectives resonate with modern simulation theories, which propose that perceived reality might be a constructed experience.

In many religious traditions, visionary experiences and divine revelations provide another layer of proto-simulative elements. Consider the biblical accounts of prophets who enter divine realms during their visions, such as Ezekiel's chariot in the Hebrew Bible. These experiences are akin to virtual journeys, where sensory perceptions are altered, and new insights are gained. The transformative power of these narratives lies in their ability to shift the believer's perception, offering a glimpse into realities governed by different rules and dimensions. This echoes the immersive quality of contemporary virtual simulations, where participants can explore environments and situations that defy everyday logic, challenging the very nature of what is real.

Furthermore, religious rituals often create immersive experiences that simulate sacred narratives and events. The Catholic Mass, for instance, reenacts the Last Supper, inviting participants to transcend time and space to connect with a pivotal moment in Christian history. Such rituals employ symbolic elements to immerse individuals in a narrative, fostering a collective experience that transcends ordinary consciousness. This parallels the objectives of modern simulations designed for collective engagement and shared experience, where multiple users can inhabit a single virtual environment, creating a sense of community and shared purpose.

Recent research into the cognitive aspects of religious experiences highlights their similarity to virtual reality. Studies suggest that spiritual practices can alter brain states, creating heightened awareness or altered perceptions akin to those experienced in virtual environments. Such findings underscore the potential for religious narratives to function as early forms of cognitive simulations, where mental states are deliberately manipulated to achieve specific insights or transformations. As cognitive science delves deeper into these phenomena, parallels between ancient religious experiences and modern virtual reality may offer new pathways for understanding consciousness and perception.

Religious narratives as proto-simulations invite a re-examination of the ways belief systems shape human understanding of reality. They challenge us to consider how storytelling and ritual have historically functioned as immersive experiences, guiding consciousness beyond the limitations of physical existence. This perspective encourages further exploration into how contemporary simulations can draw from these ancient traditions to craft experiences that not only entertain but also enlighten and transform. As we continue to create and inhabit increasingly sophisticated virtual worlds, the wisdom embedded in these narratives may offer valuable insights into the ethical and philosophical dimensions of simulated realities.

Cultural Fabrications and Virtual Realities in Folklore

Cultural fabrications and virtual realities in folklore offer a rich tapestry of narratives that mirror the concept of simulated realities. Folklore, with its myriad of tales and legends, often blurs the line between the tangible and the ethereal, creating worlds where the ordinary transforms into the extraordinary. These narratives, passed down through generations, serve as early examples of humans' innate desire to imagine and inhabit alternate realities. They reveal a collective yearning to explore dimensions beyond the mundane, reflecting a fundamental aspect of human consciousness—the quest for experiences that transcend the limitations of our physical world.

In many cultures, folklore is replete with stories of enchanted lands and mystical creatures, conjuring worlds that operate under their own sets of rules and logic. These tales, much like modern simulations, allow audiences to suspend disbelief and engage with realities that challenge our conventional understanding of existence. For instance, the Irish legend of Tír na nÓg, a mythical land of eternal youth and beauty, can be seen as an ancient form of virtual reality—an imagined realm that offers an escape from the constraints of time and mortality. Similarly, the concept of the "Otherworld" in Celtic folklore presents a parallel dimension accessible through certain rituals or geographical portals, akin to entering a simulated environment with its own unique parameters.

The narrative structures within folklore often employ elements akin to modern-day game design, where protagonists must navigate complex worlds, solve puzzles, or fulfill quests. These stories not only entertain but also serve educational purposes, imparting moral lessons and cultural values to their audiences. The labyrinthine journey of Theseus in Greek mythology, where he navigates the Minotaur's maze, echoes the immersive challenges found in contemporary video games. Such tales highlight the timeless appeal of navigating constructed environments, offering insights into how humans have continually sought to create and explore scenarios that extend beyond the tangible.

Recent interdisciplinary studies suggest that these folklore narratives may serve as cognitive tools, enhancing our mental faculties by encouraging imaginative problem-solving and abstract thinking. By engaging with these stories, individuals can develop a more nuanced understanding of the world, enhancing their capacity for empathy and creativity. This perspective aligns with cognitive science research, which posits that the act of storytelling and engagement with fictional worlds can strengthen neural pathways associated with imagination and empathy. As such, folklore can be seen as an early precursor to the cognitive benefits we now associate with virtual environments and simulations.

In contemplating the implications of cultural fabrications as proto-simulations, we are invited to ponder the enduring relationship between storytelling and technology. As we continue to refine our ability to create immersive digital worlds, these ancient narratives remind us of the power of the human imagination and its capacity to shape not only our cultural heritage but also our technological future. By drawing from this rich well of folklore, we can better understand the psychological and cultural underpinnings of our fascination with simulations, providing a historical context that enriches our appreciation of modern virtual realities.

Technological advancements making simulations plausible

In the ever-evolving landscape of human innovation, few realms hold as much intrigue and potential as the field of simulation technology. As we stand on the precipice of a new era, the tools and techniques that once seemed confined to the pages of science fiction are rapidly becoming our reality. The convergence of computational power, immersive interfaces, and artificial intelligence is creating a fertile ground for simulations that are not only plausible but are beginning to blur the lines between the virtual and the tangible. This transformation is more than a technical feat; it's a revolution that promises to reshape how we perceive and interact with the world around us.

At the heart of this revolution lies a confluence of technological advancements that are making once-unimaginable simulations attainable. The relentless march of computational power and real-time processing capabilities is allowing for the creation of complex and responsive virtual environments. Meanwhile, breakthroughs in virtual and augmented reality interfaces are offering unprecedented levels of immersion, drawing users into worlds that feel as real as their own. Complementing these developments, the integration of artificial intelligence is enabling dynamic world-building, where virtual landscapes can evolve and respond in ways that mimic the unpredictability of life itself. Together, these innovations are not just enhancing the fidelity of simulated experiences; they are opening doors to new possibilities, inviting us to explore realities limited only by the edges of human imagination.

Advancements in Computational Power and Real-Time Processing

In the realm of simulation, the rapid advancement in computational power stands as a cornerstone, enabling the creation of intricate and lifelike digital realities. The exponential growth in processing capabilities, often described by Moore's Law, has fueled this evolution, allowing for the complex calculations required to render detailed virtual environments in real-time. High-performance GPUs, once primarily the domain of gaming, now hold critical roles in the development of simulations, driving the sophisticated graphics and physics engines that underpin these digital worlds. This leap in computational prowess has not only enhanced the fidelity of simulations but also expanded their scale, supporting vast, interconnected environments that were once the stuff of science fiction.

The shift towards distributed computing and cloud-based platforms has further propelled the scope of simulations, breaking traditional limitations imposed by local hardware. By harnessing the collective power of networks of computers, simulations can now be run on a scale previously unimaginable. This has opened doors for massively multiplayer online simulations and complex, persistent virtual worlds that continue to evolve independently of user interaction. Researchers and developers are exploring edge computing to bring even greater immediacy and responsiveness to simulations, minimizing latency and enhancing user immersion in these expansive digital landscapes.

As real-time processing becomes increasingly sophisticated, the line between virtual and physical realms begins to blur, facilitating experiences that are not only visually convincing but also dynamically responsive to user actions. Advances in machine learning algorithms have played a pivotal role in this transformation, empowering simulations to adapt and evolve in real time. These algorithms enable simulations to anticipate user behavior and modify the environment accordingly, creating a sense of agency and interactivity that is critical for educational and training applications. The integration of natural language processing and voice recognition technologies further enhances realism, allowing users to interact with simulations in more intuitive and human-like ways.

The ongoing refinement of simulation technology continues to push boundaries, fostering innovation across various fields. In architecture and engineering, real-time simulations allow professionals to visualize and adjust designs dynamically, improving efficiency and accuracy in the design process. In healthcare, simulations offer immersive training environments where medical professionals can practice and refine skills, reducing the risk of errors in real-world scenarios. The entertainment industry, too, benefits immensely from these advancements, crafting experiences that are both visually stunning and emotionally engaging, drawing users deeper into the narrative worlds.

With these advancements, the potential applications of simulations appear limitless, yet they also raise important questions about the future of human interaction with technology. As simulations become more pervasive and realistic, the need for ethical considerations and responsible design grows ever more pressing. How will society navigate the balance between virtual escapism and real-world engagement? What safeguards can be implemented to ensure simulations are used for enrichment rather than detriment? These questions invite readers to critically examine the trajectory of simulation technology and its place in shaping the human experience.

Innovations in Virtual and Augmented Reality Interfaces

The technological landscape of virtual and augmented reality interfaces has undergone a remarkable transformation, opening new horizons for realism and immersion in simulated environments. These advancements have been propelled by a quest for authenticity, merging the tactile with the virtual to create experiences that blur the lines between digital illusions and tangible reality. Recent innovations in haptic feedback and spatial audio have revolutionized how users interact with virtual worlds, adding layers of sensory engagement that elevate the authenticity of the experience. Haptic suits, for instance, now allow users to "feel" the virtual environment, providing physical sensations that correspond to digital interactions. Meanwhile, spatial audio technology creates an immersive soundscape that adjusts based on the user's movements, enhancing the perception of depth and presence within the simulation.

One of the most significant breakthroughs in this arena is the development of lightweight, high-resolution headsets that offer unprecedented visual fidelity. These devices, often equipped with eye-tracking technology, enable a seamless and intuitive interface between the user and the virtual world. Eye-tracking not only enhances navigation within the simulation but also allows for more nuanced interaction with virtual elements, as the system can respond to the user's gaze and focus. This technology is pivotal in creating environments that feel intuitive and responsive, bridging the gap between human cognition and machine interpretation. As a result, users experience a more natural and engaging interaction, fostering deeper immersion and connection with the simulated reality.

The integration of artificial intelligence into virtual and augmented reality interfaces has further expanded the potential of these technologies. AI-driven algorithms can dynamically adapt the virtual environment based on user preferences and behavior, creating personalized and evolving experiences. This adaptability is crucial for maintaining engagement and providing meaningful interactions that resonate with individual users. For instance, AI can adjust the complexity of a virtual task or alter the narrative flow of a simulation to match the user's skill level or emotional state, ensuring that the experience remains challenging yet accessible. This level of customization not only enhances user satisfaction but also opens avenues for innovative applications in education and training, where adaptive learning environments can cater to diverse learning styles and needs.

Beyond individual experiences, virtual and augmented reality interfaces are increasingly being utilized for collaborative and social purposes. These technologies enable multiple users to interact within the same virtual space, fostering a sense of community and shared presence despite geographical separation. Platforms that support multiplayer interactions are paving the way for virtual conferences, remote team collaboration, and social gatherings, transforming how people connect and communicate. This connectivity is particularly valuable in contexts where physical presence is impractical or impossible, offering an alternative means of interaction that retains the richness and nuance of in-person communication.

As we contemplate the future of virtual and augmented reality interfaces, it is essential to consider the ethical and societal implications of these technologies. While the potential benefits are vast, there are also challenges to address, such as ensuring accessibility for diverse populations and protecting user privacy in immersive environments. Thought-provoking questions arise: How do we balance the allure of virtual escapism with the need for real-world engagement? What safeguards can be implemented to prevent misuse of these powerful technologies? By critically examining these issues, we can harness the transformative potential of virtual and augmented reality interfaces, ensuring they contribute positively to the fabric of human experience. As these technologies continue to evolve, they promise to redefine our understanding of reality itself, offering new ways to explore, learn, and connect.

Integration of Artificial Intelligence for Dynamic World-Building

Artificial intelligence has become a cornerstone in the development of dynamic simulated environments, revolutionizing the way virtual worlds are constructed and experienced. By harnessing sophisticated AI algorithms, designers can create complex, adaptive ecosystems that respond to user interactions in real-time. These intelligent agents not only populate virtual landscapes but also evolve alongside the user, offering a deeply immersive experience that mirrors the unpredictability and richness of the physical world. The integration of AI into simulation design allows for the creation of worlds that feel alive, enabling users to interact with environments and characters that display realistic behaviors, emotions, and decision-making processes. This advancement marks a significant leap from static, pre-programmed environments to dynamic, responsive worlds that can offer infinite possibilities for exploration and engagement.

Incorporating AI into simulations transcends mere visual enhancement; it introduces a level of realism that blurs the line between digital and physical realities. Machine learning techniques enable simulations to adapt and improve over time, learning from user interactions to provide personalized experiences. This adaptability is crucial in educational simulations, where AI can tailor challenges and feedback to individual learning styles, ensuring that each user receives a unique and effective learning journey. In entertainment, AI-driven simulations can offer narratives that shift and evolve based on player choices, creating personalized storylines that enhance engagement and replayability. The potential for AI to transform simulations into training grounds for complex problem-solving and critical thinking skills cannot be overstated, offering profound implications for personal and professional development.

Recent advancements in AI, such as generative adversarial networks and reinforcement learning, have unlocked new possibilities in world-building. These technologies allow for the creation of vast, procedurally generated landscapes that can be continuously modified and expanded. By employing AI to simulate weather patterns, ecological systems, and even societal dynamics, designers can craft worlds that are not only visually stunning but also functionally complex. This capability opens the door to simulations that can be used as testbeds for real-world scenarios, offering insights into urban planning, environmental management, and social dynamics. The ability to simulate such intricate systems with a high degree of accuracy provides valuable tools for researchers and policymakers seeking to understand and address complex global challenges.

While the integration of AI in simulations offers extraordinary potential, it also raises important questions about the ethical implications of such technology. As simulations become more lifelike, the line between real and artificial blurs, prompting considerations about the moral responsibilities of creating and interacting with these worlds. Designers and users alike must grapple with questions of agency, autonomy, and the potential for AI to develop beyond its intended purposes. These considerations are pivotal as we move toward a future where simulations play an increasingly central role in daily life. The challenge lies in balancing innovation with ethical stewardship, ensuring that these powerful tools are used to enhance human experience without compromising our values or well-being.

AI-driven simulations invite us to envision futures where the boundaries of reality are continuously redefined. As technology advances, the potential for virtual worlds to become indistinguishable from the physical realm grows, challenging our perceptions of existence and identity. Thought-provoking scenarios arise: What happens when virtual experiences become preferable to real ones? How do we navigate a world where our perceptions can be manipulated by intelligent systems? These questions urge us to consider the role of AI in shaping our future realities and the responsibilities that come with such power. By contemplating these possibilities, we prepare ourselves to harness the full potential of AI in simulations, ensuring that this technology serves as a force for positive transformation in society.

The exploration of simulation theory in this chapter unveils a rich tapestry of ideas that challenge our understanding of reality and perception. By traversing philosophical musings and scientific inquiries, we see how the notion of simulated realities has fascinated thinkers throughout history, from ancient myths to contemporary hypotheses. The simulation hypothesis, in particular, invites us to reconsider the nature of existence, suggesting that our universe might not be the base reality we assume it to be. Historical precedents in literature and culture reveal humanity's perennial interest in alternate worlds, while recent technological advancements bring these once-fanciful ideas closer to feasibility. As we stand on the brink of creating expansive virtual environments, the implications are profound, offering both opportunities and ethical dilemmas. This foundation sets the stage for further exploration, inviting us to consider how simulations might not only reflect but also transform our reality. With these concepts in mind, the journey continues into the technical and perceptual intricacies that make these simulated worlds possible, prompting reflection on how deeply these virtual experiences could intertwine with human consciousness.

Chapter Two

Building Blocks Of A Simulated Reality

Step into the world of simulated realities, where the boundaries between the tangible and the virtual blur, and the impossible becomes possible with a mere flick of a digital switch. Imagine a universe meticulously crafted from lines of code, where every sensation and interaction is designed to mimic the nuances of our physical world. This realm is not just a playground for the imagination but a frontier of technological artistry, where architects of the digital age lay down the foundations of alternate realities. As you venture deeper, consider the ancient human yearning to create worlds beyond our own—a dream now within reach thanks to the interplay of advanced physics engines, sophisticated artificial intelligence, and immersive sensory technologies.

In this digital landscape, what makes a simulation truly indistinguishable from reality? The secret lies in the delicate art of perception. Just as a magician uses sleight of hand to captivate an audience, simulation architects employ a blend of psychological insights and technical wizardry to craft experiences that are both believable and compelling. These virtual worlds are underpinned by intricate data models and powerful algorithms, forming the bedrock upon which entire universes are constructed. Each detail, from the rustle of leaves in a virtual breeze to the distant echo of a simulated thunderstorm, is meticulously rendered to engage the human senses fully.

Yet, all this splendor requires a robust foundation, driven by cutting-edge hardware and infrastructure capable of sustaining high-fidelity experiences. The technology powering these simulations is as awe-inspiring as the worlds they create, pushing the boundaries of what is possible and challenging our understanding of reality itself. As we journey through the components that bring simulated realities to life, we reflect on the profound implications these digital creations hold for the future of human experience. Prepare to explore a realm where the lines between creator and creation, observer and participant, begin to dissolve.

Core components: Physics engines, AI, and sensory immersion

Visualize a future where the boundaries between the tangible and the virtual blur seamlessly. In this world, the intricate dance of technology and creativity gives rise to experiences so vivid and authentic that they challenge our very perception of reality. At the heart of these compelling simulations lie the core components that breathe life into digital realms: physics engines, artificial intelligence, and sensory immersion. These elements are not mere tools; they are the architects of worlds, crafting elaborate tapestries of existence where the rules of physics, the spontaneity of interactions, and the richness of sensory input converge to create environments indistinguishable from our own. Their significance stretches beyond mere entertainment, laying the groundwork for profound changes in how we learn, explore, and interact with the universe around us.

Physics engines act as the fundamental scaffolding, orchestrating the laws that govern these virtual worlds with precision and nuance. Simultaneously, artificial intelligence emerges as the maestro, infusing simulations with life, adaptability, and complexity, offering dynamic experiences that evolve with the participant's engagement. Meanwhile, the pursuit of sensory immersion endeavors to captivate our senses fully, endeavoring to replicate the subtle textures of reality through innovative techniques and cutting-edge technology. Together, these components form a harmonious symphony, each playing a crucial role in the grand design of simulated realities. As we explore their individual contributions, a deeper understanding of their collective impact on crafting believable and immersive experiences unfolds, setting the stage for examining their potential to reshape the fabric of human experience.

The Role of Physics Engines in Creating Realistic Virtual Environments

Physics engines serve as the invisible architects of virtual worlds, crafting the laws of nature that govern every interaction within a digital environment. These engines form the foundational layer upon which realism is built, simulating the intricacies of motion, force, and collision with remarkable precision. By mimicking the principles of classical mechanics, physics engines endow virtual spaces with a sense of authenticity that is crucial for immersive experiences. Recent advances in computational power and algorithm design have pushed the boundaries of what these engines can achieve, enabling the simulation of phenomena as complex as fluid dynamics and soft-body deformation in real time. Such developments are pivotal for applications ranging from realistic gaming environments to high-fidelity training simulations used in industries like aviation and medicine.

The sophistication of a physics engine often dictates the level of detail and realism that can be achieved within a simulation. High-end engines, like NVIDIA's PhysX, employ complex mathematical models to simulate not only basic rigid body physics but also more nuanced interactions like cloth tearing, smoke diffusion, and water flow. These capabilities allow developers to create environments where the virtual and the physical blur, offering users experiences that closely mirror the unpredictability and complexity of the real world. This level of realism is not just about visual fidelity; it profoundly affects user engagement, as the brain's perceptual systems are finely attuned to the subtleties of physical interactions. When a virtual world behaves as expected, it fosters a deeper sense of presence, enhancing both the educational and entertainment potential of simulations.

The role of physics engines extends beyond mere replication of physical laws; they are crucial in the creative process, offering designers a sandbox to experiment with and manipulate the parameters of reality itself. By altering gravitational forces or material properties, creators can construct worlds that defy earthly limitations, inspiring awe and encouraging exploration. This flexibility is not only vital for crafting fantastical game worlds but also for educational purposes, such as teaching complex concepts in physics or engineering through interactive simulations. For instance, virtual reality simulations that allow users to adjust variables and observe outcomes can provide a more intuitive understanding of scientific principles than traditional methods.

Recent research has also explored the integration of machine learning algorithms with physics engines, paving the way for more adaptive and intelligent virtual environments. This amalgamation enables simulations to predict and adapt to user behavior, creating dynamic interactions that feel organically responsive. By leveraging artificial intelligence, physics engines can optimize the balance between computational load and visual fidelity, ensuring smooth performance even in the most intricate simulations. This synergy also opens doors to novel applications, such as personalized training programs that adjust difficulty based on a user's learning curve, thereby enhancing both efficiency and engagement.

As we continue to advance towards increasingly complex simulations, the potential of physics engines remains vast and largely untapped. Their ability to replicate and even transcend natural laws holds promise for both practical applications and creative endeavors. By harnessing these engines, developers can craft experiences that not only entertain but also educate and inform, pushing the limits of what is possible in virtual reality. As these technologies evolve, they invite us to rethink our relationship with the digital and physical worlds, challenging our perceptions and expanding the horizons of human creativity.

Artificial Intelligence as the Driving Force Behind Dynamic Simulations

Artificial intelligence stands as a central pillar in the construction of dynamic simulations, providing the lifelike behaviors and complex interactions that enchant users. At its core, AI in simulations is designed to replicate human-like cognition, imbuing virtual entities with the capacity to learn, adapt, and make decisions. This capability is achieved through sophisticated algorithms that allow simulated characters, or agents, to respond to environmental stimuli in a nuanced manner. Recent advancements in machine learning and neural networks have significantly enhanced the realism of these interactions, enabling AI to not only react to changes in the virtual environment but also predict and anticipate user actions, creating a seamless and intuitive experience.

One of the groundbreaking developments in AI for simulations is the use of reinforcement learning, where agents learn optimal behaviors by receiving feedback from the environment through rewards or penalties. This technique mirrors the way humans and animals learn from consequences, resulting in increasingly autonomous and intelligent virtual beings. For instance, in gaming simulations, AI opponents can evolve their strategies based on a player's tendencies, ensuring that no two encounters are the same and keeping users engaged. Beyond entertainment, these AI systems have profound implications for training simulations, where they can simulate complex scenarios, such as emergency responses or military operations, providing invaluable hands-on experience in a controlled setting.

The integration of AI with procedural generation techniques further amplifies the potential for creating endlessly varied and rich virtual worlds. By leveraging AI to autonomously generate landscapes, architecture, and even entire ecosystems, simulations can provide users with environments that are not only visually stunning but also constantly evolving. This dynamic world-building allows for a more organic exploration experience, where users can discover new elements each time they enter the simulation. This continuous novelty is essential for maintaining user interest and immersion, as it mirrors the unpredictability and diversity of the real world, challenging users to adapt and engage with the unfolding narratives.

As AI continues to evolve, its role in simulations is expanding beyond traditional applications. Emerging research in affective computing is exploring ways to enable AI to recognize and respond to user emotions, crafting personalized experiences that resonate on a deeper emotional level. Imagine a simulation that adjusts its difficulty based on the user's frustration levels, or an AI companion that offers support and encouragement during challenging tasks. These emotion-sensitive systems hold the promise of creating more empathetic and responsive virtual environments, where simulations become not just tools for entertainment or education, but companions that foster personal growth and wellbeing.

The potential of AI in simulations also raises intriguing ethical and philosophical questions about the nature of intelligence and consciousness. As AI entities become more sophisticated, the line between programmed responses and genuine understanding blurs, prompting us to reconsider our definitions of life and awareness. This conundrum invites a broader discussion about our responsibilities toward these virtual beings and the ethical frameworks that should guide their development and use. By engaging with these questions, we can ensure that the advancement of AI in simulations is not only technically impressive but also aligned with the values and principles that define our humanity.

Techniques for Achieving Immersive Sensory Experiences in Virtual Worlds

Crafting immersive sensory experiences in virtual worlds requires a synthesis of cutting-edge techniques, each harmonizing to blur the line between the digital and the tangible. At the forefront are haptic technologies, which have evolved dramatically, bringing a new dimension of tactile feedback to users. Modern haptic devices, such as gloves and suits equipped with actuators, simulate the sensation of touch, allowing individuals to feel textures, pressure, and even temperature variations in a virtual environment. This tactile engagement enhances the realism of simulations, creating a profound sense of presence that captivates and grounds users within the virtual realm. The ongoing advancements in nanotechnology promise to further refine these devices, potentially leading to even more precise and nuanced feedback systems.

Parallel to haptics, the auditory dimension plays a pivotal role in crafting convincing virtual experiences. Spatial audio technology has achieved remarkable sophistication, enabling sound to be perceived from specific directions and distances. This directional audio contributes to the illusion of depth and space, essential for creating environments that feel expansive and alive. Techniques such as binaural recording and ambisonics allow for the recreation of soundscapes that adjust dynamically based on user movement and interaction. Consider a bustling cityscape simulation where the honking of cars, distant chatter, and the rustle of leaves are not just heard but felt, creating an immersive tapestry of sound that draws users deeper into the experience.

The visual component of sensory immersion continues to advance with the development of high-resolution displays and sophisticated rendering techniques. Virtual reality headsets now boast eye-tracking capabilities that enhance focus and detail through foveated rendering, which prioritizes processing power on the area directly observed by the user. This not only improves visual fidelity but also reduces latency, making interactions within the simulation more seamless and intuitive. Moreover, innovations in graphics processing and ray tracing allow for real-time rendering of complex light interactions, shadows, and textures, resulting in breathtakingly realistic environments that challenge the boundaries of what can be perceived as real.

Olfactory and gustatory technologies, while still emerging, hold promise for expanding the sensory spectrum of virtual experiences. Devices capable of releasing specific scents or simulating taste through electrical stimulation introduce new layers of interaction. Imagine a culinary simulation where users can not only see and hear the sizzling of a dish but also smell its aroma and taste its flavors. While these technologies are in their nascent stages, research into their applications continues to grow, offering tantalizing glimpses into a future where the full range of human senses can be engaged within virtual spaces.

The integration of these sensory technologies is not without its challenges. The complexity of human perception means that achieving a truly convincing simulation requires a delicate balance between various sensory inputs. Researchers are exploring the concept of sensory congruence, where aligning stimuli across different senses enhances the believability of the virtual experience. This interdisciplinary endeavor involves collaboration among engineers, neuroscientists, and designers, each contributing insights to refine these systems. As this field progresses, the potential for simulations to mimic reality with astonishing fidelity grows, inviting both excitement and contemplation about the implications of living in worlds that are indistinguishable from our own.

Designing perception: Tricks to make simulations indistinguishable from reality

Imagine stepping into a world where the boundary between the digital and the tangible blurs so seamlessly that your senses are convinced of its authenticity. The allure of crafting such simulations lies not merely in their visual splendor but in their ability to deceive the mind into believing the impossible is real. As we embark on this exploration of perception design, we uncover the art and science behind making simulations indistinguishable from reality. The journey begins with the mastery of sensory integration, an intricate dance of sight, sound, touch, and even smell, harmonized to immerse the user entirely. Each sense, when tuned with precision, expands the depth and richness of the simulated experience, pulling the participant into an alternate realm that feels as natural as breathing.

Yet, sensory trickery is only one facet of this fascinating puzzle. The construction of realistic physics and environmental interactions further enhances the illusion, ensuring that every movement, every ripple, adheres to the laws of nature—or bends them convincingly. Meanwhile, the role of AI becomes pivotal, crafting dynamic and adaptive environments that respond intelligently to the user's actions, creating an ever-evolving tapestry of experience. Together, these elements forge a reality so convincing that the line between the simulated and the authentic becomes a mere whisper, challenging the observer to discern where one ends and the other begins. As we dive deeper into these subtopics, we unravel the techniques and technologies that bring these virtual tapestries to life, each thread meticulously woven to mimic the essence of reality itself.

Leveraging Sensory Integration for Enhanced Immersion

In the intricate tapestry of creating simulated realities, sensory integration stands as a linchpin that elevates virtual experiences from mere visual spectacles to fully immersive environments. By fusing auditory, tactile, and olfactory cues with visual elements, developers craft worlds that captivate the human psyche, fostering a sense of presence that rivals actual experiences. Recent advances in haptic technology exemplify this endeavor, offering users tactile feedback that mimics the real-world texture and resistance. For instance, gloves embedded with micro-actuators can simulate the sensation of picking up a pebble or feeling the wind's subtle resistance, enhancing the illusion of a tangible environment. This multisensory approach not only amplifies user engagement but also fosters a more profound emotional connection to the virtual world.

Auditory elements, often underestimated, play a crucial role in shaping perception within simulations. Cutting-edge sound design leverages spatial audio technologies to create a three-dimensional soundscape that responds dynamically to user movements. As users navigate through virtual environments, sounds shift in response to their position, creating a realistic auditory experience. This sonic dynamism is crucial in reinforcing spatial orientation and depth, enabling users to perceive distant thunder or the whisper of leaves with uncanny realism. Such auditory precision not only enriches the experience but also aids in cognitive mapping, allowing users to intuitively navigate and interact within the virtual space.

In tandem with auditory and tactile enhancements, visual fidelity remains paramount in constructing believable simulations. High-resolution displays and advanced rendering techniques, such as ray tracing, deliver unparalleled realism by accurately simulating light interactions with surfaces. This technology allows for the creation of lifelike shadows, reflections, and refractions, which are essential in tricking the brain into perceiving virtual environments as genuine. Coupled with advancements in eye-tracking technology, simulations now adjust visual focus and depth of field dynamically, mirroring the natural human gaze and further blurring the line between reality and illusion.

The integration of olfactory stimuli, though still nascent, represents a frontier with immense potential to deepen immersion. Emerging scent delivery systems are beginning to introduce accurate olfactory cues into virtual settings, allowing users to experience the aroma of a forest trail or the scent of ocean air. While challenges remain in replicating complex scents and synchronizing them with visual and auditory elements, the ability to engage another sensory dimension promises to unlock new levels of immersion. This development invites speculation about the future of simulations as multi-sensory experiences that engage all facets of human perception.

As simulations grow more sophisticated, the ethical implications of sensory manipulation warrant consideration. While the potential for heightened immersion is vast, developers must navigate the fine line between enhancing experience and overwhelming the senses. The risk of sensory overload or emotional manipulation necessitates a framework for ethical design, ensuring that simulated experiences enrich rather than exploit. By fostering an open dialogue about these considerations, creators can responsibly harness the power of sensory integration, crafting environments that not only captivate but also respect the agency and well-being of their participants. Through innovative design and thoughtful application, sensory integration can transform simulations into profound tools for exploration and connection.

Creating Realistic Physics and Environmental Interactions

In the intricate tapestry of simulated realities, crafting believable physics and environmental interactions is a cornerstone for achieving immersive experiences. At the heart of this endeavor lies the creation of physics engines capable of replicating the nuanced dynamics of the real world. These engines simulate the laws of motion, gravity, and collision, enabling virtual objects to behave with a semblance of authenticity. The challenge is to transcend mere imitation by integrating advanced algorithms that can account for complex variables like fluid dynamics, frictional forces, and material properties. For instance, the latest advancements in soft-body dynamics allow virtual materials to deform and react as they would in reality, enhancing the illusion of tangibility. By pushing the boundaries of what can be simulated, developers can engender a sense of presence that blurs the line between the digital and the corporeal.

To further enrich these simulations, environmental interactions must be meticulously designed to respond dynamically to user input and environmental changes. This involves not only the physical behaviors of objects but also the atmospheric conditions that influence them. Techniques like procedural generation are employed to create vast, ever-changing landscapes that mimic the unpredictability of nature. These methods enable environments to adapt in real-time, offering a unique experience with each interaction. Consider the use of dynamic weather systems that adjust based on in-game variables or user actions. Such systems incorporate real-world data and sophisticated models to simulate phenomena like rain, wind, and fog, each affecting the physics of the environment in distinct ways. By fostering an ecosystem where every element is interdependent, developers can craft worlds that feel genuinely alive.

In addition to physical realism, the integration of sensory feedback plays a pivotal role in reinforcing the authenticity of simulations. Haptic technologies, for instance, provide tactile feedback that corresponds with virtual interactions, allowing users to "feel" the weight or texture of an object. This multisensory approach augments visual and auditory cues, creating a more holistic experience. Recent innovations in this field have seen the development of wearable devices that can simulate temperature changes or vibrations, adding layers of realism that were previously unimaginable. When users can not only see but also feel the simulated world around them, the line between reality and virtuality becomes increasingly indistinct.

Artificial intelligence emerges as a key player in creating adaptive environments that respond intelligently to user behavior. AI-driven systems can generate non-player characters (NPCs) with lifelike behaviors, capable of learning and evolving based on user interactions. This adaptability ensures that no two experiences are the same, offering a personalized narrative that aligns with the user's actions and decisions. Advanced AI algorithms can also simulate environmental changes over time, replicating the impact of user actions on the ecosystem. For example, an AI-driven forest might grow denser or become barren based on how the user interacts with it, offering a dynamic storytelling element that is both engaging and immersive.

As we ponder the possibilities of these advancements, one must consider the ethical and practical implications of such realistic simulations. Are we prepared for environments so convincing they might challenge our perception of what is real? How do we ensure these simulations serve to enhance our lives rather than detract from genuine human experiences? These thought-provoking questions invite reflection on the balance between technological innovation and its impact on society. By understanding and navigating these complexities, we can harness the power of simulations to create not just convincing illusions but transformative experiences that extend beyond the virtual realm.

Utilizing AI for Dynamic and Adaptive Simulation Environments

Artificial intelligence serves as the dynamic lifeblood of simulation environments, breathing life into static virtual worlds by adapting them to the actions and preferences of the users. These advanced systems employ complex algorithms to model behaviors and interactions, creating simulations that feel responsive and alive. The integration of AI within these environments allows for a seamless blend of pre-defined scenarios and emergent narratives, where users can engage with a world that feels both familiar and unpredictable. For instance, non-playable characters in a virtual city might exhibit behaviors that mirror human responses, reacting to environmental changes or user interactions in ways that are not pre-scripted but learned through sophisticated machine learning techniques.

Harnessing AI for adaptive simulations involves embedding neural networks and decision-making frameworks capable of processing vast amounts of data in real time. These frameworks interpret user input and environmental variables to generate outcomes that are contextually relevant and varied. An exciting development in this arena is the use of reinforcement learning, where AI agents learn optimal behaviors through trial and error, much like humans. This approach not only enhances the realism of virtual worlds but also allows the simulation to evolve organically, presenting users with a unique experience each time they engage. Reinforcement learning has demonstrated remarkable success in applications such as autonomous vehicles and game-playing AI, showcasing its potential to refine user experiences in simulations.

Beyond mere technical prowess, AI's role in simulations extends to crafting emotionally resonant and personalized experiences. By analyzing user behavior and preferences, AI systems can tailor narratives and challenges that align with individual needs and desires, creating a bespoke interaction. This customization can be seen in virtual training environments where AI adjusts the difficulty of scenarios based on the user's performance, ensuring a balanced and engaging learning curve. Such adaptability not only enriches the user experience but also enhances the educational value of simulations, as users are more likely to remain engaged and motivated when the content resonates with their personal learning style.

In the realm of dynamic simulations, AI also serves as a bridge between the virtual and physical worlds, enabling simulations to respond to real-world data and events. This application is particularly relevant in fields such as urban planning and disaster management, where simulations can provide real-time insights and predictive analytics. By continuously integrating data from sensors and IoT devices, AI-driven simulations can anticipate changes and suggest interventions, thus becoming invaluable tools for decision-makers. This capability underscores the transformative potential of AI in simulations, as it extends the reach of these virtual environments into tangible societal applications.

The evolution of AI in simulation environments invites us to ponder the ethical and philosophical implications of creating worlds that mirror our own. As these virtual realms become increasingly indistinguishable from reality, questions arise about the authenticity of our experiences and the nature of our interactions within them. Are the emotions and connections we form in these environments as valid as those in the physical world? What responsibilities do creators hold in ensuring that these simulated experiences contribute positively to human well-being? These inquiries challenge us to consider the broader impact of AI-driven simulations and encourage a thoughtful approach to their development and implementation.

Data models and algorithms: The backbone of simulated universes

In the captivating realm of simulated realities, data models and algorithms serve as the unseen architects, intricately weaving the fabric of entire universes. These mathematical frameworks and computational methods are not merely tools; they are the very essence of what makes virtual worlds tick, pulse, and breathe with life. Imagine a vast, uncharted canvas where every brushstroke is guided by a sophisticated algorithm, crafting landscapes that respond in real-time to the whims of the explorer. The seamless integration of these elements not only enhances the believability of the experience but also ensures that each simulated environment is as rich and dynamic as the imagination itself. At their core, these data models are the silent puppeteers, orchestrating a delicate balance between complexity and coherence, ensuring that every virtual leaf catches the wind and every wave crashes upon the shore with a sense of purpose.

As we venture deeper, the intricate dance between data and perception becomes evident. The same algorithms that simulate the rustle of leaves can also mimic the neural networks of human thought, creating complex ecosystems where artificial intelligence and machine learning thrive. These components are not isolated; they are part of an elaborate puzzle that, when pieced together, creates a vivid tapestry of reality within the digital realm. By understanding the fundamental concepts of data modeling, exploring advanced algorithmic techniques, and integrating AI into these ecosystems, we unlock the potential for simulations that not only mirror our reality but enhance it. The journey into this digital genesis invites us to question the boundaries of our creations and to ponder the endless possibilities that lie within the coded heart of these virtual worlds.

Fundamental Concepts of Data Modeling in Virtual Environments

In the realm of virtual environments, data modeling serves as the intricate scaffolding upon which simulated realities are constructed. At its core, data modeling involves the systematic organization of digital representations, structuring the information to simulate real-world phenomena with precision and fidelity. This foundational process requires the careful consideration of spatial relationships, object hierarchies, and interactive dynamics, creating a virtual tapestry that mirrors the complexity of the natural world. Advanced data modeling techniques leverage multidimensional databases and spatial data structures, allowing creators to render expansive environments that are both richly detailed and highly interactive. By utilizing cutting-edge tools such as procedural generation, developers can craft vast landscapes and intricate ecosystems that evolve in response to user interactions, simulating the unpredictability and diversity of real-life environments.

The sophistication of modern data models is further enhanced by the integration of real-time analytics and contextual intelligence, which enable simulations to adapt dynamically to user behavior and environmental changes. The use of predictive modeling and data analytics, for instance, allows simulations to anticipate user needs and modify scenarios accordingly, creating an experience that feels uniquely personalized and responsive. This adaptability is crucial not only for gaming and entertainment but also for educational and training simulations where real-time feedback and adjustment can significantly enhance learning outcomes. By drawing on recent advancements in big data and analytics, developers can harness vast datasets to inform the behavior of simulated entities, ensuring that virtual environments remain engaging and relevant.

In crafting these complex models, developers often face the challenge of balancing realism with computational efficiency. To achieve this, they employ a range of optimization techniques, such as level-of-detail rendering and occlusion culling, which ensure that system resources are allocated effectively without compromising on visual fidelity. These techniques allow simulations to maintain high-performance levels even in resource-intensive scenarios, such as large-scale multiplayer environments or simulations requiring intricate physics calculations. The ongoing evolution of graphics processing units (GPUs) and parallel computing further amplifies these capabilities, enabling the creation of simulations that are both visually stunning and operationally efficient.

The interplay between data models and algorithms is pivotal in driving the realism of simulated worlds. Algorithms serve as the engines that power the behavior of simulated objects and environments, dictating how they respond to user inputs and interact with one another. Innovations in algorithmic design, including those inspired by biological systems and natural processes, have led to more lifelike and adaptable simulations. For instance, swarm intelligence and genetic algorithms are employed to simulate complex behaviors such as crowd movements and ecosystem interactions, providing a deeper level of immersion and authenticity. As algorithmic techniques continue to evolve, they unlock new possibilities for creating simulations that not only mimic reality but also extend beyond its boundaries.

As we explore these sophisticated models and algorithms, it is essential to ponder the implications of their application. Questions about ethical usage, data privacy, and the potential for bias in data models prompt ongoing discourse within the field. Developers and researchers must navigate these challenges thoughtfully, ensuring that the simulated realities they create contribute positively to society. By embracing a multidisciplinary approach and fostering collaboration across fields such as computer science, psychology, and ethics, the simulation community can work toward creating environments that are not only technologically advanced but also socially responsible. This collaborative effort will be vital in shaping the future of simulated realities, ensuring they serve as tools for empowerment and enrichment, rather than sources of escapism or division.

Advanced Algorithmic Techniques for Real-Time Simulation

In the realm of real-time simulation, algorithms perform as the silent architects, crafting intricate worlds that respond with immediacy and authenticity. At the heart of this endeavor lies the necessity for algorithms that can process massive datasets and execute complex computations without hesitation. These algorithms must not only function efficiently but must also accommodate the dynamic nature of virtual environments, adapting in real time to the myriad interactions and changes occurring within the simulation. This requires a symbiotic relationship between the algorithmic processes and the underlying data structures, where each algorithm is meticulously tailored to optimize performance and maintain the illusion of a seamless reality.

Recent strides in algorithmic development have ushered in innovative tech-niques that enhance the fidelity and responsiveness of simulations. One such advancement is the deployment of procedural generation, which allows for the creation of vast, detailed landscapes and intricate environmental conditions using relatively simple rule sets. By dynamically generating content on-the-fly, procedural algorithms can produce diverse and expansive virtual worlds with-out the prohibitive resource demands of pre-designed models. This not only enriches the user's experience but also opens new avenues for creativity and exploration in simulation design, providing a canvas that is both vast and varied.

Moreover, the integration of parallel processing techniques has elevated the capabilities of real-time simulations. By distributing computational tasks across multiple processors or cores, simulations can handle complex interactions and render high-quality graphics simultaneously. This approach not only increases the speed and efficiency of simulations but also enables more sophisticated be-haviors and interactions within the virtual environment. As a result, simulations can offer richer, more immersive experiences that captivate users and push the boundaries of what is possible in a digital realm.

Incorporating machine learning algorithms into real-time simulations has also been transformative. These algorithms can analyze and predict user be-havior, allowing the simulation to adapt dynamically to individual preferences and actions. By learning from user interactions, simulations can become more intuitive and personalized, providing an experience that feels uniquely tailored to each participant. Furthermore, machine learning can enhance the realism of non-player characters and environmental responses, creating a more believable and engaging world that mirrors the complexities of reality.

As we continue to explore the potential of these advanced algorithmic tech-niques, it is crucial to consider the broader implications and possibilities they present. How might these innovations reshape our understanding of interac-tion within digital spaces? What ethical considerations arise when simulations become indistinguishable from reality? These questions challenge us to think critically about the future of simulation technology and its impact on society. By embracing diverse perspectives and pushing beyond conventional boundaries, we can unlock new potentials and navigate the uncharted territories of virtual existence.

Integrating AI and Machine Learning in Complex Simulated Ecosystems

Amidst the growing sophistication of simulated ecosystems, the integration of artificial intelligence and machine learning stands as a transformative frontier. These technologies act as the cerebral core of virtual environments, orchestrating the myriad interactions that unfold within them. AI, in particular, brings an unparalleled level of dynamism and adaptability, endowing simulated entities with behaviors that can evolve over time. Machine learning algorithms, on the other hand, enable these entities to glean insights from their virtual surroundings, adapting to changing scenarios with a level of nuance previously unattainable. This symbiotic relationship between AI and machine learning elevates simulations from static constructs to vibrant, ever-evolving universes, facilitating a level of complexity and realism that captures the imagination.

In the realm of complex simulations, one finds intriguing applications of neural networks and reinforcement learning. These advanced methodologies enable virtual entities to learn from their interactions, optimizing their actions to achieve specific goals within the simulation. For instance, in a simulated cityscape, AI-driven characters could learn optimal routes through bustling streets, responding intelligently to changes in traffic patterns and environmental conditions. Such capabilities not only enhance the realism of the simulation but also provide invaluable insights for urban planning and crisis management in the tangible world. By observing the adaptive behaviors of AI within these virtual ecosystems, designers and researchers can glean lessons that inform real-world decision-making.

The role of AI is further amplified when considering the integration of natural language processing within simulations. This technology empowers virtual inhabitants to engage in meaningful dialogue with users, creating an immersive experience that blurs the line between the simulated and the real. Through conversational AI, users can interact with characters in a manner that feels organic and authentic, fostering deeper engagement and emotional connection. This capacity for nuanced communication can be leveraged in educational simulations, where learners engage with historical figures or fictional characters, enhancing their understanding through interactive storytelling and dialogue.

One cannot overlook the impact of AI-driven procedural generation on the richness of simulated environments. This technique allows for the creation of vast, intricate worlds that are not painstakingly crafted by human designers, but rather generated algorithmically, with endless possibilities. By employing AI to analyze patterns and preferences, these environments can be tailored to suit the unique inclinations of each user, offering personalized experiences that resonate on a deeply individual level. The potential for such customization opens new avenues for exploration, allowing users to embark on journeys that are as distinct as their own imaginations.

As AI and machine learning continue to evolve, the horizon for simulated ecosystems expands, inviting us to ponder the ethical and practical ramifications of these technologies. The capacity for AI to learn and adapt raises questions about agency and autonomy within simulated worlds. How do we ensure that these virtual beings act in ways that align with human values and ethics? Such inquiries are not merely academic; they hold profound relevance for the future of simulations as tools for education, entertainment, and societal advancement. By engaging with these questions, readers are encouraged to contemplate the role of AI as both a tool and a creator within the simulated realms, shaping experiences that transcend the boundaries of what is currently possible.

Hardware and infrastructure: Powering high-fidelity experiences

What makes this fascinating is the intricate dance of technology and creativity that underpins the magic of high-fidelity simulations. As we step into these virtual realms, a seamless blend of hardware and infrastructure works tirelessly behind the scenes, orchestrating experiences that blur the lines between reality and illusion. Imagine standing on the precipice of a breathtaking landscape, every detail rendered with astonishing clarity, or engaging in a virtual conversation where distance and latency vanish into thin air. These experiences, rich with sensory depth and interactivity, owe their existence to the sophisticated machinery and networks that power them.

At the heart of these immersive worlds lies a symphony of advanced graphics processing and rendering techniques, pushing pixels to their limits to craft lifelike visuals. But visuals are only part of the equation. The backbone of these virtual interactions extends further, into the realm of network architectures that ensure seamless communication and connectivity, allowing users to share experiences without interruption. And on the horizon, quantum computing promises to revolutionize simulation power, unlocking possibilities that were once the stuff of science fiction. As we journey through this chapter, we will explore how these components interweave to create the high-fidelity experiences that captivate our senses and expand our perception of reality.

Advanced Graphics Processing and Rendering Techniques

The realm of advanced graphics processing and rendering techniques is revolutionizing the fidelity of simulated realities, pushing the boundaries of what we perceive as real. At the heart of this transformation lie graphics processing units (GPUs) that have evolved into powerhouses capable of handling complex computations with unparalleled speed and efficiency. Modern GPUs employ parallel processing architectures that allow for simultaneous calculations, rendering intricate visuals with astonishing detail. This capability is further enhanced by ray tracing technology, which simulates the way light interacts with objects, producing lifelike reflections, shadows, and textures. These advancements enable simulations to mimic the subtle nuances of the physical world, blurring the line between digital and tangible experiences.

Cutting-edge rendering techniques also integrate machine learning algorithms to optimize the creation of realistic environments. Neural networks are now being trained to predict and generate visual data, significantly reducing the computational load traditionally required for high-fidelity graphics. This approach allows for dynamic adaptation of scenes in real-time, creating immersive experiences that respond fluidly to user interactions. Furthermore, procedural generation, powered by AI, is being used to craft expansive and detailed virtual landscapes without the need for manual design, offering vast and diverse environments that evolve based on user engagement. These techniques are not only enhancing visual realism but also providing a canvas for creativity that was previously unimaginable.

The push towards hyper-realistic simulations has also sparked interest in novel rendering paradigms such as voxel rendering and point-based graphics. These methods offer alternative ways to represent three-dimensional objects, each with unique advantages in terms of memory efficiency and the ability to depict fine details. Voxel rendering, for instance, excels at representing complex volumetric data, making it ideal for simulations that require intricate modeling of natural phenomena like smoke or fire. Meanwhile, point-based graphics offer a scalable approach to rendering that accommodates varying levels of detail, ensuring that simulations remain visually coherent across diverse hardware configurations. These innovative approaches highlight the diversity of techniques available to simulation architects and underscore the potential for continued evolution in rendering technologies.

As we advance, quantum computing emerges as a potential game-changer in the landscape of graphics processing. While still in its nascent stages, quantum computing promises exponential increases in processing power, which could unlock new possibilities for rendering techniques that were previously constrained by classical computational limits. The ability to process vast amounts of data simultaneously could lead to simulations with unprecedented complexity and realism. Researchers are already exploring quantum algorithms that could enhance rendering processes, hinting at a future where the visual fidelity of simulations reaches new heights, further challenging our perceptions of reality.

The relentless pursuit of visual perfection also necessitates consideration of the ethical and philosophical dimensions of hyper-realistic simulations. As these technologies evolve, so too do questions about authenticity and the potential for deception. In crafting simulations that are indistinguishable from reality, creators must grapple with the implications of their work, ensuring that these digital experiences serve to enrich rather than mislead. Thoughtful design and

transparency become paramount in navigating these challenges, guiding the responsible development of simulations that honor the delicate balance between
technological innovation and ethical stewardship.

Network Architectures for Seamless Virtual Interactions

The evolution of network architectures has been nothing short of transformative, propelling virtual interactions to dizzying levels of realism and accessibility.
At the heart of this revolution lies the quest for seamlessness, a pursuit fueled
by the need to create virtual environments that mirror the fluidity of our
physical world. Distributed computing models, such as edge computing, have
emerged as pivotal in this landscape. By processing data closer to the user, edge
computing reduces latency, ensuring that virtual experiences are not only vivid
but also immediate. This advancement is particularly crucial in multiplayer
simulations, where lag can disrupt immersion and diminish the sense of shared
reality.

In tandem with edge computing, the integration of 5G technology marks
a significant leap forward. This new generation of wireless technology offers
unprecedented speed and bandwidth, essential for supporting the high data
throughput required by sophisticated simulations. 5G networks enable rapid
data exchange between users and servers, facilitating the smooth rendering of
complex environments and interactions in real-time. As simulations grow in
intricacy and scale, the low latency and high reliability of 5G become indispensable, laying the groundwork for more intricate and interactive virtual worlds.

Yet, as the frontiers of simulation expand, the challenge of data management
becomes more pronounced. The vast amounts of data generated and con-
sumed in virtual spaces necessitate innovative solutions for storage and retrieval.
Blockchain technology, with its decentralized and secure framework, presents
a novel approach to this challenge. By offering a transparent and tamper-proof
method of data verification, blockchains allow for a more trustworthy and
efficient management of virtual transactions and interactions. This not only
enhances data integrity but also fosters new paradigms of user interaction and
collaboration within simulations.

While the technological underpinnings are compelling, the human aspect
remains paramount. Network architectures must be designed with user experience in mind, ensuring that interactions are intuitive and engaging. Virtual
Reality (VR) and Augmented Reality (AR) interfaces are leading this charge,
transforming how users navigate and engage with simulated environments.
These interfaces capitalize on natural human movements, reducing barriers to
entry and making virtual interactions feel more instinctive. As VR and AR
technologies continue to mature, they promise to bridge the gap between the

digital and physical realms, offering users an ever more immersive and authentic experience.

As we stand on the cusp of further advancements, it is essential to consider the broader ramifications of these technologies. How will seamless virtual interactions redefine our social structures, economies, and daily lives? What ethical frameworks must we establish to navigate the complexities of privacy and security in these interconnected spaces? These questions beckon us to look beyond the technical marvels and consider their societal implications, prompting a dialogue that balances innovation with responsibility. By fostering such discussions, we can ensure that the virtual worlds we build are not only technologically advanced but also aligned with our collective values and aspirations.

Quantum Computing and the Future of Simulation Power

Quantum computing stands at the frontier of technological advancements, poised to revolutionize the way we power simulated realities. Unlike classical computers, which process information in binary bits, quantum computers utilize qubits that exist in superposition, allowing them to perform complex calculations at unprecedented speeds. This capability is particularly significant for simulations, where vast amounts of data need to be processed simultaneously to create lifelike experiences. The potential of quantum computing to enhance the computational power required for high-fidelity simulations is immense, offering a glimpse into a future where virtual worlds are indistinguishable from the physical realm.

One of the most promising aspects of quantum computing in simulations is its ability to optimize physics engines and artificial intelligence algorithms. Physics engines, which simulate realistic interactions in virtual environments, require intense computational resources to achieve the nuance and detail seen in real-world physics. Quantum computers, with their ability to handle complex, probabilistic scenarios, can significantly improve these engines' efficiency and accuracy. Similarly, quantum-enhanced AI can manage more sophisticated decision-making processes, leading to more intelligent and responsive virtual entities that enrich the simulated experience.

Incorporating quantum computing into network architectures could redefine the landscape of virtual interactions. Current simulations rely heavily on classical networks, which can suffer from latency issues and bottlenecks, particularly in massively multiplayer online environments. Quantum networks, leveraging principles like entanglement and quantum teleportation, promise near-instantaneous data transmission and robust security protocols. This advancement would ensure seamless interactions within virtual worlds, fostering a sense of presence and immediacy that classical systems struggle to achieve.

While the potential of quantum computing is dazzling, it also presents unique challenges and ethical considerations. The sheer power of quantum simulations could lead to issues of hyper-realism, where distinguishing between simulated and real experiences becomes increasingly difficult. This raises profound questions about consent, identity, and the nature of reality itself. As researchers and developers push the boundaries of quantum technology, a parallel dialogue must occur regarding its responsible application, ensuring that the benefits of these advancements are realized without compromising ethical standards.

Imagining a future where quantum computing has fully integrated with simulation technologies invites exciting possibilities. Consider the scenario of fully immersive historical recreations, where quantum-powered simulations allow individuals to experience past events with unparalleled authenticity. This could transform education, offering visceral understanding through firsthand virtual experiences. Such applications not only underscore the transformative potential of quantum computing but also challenge us to think critically about its role in shaping the future of human experience. As we stand on the brink of this quantum revolution, the path forward demands both innovation and thoughtful deliberation, ensuring a harmonious blend of technology and humanity.

Bringing this chapter to a conclusion, the exploration of the building blocks of simulated reality reveals a tapestry woven from the threads of physics engines, AI, sensory immersion, and robust hardware infrastructure. These elements work in harmony to craft experiences that blur the line between the virtual and the tangible, underscoring the ingenuity and complexity inherent in simulation design. The sophisticated data models and algorithms serve as the backbone, ensuring that these digital realms are both believable and captivating. By delving into the tricks of perception, one gains insight into the nuanced art of making the unreal feel real. This intricate dance between technology and human perception is not just a technical feat but a profound reflection on our desire to transcend the boundaries of the known world. As we ponder the potential of these digital constructs, it invites us to question the very fabric of our reality and the future it holds. With a firm grasp on these foundational concepts, readers are well-prepared to journey forward, contemplating how these building blocks will influence not just individual experiences but also reshape the societal landscapes explored in subsequent chapters.

Chapter Three

Cognitive Science And Perception In Simulations

At the dawn of a new era in technological evolution, a young game designer named Alex found themselves lost in the intricate landscapes of a virtual reality they had painstakingly crafted. As Alex navigated these digital realms, they marveled at how effortlessly their senses were beguiled, each pixel and sound wave interwoven to mimic the essence of life. This world, though artificial, felt astonishingly real, urging the question: What is reality if not the tapestry woven by our perceptions? This question, a beacon of curiosity, invites us to explore the profound relationship between our cognition and the simulated worlds we create.

Our brains, those enigmatic conductors of experience, hold the key to understanding how we interpret both the tangible and the virtual. By deciphering the brain's role in constructing reality, we unlock the secrets to creating simulations that not only entertain but deeply engage our senses. These virtual experiences, crafted with precision, tap into our sensory perceptions, manipulating them to conjure environments that feel as genuine as our own world. As we journey through this chapter, we will unravel the mechanisms that allow simulations to hijack our senses, crafting believable experiences that blur the line between the real and the imagined.

Yet, the allure of simulated realities extends beyond mere sensory trickery. Within their digital confines, questions of memory and identity surface, challenging our self-conception. As we immerse ourselves for extended periods, these virtual environments shape not just what we see or hear, but our very sense of self. This chapter delves into the psychological effects of such immersion, exploring the impact on our psyche and the deeper philosophical implications for our understanding of identity. As we venture into this exploration, we begin to see how simulations hold the potential not only to reflect our reality but to transform it, reshaping the human experience in ways we are only beginning to comprehend.

The brain's role in interpreting reality

Reflect on a time when you were so engrossed in a movie or a video game that the boundary between the screen and reality seemed to blur. This moment of deep immersion is not merely a trick of the mind but a testament to the brain's remarkable ability to interpret and construct reality. Our brains act as master architects, weaving sensory inputs into coherent worlds, whether they come from the physical environment or a digital one. This fascinating dance between perception and reality is at the heart of our experience, and understanding it is crucial in the age of simulations. As we venture further into creating virtual realities, the brain's role becomes even more significant, serving as both a canvas and a critic of these constructed worlds.

The brain's interpretation of reality is a complex symphony of neural mechanisms, cognitive biases, and adaptive capabilities. It processes sensory information with astonishing speed and accuracy, yet remains susceptible to illusions and biases that can be exploited by simulations. Cognitive biases, those mental shortcuts that shape our perception, play a pivotal role in how we perceive simulated environments, often enhancing their believability. Meanwhile, the brain's neuroplastic nature allows it to adapt to these artificial contexts, sometimes with surprising ease. This interplay between the brain's natural processes and the engineered experiences of simulations sets the stage for a deeper exploration of how our sensory and cognitive faculties are engaged, and sometimes challenged, in virtual environments.

Neural Mechanisms of Sensory Processing in Virtual Environments

In the realm of virtual environments, the brain's ability to process sensory information takes center stage, offering a fascinating window into the interplay between technology and human perception. At the heart of this relationship are neural mechanisms that decipher a barrage of stimuli, both real and artificially generated. The human brain operates as a sophisticated interpreter, transforming electrical signals from sensory organs into coherent experiences. In virtual settings, this process is manipulated to create believable illusions, immersing users in worlds crafted from pixels and codes. Advanced techniques in virtual reality (VR) capitalize on the brain's inherent tendencies, such as its proclivity for pattern recognition and spatial awareness, to fabricate environments that feel tangibly real. By harnessing the brain's neural circuitry, designers can craft experiences that are not only visually convincing but also resonate on an emotional and cognitive level.

Central to this sensory processing is the concept of presence, a psychological state where individuals perceive themselves as being part of a virtual environment. This is achieved through meticulously synchronized multisensory inputs that engage the brain's capacity for integration. When visual, auditory, and tactile signals are harmonized, the brain constructs a seamless narrative that blurs the line between actual and virtual. Cutting-edge VR systems employ techniques such as binaural audio, haptic feedback, and motion tracking to amplify this sensation of presence. For instance, the use of spatial audio, which replicates the way sound waves interact with physical space, tricks the auditory system into believing sounds are emanating from specific directions, enhancing the spatial realism of a virtual scenario.

Neuroplasticity, the brain's remarkable ability to reorganize itself by forming new neural connections, plays a pivotal role in adapting to virtual contexts. As individuals spend more time in simulated environments, their brains begin to adjust, refining sensory processing pathways to better navigate these novel experiences. This adaptability is not only a testament to the brain's resilience but also a cornerstone for developing more immersive simulations. Researchers are exploring how prolonged exposure to virtual realities can induce long-term changes in neural architecture, potentially offering therapeutic applications such as rehabilitation for sensory processing disorders. By understanding and leveraging neuroplasticity, simulation architects can design environments that cater to specific cognitive and sensory needs, tailoring experiences that facilitate learning and rehabilitation.

The influence of cognitive biases on sensory processing in virtual environments cannot be overlooked. These biases, which are mental shortcuts our brains use to make sense of complex information, can be exploited to enhance or manipulate the perception of reality. For example, the brain's tendency to fill in gaps in visual information, known as the Gestalt principle, can be used to create the illusion of completeness in virtual spaces, even when graphical details are sparse. By understanding these biases, designers can create more efficient and resource-effective simulations that maintain high levels of immersion without requiring exhaustive detail. This understanding also opens avenues for creating experiences that challenge and expand cognitive perceptions, offering users new ways of interacting with and understanding virtual worlds.

As virtual environments become increasingly sophisticated, the psychological impact of extended immersion becomes a critical area of exploration. The
brain's continuous engagement with virtual stimuli can lead to profound shifts
in perception and cognitive function. While these changes present exciting
opportunities for enhancing creativity and learning, they also pose potential
risks, such as sensory overload or altered real-world perception. By studying
the neural mechanisms at play, researchers can develop strategies to mitigate
these effects, ensuring that the benefits of virtual experiences are maximized
while minimizing potential drawbacks. This balance between innovation and
caution is vital in the evolving landscape of simulation technology, guiding the
development of environments that are both exhilarating and safe.

The Influence of Cognitive Biases on Perceived Reality

Cognitive biases, those mental shortcuts our brains use to process information,
play a fascinating role in how we perceive reality, and their influence becomes
even more pronounced within virtual environments. These biases are deeply
ingrained in our cognitive architecture, shaping the way we interpret sensory
data and make decisions. When immersed in simulations, our brains apply these
biases to the virtual stimuli, often leading to experiences that feel as authentic as
those in the physical world. Consider the confirmation bias, where individuals
tend to favor information that aligns with their preexisting beliefs. In a virtual
setting, this bias can lead users to interpret simulated events in a way that reinforces their expectations, making the experience more convincing and engaging.
This intertwining of cognitive biases with virtual stimuli not only enhances
realism but also opens doors to more personalized and impactful simulations.

The malleability of perception through cognitive biases is not merely theoretical; it has practical applications that can be harnessed to craft more effective simulations. For instance, the anchoring effect, where initial information
disproportionately influences subsequent judgments, can be strategically employed in educational simulations to guide learning outcomes. By presenting
foundational concepts early in a simulation, users are more likely to integrate
and build upon this knowledge throughout their experience. Similarly, the
availability heuristic, which relies on immediate examples that come to mind,
can be used in virtual training scenarios to enhance decision-making processes. By designing simulations that highlight critical events or outcomes, users
can develop a more intuitive grasp of complex subjects, leading to improved
real-world application.

Recent advancements in cognitive science have shed light on how these biases
can be both a limitation and a tool within simulated environments. Research
reveals that while biases can distort reality, they also offer a framework for

understanding and predicting user behavior. In therapeutic simulations designed for mental health, for example, awareness of cognitive biases is crucial. Through carefully crafted virtual interactions, individuals can be guided to recognize and challenge their biases, leading to therapeutic breakthroughs. This approach leverages the same biases that might initially distort perception to facilitate personal growth and cognitive flexibility. By understanding the dual nature of biases as both challenges and opportunities, simulation architects can create environments that not only replicate reality but also serve as platforms for cognitive transformation.

As we explore the frontier of virtual experiences, it's essential to consider the ethical implications of manipulating cognitive biases. While simulations offer unprecedented opportunities for education, entertainment, and therapy, they also raise questions about consent and manipulation. Can virtual environments that exploit biases to create more immersive experiences inadvertently lead to manipulation or misinformation? Addressing these questions requires a nuanced understanding of both the power and responsibility inherent in simulation design. The challenge lies in balancing the potential benefits of bias-driven realism with the ethical obligation to protect users from unintended consequences. This delicate equilibrium underscores the importance of ethical frameworks in guiding the development and deployment of simulations.

Imagining the future, one might envision simulations that not only accommodate but actively adapt to individual cognitive biases, creating tailor-made experiences that resonate deeply with each user. Imagine a virtual museum tour that adjusts its narrative based on the visitor's interests and preconceptions, or an educational simulation that dynamically alters its complexity to match the learner's cognitive profile. Such innovations could revolutionize personalized learning and interactive storytelling, transforming how we engage with digital content. By embracing the complexity of cognitive biases, simulation architects have the opportunity to craft experiences that are not only more authentic but also profoundly transformative, bridging the gap between virtual and tangible realities in ways that were once unimaginable.

Neuroplasticity and Adaptation to Simulated Contexts

In the fascinating realm of virtual environments, the concept of neuroplasticity emerges as a pivotal force that enables the human brain to adapt and thrive within simulated contexts. Neuroplasticity refers to the brain's remarkable ability to reorganize itself by forming new neural connections throughout life. This adaptability is the cornerstone of how individuals can acclimate to virtual realities that, at first glance, may seem foreign or unconventional. As we engage with simulated environments, our brains are not merely passive observers but active participants that continuously evolve, enabling us to navigate and interact with these digital landscapes more effectively.

Recent studies in cognitive neuroscience reveal that repeated exposure to virtual environments can lead to structural and functional changes in the brain. For instance, research has demonstrated that individuals who frequently immerse themselves in virtual reality games or simulations exhibit enhanced spatial navigation skills and improved hand-eye coordination. These cognitive enhancements are attributed to changes in the brain's neural circuitry, showcasing the tangible benefits of neuroplasticity. The brain's capacity to adapt means that virtual environments can be designed to not only entertain but also educate and rehabilitate, offering promising avenues for therapeutic applications such as cognitive rehabilitation and skill acquisition.

Understanding the brain's adaptability opens up intriguing possibilities for crafting virtual experiences that cater to individual needs. Personalized simulations that adjust based on real-time feedback from neural activity could revolutionize how we approach learning and development. Imagine simulations that dynamically evolve as they gauge a user's cognitive state, offering tailored challenges and stimuli to optimize engagement and growth. Such innovations could harness neuroplasticity to foster accelerated learning and skill mastery, pushing the boundaries of what education and training can achieve in a digital age.

The implications of neuroplasticity in virtual environments extend beyond individual growth to societal applications. As our brains adapt to simulated realities, there is potential for fostering greater empathy and understanding across diverse cultures and perspectives. Virtual experiences designed to simulate life in different cultural contexts could lead to profound shifts in perspective, promoting global empathy and collaboration. The brain's capacity to change suggests that simulations can be powerful tools for bridging divides and fostering a more interconnected world, where understanding and cooperation are paramount.

Yet, as we marvel at the brain's adaptability, it is crucial to consider the ethical dimensions of such profound changes. Prolonged exposure to virtual environments raises questions about the long-term impacts on mental health and identity. While neuroplasticity offers vast potential for growth and development, it also necessitates a careful balance to prevent adverse effects such as addiction or detachment from reality. As we continue to explore the frontiers of virtual experiences, a thoughtful approach that prioritizes mental well-being and ethical considerations will be essential to harnessing the full potential of neuroplasticity for human benefit. In this dynamic interplay between brain and simulation, the path forward is one of discovery, responsibility, and boundless possibility.

Creating believable experiences: How simulations hack human senses

Let's dive into the heart of how simulations craft experiences so convincingly real that they blur the lines between the tangible and the virtual. At the core of this mesmerizing dance is the human brain, a master of perception and interpretation. Our senses, gateways to the world, become pliable tools in the hands of simulation architects. These designers employ sophisticated sensory deception techniques, weaving intricate tapestries of sight, sound, touch, and even smell to construct alternate realities. By commandeering these senses, simulations create an illusion so seamless that the mind readily accepts the virtual as genuine. This manipulation of perception is not merely a technological feat; it's a profound exploration of cognitive science and the plasticity of human experience.

As we transition deeper into this topic, the interplay between multisensory integration and neurological pathways reveals the delicate balance required to maintain the illusion of presence. Understanding the brain's role in synthesizing various sensory inputs is crucial for crafting environments where virtual and real worlds converge. Each sensory thread, meticulously woven, contributes to a rich tapestry that captivates and engages the mind. Yet, this raises intriguing questions about the psychological implications of sustained immersion in these crafted worlds. The journey through these subtopics will illuminate the sophisticated symphony of sensory manipulation, offering insights into how simulations hack our senses to construct believable, compelling experiences.

Sensory Deception Techniques and Their Psychological Impact

Human perception is a remarkable interplay between sensory input and cognitive processing, creating the illusion of a seamless reality. In simulated environments, sensory deception techniques exploit this intricate relationship, crafting experiences that are both convincing and immersive. By manipulating visual, auditory, and tactile inputs, simulations can effectively "trick" the brain into perceiving a fabricated world as genuine. This is achieved through advanced algorithms that synchronize sensory cues, creating a cohesive and believable experience. For instance, virtual reality headsets employ high resolution displays and spatial audio to envelop users in a 360-degree environment, while haptic feedback devices simulate texture and force, enhancing the sensation of touch. These techniques not only heighten realism but also deepen user engagement, allowing for a more profound connection with the virtual landscape.

The psychological impact of these sensory deceptions is profound, as they tap into the brain's natural propensity to fill gaps in sensory information. This phenomenon, known as perceptual filling-in, allows simulations to present incomplete data that the mind automatically completes, creating a full-fledged experience. For example, in a virtual forest, the rustling of leaves might be suggested by sound rather than visual cues, yet the brain integrates these inputs to produce a vivid mental image. Such multisensory integration is essential for maintaining the illusion of presence and continuity within a simulated setting. However, the reliance on these techniques raises questions about the line between perception and reality, challenging users to discern where one ends and the other begins.

Recent advances in neuroscience have uncovered specific neural pathways responsible for processing sensory information, offering insights into how simulations can more effectively engage the brain. By understanding these pathways, designers can tailor experiences to align with the brain's natural processing patterns, enhancing the illusion of presence. One emerging technique involves leveraging predictive coding, where the brain anticipates sensory input based on past experiences. By aligning simulations with these predictive mechanisms, designers can create environments that feel intuitive and familiar, even when entirely novel. This approach not only enhances user satisfaction but also opens up new avenues for personalized experiences that adapt to individual perceptual tendencies.

The potential applications of sensory deception techniques extend beyond entertainment and into realms such as education and therapy. In educational settings, simulations can create immersive learning environments that stimulate curiosity and engagement, allowing students to explore complex concepts through experiential learning. Meanwhile, therapeutic applications can harness these techniques to provide exposure therapy for phobias or to simulate social interactions for individuals with autism, offering controlled environments where users can safely confront and overcome challenges. By carefully calibrating sensory inputs, these applications can create transformative experiences that yield lasting benefits, illustrating the vast potential for positive impact.

As the field of simulation continues to evolve, it is crucial to consider the ethical implications of sensory deception. While the ability to create immersive experiences offers numerous benefits, it also poses risks such as addiction and detachment from the physical world. To mitigate these concerns, designers and researchers must establish ethical guidelines that prioritize user well-being, ensuring that simulations remain tools for enhancement rather than escapism. Encouraging users to reflect on their experiences and maintain a balanced relationship with both virtual and real-world environments can foster a healthier interaction with simulation technology. By embracing a holistic approach that considers both the psychological and ethical dimensions, the future of sensory deception in simulations holds the promise of enriching human experience while safeguarding against potential pitfalls.

Multisensory Integration in Virtual Environments

In the intricate dance of virtual environments, multisensory integration emerges as a pivotal element in crafting convincingly immersive experiences. This process—the brain's seamless fusion of sensory inputs—enables users to perceive virtual worlds as tangible and authentic. Researchers have made significant strides in understanding how to manipulate these sensory cues to create a cohesive illusion of presence. By synchronizing auditory, visual, tactile, and even olfactory stimuli, simulations can transcend the limitations of individual senses, achieving a holistic experience that feels remarkably real. This meticulous orchestration of sensory data not only enhances immersion but also facilitates deeper engagement with the virtual environment, fostering a connection that is both visceral and intellectual.

One fascinating application of multisensory integration is in virtual reality therapies, where patients experience environments that stimulate healing or relaxation. For instance, virtual nature walks that combine realistic sounds of rustling leaves with gentle breezes from strategically placed fans can reduce stress and improve mental well-being. The synergy between senses amplifies the therapeutic effects, proving more effective than traditional methods. This integration is not just about layering sensory inputs but about understanding the nuances of how they interact to produce a compound experience greater than the sum of its parts. Such knowledge has profound implications for designing educational tools, where engaging multiple senses can lead to more effective and memorable learning experiences.

The science behind multisensory integration leverages the brain's inherent capacity to resolve discrepancies between conflicting sensory information. The McGurk effect, a well-documented phenomenon, illustrates how visual and auditory inputs can merge to create a perception that aligns with neither input alone. Virtual simulations exploit such phenomena to enhance realism, ensuring that even minor inconsistencies do not disrupt the user's sense of immersion. By precisely calibrating these sensory elements, developers can guide users' perceptions, crafting environments that convincingly blur the line between virtual and physical realms. This manipulation of perception is a testament to the intricate interplay between technology and neuroscience, where understanding the brain's processing mechanisms unlocks new dimensions of experience.

Emerging technologies like haptic feedback and scent generators are pushing the boundaries of multisensory integration further. These innovations allow users to feel textures or smell environments, deepening the illusion of reality. Haptic suits, for example, provide tactile responses that mimic real-world sensations, such as the resistance of a virtual object or the impact of a virtual projectile. These advancements are transforming fields such as gaming and training simulations, where the addition of tactile and olfactory cues can lead to more immersive and effective scenarios. As technology continues to evolve, the potential for creating experiences that engage all senses becomes increasingly feasible, opening new avenues for exploration and interaction.

As we venture into this multisensory frontier, it is essential to consider the broader implications of our creations. Questions arise about the ethical responsibilities in crafting environments that can so profoundly affect human perception and behavior. How should developers balance immersion with potential sensory overload? What safeguards are necessary to prevent manipulation or misuse of these technologies? These considerations remind us that while the allure of multisensory integration is undeniable, the power it wields must be harnessed with care and foresight. By engaging with these questions, we not only enrich our understanding of virtual environments but also ensure that the advancements we pursue ultimately serve the greater good.

Neurological Pathways and the Illusion of Presence

The tantalizing domain of neurological pathways and the illusion of presence in simulations offers a fascinating glimpse into how our brains construct reality. At the heart of this exploration lies the concept of presence— the sensation of being truly 'there' in a virtual environment. This profound feeling is a result of intricate interactions within our neural networks, which translate sensory inputs into immersive experiences. As the brain strives to make sense of the information it receives, it employs mechanisms honed by thousands of years of evolution, which simulations can skillfully manipulate. By understanding these neural processes, creators of virtual worlds can craft experiences that blur the line between the tangible and the virtual, offering users an unparalleled sense of immersion.

One of the cornerstones of achieving presence is the brain's ability to synthesize multisensory information into a cohesive whole. This process, known as multisensory integration, relies heavily on the brain's ability to reconcile disparate sensory data into a unified experience that feels real. When virtual environments adeptly synchronize visual, auditory, and tactile stimuli, they can activate the brain's natural predilection for creating a reality from these inputs. For instance, when the visual cues of a virtual landscape are paired with spatial audio and haptic feedback, the brain weaves these into a tapestry that feels authentic, making users believe they are indeed part of the simulation.

Cutting-edge research has delved into the specific neurological pathways that underpin this phenomenon, revealing how certain brain regions are pivotal in sustaining the illusion of presence. The parietal cortex, for example, plays a crucial role in integrating sensory information, while the prefrontal cortex helps manage the expectations and predictions that guide our perception. Recent studies employing functional MRI scans have shown how these regions light up in response to well-designed simulations, highlighting their involvement in constructing a convincing sense of presence. As scientists continue to unravel these complexities, they provide simulation architects with invaluable insights into how to push the boundaries of immersive technology.

Yet, the art of crafting presence in simulations is not without its challenges. The human brain is remarkably skilled at detecting inconsistencies, and even minor discrepancies between sensory inputs can shatter the illusion of being in a virtual world. This demands a meticulous attention to detail from simulation designers, who must ensure that elements such as latency, resolution, and sensory feedback are harmonized to maintain the suspension of disbelief. Emerging technologies, such as advanced haptic devices and real-time rendering algorithms, offer promising avenues to address these challenges, enabling creators to construct simulations that are not only visually stunning but also neurologically convincing.

The quest to perfect the illusion of presence raises intriguing questions about the nature of reality and perception. If simulations can evoke such convincing sensations of presence, what does this imply about the malleability of our perceived reality? Could these virtual experiences alter our perceptions of the physical world, or even our understanding of self? By inviting readers to ponder these questions, we not only deepen our appreciation of the neurological underpinnings of presence but also inspire contemplation on the broader implications of living in a world where the virtual and the real increasingly intertwine.

Memory and identity in virtual environments

Think about an instance where you found yourself lost in a story, so engrossed that the line between the narrative and your reality blurred. In simulated environments, this boundary is not merely crossed but redefined, as virtual worlds become arenas where memory and identity are not only experienced but actively constructed and reconstructed. In these crafted realities, individuals weave personal narratives that can be as vivid and meaningful as those formed in the tangible world. Simulations offer a unique canvas for the human mind, allowing for the creation of experiences that can impact one's sense of self. As users navigate these digital landscapes, they engage in a delicate dance between what is real and what is imagined, challenging the very essence of identity. These virtual experiences, laden with emotional and cognitive significance, beckon us to question how memories formed in such spaces influence who we are and who we might become.

As we journey deeper into the realm of virtual environments, the persistence of these digital memories emerges as a powerful force, shaping identity in unexpected ways. The fluidity of self within these spaces offers a playground for experimentation, where altered identities can be explored without the constraints of physical reality. This malleable sense of self raises intriguing questions about the continuity of identity and the potential for transformation within the digital sphere. How do these experiences inform our understanding of memory and identity, and what implications do they hold for the future of human consciousness? By examining these themes, we gain insight into the profound psychological impact of extended immersion in virtual environments, setting the stage for a rich exploration of personal and collective identity in the age of simulation.

Constructing Personal Narratives in Simulated Worlds

In the realm of simulated environments, the creation of personal narratives is a pivotal aspect of user experience, offering individuals the opportunity to craft identities and stories that transcend their everyday lives. This process taps into our innate desire to construct and convey personal histories, a fundamental aspect of human nature that simulations enhance by providing a malleable canvas for self-expression. With the rapid progression of technology, simulations have become increasingly adept at facilitating these narratives, offering a myriad of possibilities for users to explore alternate identities and scenarios. Through intricate world-building and interactive storytelling, simulations enable users to weave complex narratives that mirror, amplify, or entirely reimagine their real-world experiences, infusing them with new dimensions of meaning and significance.

Advancements in artificial intelligence and machine learning further enrich these narrative experiences by allowing simulations to adapt dynamically to user inputs. These technologies can tailor storylines to fit individual preferences, creating a personalized experience that feels uniquely authentic to each user. As a result, users are not only participants but co-creators of their virtual narratives, a phenomenon that significantly enhances engagement and emotional investment. Moreover, such personalized storytelling can foster a deeper understanding of one's own desires, motivations, and personal growth by presenting challenges and outcomes that reflect the user's choices and actions within the simulated environment.

The persistence of virtual memories plays a crucial role in shaping these personal narratives, as they often become interwoven with one's sense of self and identity. Virtual experiences, particularly when they evoke strong emotions or involve significant achievements, can leave lasting impressions that influence an individual's perception of themselves and their capabilities. This blurring of virtual and real memories can have profound implications for identity formation, encouraging users to reflect on how these experiences contribute to their overall life story. It raises intriguing questions about the nature of memory and reality, prompting considerations of whether virtual experiences hold the same weight as their real-world counterparts in shaping who we are.

The concept of altered identity within virtual realms introduces a fascinating dynamic, where users can experiment with different facets of their personality or entirely new personas. This fluidity allows for exploration and experimentation, challenging traditional notions of fixed identity and presenting opportunities for personal growth and self-discovery. By embodying various roles, users can gain insights into different perspectives and social dynamics, fostering empathy and resilience. This transformative potential underscores the value of simulations as tools for reflection and self-improvement, offering a safe space for users to navigate complexities of identity without real-world repercussions.

Despite the myriad benefits, constructing personal narratives in simulated worlds also invites contemplation of ethical and psychological considerations. The potential for virtual experiences to overshadow real-life interactions or lead to dependency raises questions about the balance between virtual and physical existence. Simulations must be designed with awareness of these challenges, ensuring they enrich users' lives without compromising their connection to reality. As we continue to explore the possibilities of simulated worlds, it is imperative to strike a harmonious balance, leveraging the creative potential of personal narratives while maintaining a grounded sense of self. Through thoughtful design and mindful engagement, simulations can become powerful platforms for personal and collective storytelling, offering users the tools to craft meaningful narratives that resonate on both virtual and real-world stages.

The Persistence of Virtual Memories and Their Impact on Identity

In the realm of virtual environments, the formation and persistence of memories have profound implications for one's sense of self. As technology advances, these digital experiences increasingly mirror the vividness and complexity of real-life memories. The human brain, with its remarkable capacity for memory, does not inherently differentiate between memories of physical events and those crafted in virtual spaces. This convergence raises intriguing questions about the extent to which virtual memories can shape identity. Recent studies suggest that virtual experiences can leave enduring impressions, influencing how individuals perceive themselves and their past. As these memories become more intertwined with personal narratives, they contribute to the evolving tapestry of identity, reshaping self-perception and personal history in significant ways.

The persistence of virtual memories is not merely a byproduct of technological immersion but a testament to the brain's adaptability. Virtual environments, designed with increasing sophistication, engage the brain's memory systems in ways similar to physical experiences. This engagement is not limited to visual stimuli; it encompasses multisensory inputs that enrich the realism of virtual encounters. By harnessing cutting-edge neuroimaging techniques, researchers have begun to map how these experiences are encoded and stored, offering insights into the neural processes that underpin memory formation. Such research has profound implications for understanding memory's fluidity, suggesting that virtual environments might serve as a canvas for memory enhancement or rehabilitation, presenting opportunities to address cognitive impairments or enhance learning.

As virtual memories imprint themselves upon identity, they also introduce new dimensions to the concept of self. The fluidity of identity in virtual spaces allows for exploration and experimentation beyond the constraints of physical reality. In these environments, individuals can craft identities that reflect aspirational aspects of themselves, fostering growth and self-discovery. This fluidity, while empowering, also presents challenges regarding authenticity and coherence in identity formation. As virtual and physical experiences intertwine, distinguishing between them becomes more complex, prompting philosophical inquiries into what constitutes the "true" self. These questions invite a reevaluation of identity, urging individuals to consider the multifaceted nature of their existence and the role of virtual experiences in shaping it.

The impact of virtual memories extends beyond individual identity, influencing social dynamics and relationships. In virtual worlds, shared experiences can foster connections and communities that transcend geographical boundaries. These connections, grounded in shared virtual memories, can be as meaningful and enduring as those formed in physical spaces. The potential for virtual environments to facilitate social bonding and empathy is significant, offering avenues for collaborative problem-solving and cultural exchange. As these virtual communities grow, they challenge traditional notions of belonging and community, prompting a reconsideration of the social fabric that binds individuals together.

As we navigate the complexities of virtual memories and identity, it is crucial to consider practical implications and strategies for harnessing their potential. One approach is to design virtual environments that prioritize positive experiences and personal growth, fostering memories that contribute constructively to identity. This involves creating spaces that encourage exploration, creativity, and collaboration, while also providing tools for reflection and self-assessment.

By consciously shaping the narratives that emerge from virtual experiences, individuals can cultivate a sense of agency and coherence in their personal development. As we continue to explore the interplay between virtual memories and identity, we are invited to envision a future where these digital experiences enrich and expand the human experience, offering new pathways for personal and societal advancement.

Altered Identity and the Fluidity of Self in Virtual Environments

As individuals immerse themselves in virtual environments, they encounter an opportunity to explore and reinvent their identities in ways that challenge traditional notions of self. These digital realms offer a playground for identity experimentation, where users can adopt new personas, roles, and characteristics distinct from those in their physical lives. This fluidity of self is facilitated by the malleability of virtual avatars, allowing individuals to transcend real-world limitations and express aspects of their personality that might otherwise remain dormant. Such flexibility can lead to profound introspection and self-discovery, as users engage with different facets of their identity, each experience contributing to a richer understanding of the self. This phenomenon is not merely theoretical; it is supported by research indicating that virtual interactions can influence self-perception and personal development in meaningful ways.

In these environments, the boundaries between the virtual and the real begin to blur, impacting how individuals perceive their own identity. Studies have shown that the experiences and memories formed in virtual spaces can be as vivid and enduring as those formed in the physical world. This persistence of virtual memories has significant implications for identity construction, as individuals begin to integrate these experiences into their self-narratives. The ability to carry memories across both digital and physical realms creates a complex tapestry of experiences that shape who we are, challenging the notion that identity is static. As users navigate multiple realities, they may find themselves developing hybrid identities, where elements from both worlds intermingle to form a cohesive sense of self.

The fluidity of identity in virtual environments also raises intriguing questions about authenticity and self-expression. Are the personas we create in virtual worlds authentic extensions of ourselves, or do they represent idealized versions shaped by the affordances of digital platforms? This question invites deeper reflection on the nature of authenticity and how it is constructed in environments that allow for limitless reinvention. Some scholars argue that virtual identities can be seen as authentic expressions, as they often reflect genuine desires and aspirations that may not be feasible in the physical world.

Conversely, others caution against equating virtual personas with authenticity, emphasizing the potential for digital environments to obscure or distort one's true self.

As virtual environments become more sophisticated, the psychological impact of inhabiting multiple identities simultaneously becomes a critical area of inquiry. Extended immersion in these worlds can lead to a phenomenon known as "digital dissociation," where individuals may struggle to reconcile their virtual and physical identities. This can result in both positive and negative outcomes, from increased empathy and understanding to potential identity confusion and detachment from reality. Understanding these dynamics is crucial for designing virtual experiences that not only entertain but also promote psychological well-being. By fostering environments that support healthy identity exploration and integration, developers can create simulations that enhance, rather than complicate, our understanding of self.

To harness the transformative potential of fluid identities in virtual environments, developers and users alike must approach these spaces with intentionality and mindfulness. Encouraging users to reflect on their digital experiences and their impact on identity can foster a more conscious engagement with virtual worlds. Developers can support this by designing experiences that encourage self-reflection and offer tools for users to document and process their virtual journeys. By doing so, the exploration of identity in virtual environments can become a powerful tool for personal growth and self-awareness, enriching our understanding of who we are in both digital and physical realms. This approach not only enhances the immersive experience but also ensures that the exploration of identity remains a beneficial and enriching endeavor.

The psychological impact of extended immersion

Imagine waking up one morning to find yourself in a world indistinguishable from your dreams, where the boundaries between the virtual and the tangible blur into oblivion. In this realm, the human mind becomes both canvas and creator, sculpting experiences that defy the laws of physics and challenge the very notion of reality. As we venture deeper into these digital landscapes, it becomes essential to understand not just how they enchant us, but also the profound psychological effects they imprint upon our consciousness. The allure of simulated environments often lies in their ability to craft compelling narratives and experiences, but what happens when the line between these experiences and our own identities begins to fade? The psychological impact of extended immersion in such worlds is a frontier that beckons exploration, offering insights into our emotional resilience and the transformative potential of virtual identities.

As the mind navigates these expansive digital realms, it faces unique challenges and opportunities. Emotional resilience is put to the test as individuals
adapt to experiences that can evoke powerful emotions and alter perceptions
of self. Meanwhile, the cognitive load imposed by these immersive experiences
can shape mental health in unexpected ways, influencing thought patterns and
emotional well-being over time. The mind's ability to distinguish between virtual and actual memories may also become compromised, leading to fascinating
yet potentially disorienting shifts in memory and perception. This journey
into the heart of digital immersion unveils a complex tapestry of psychological
effects, inviting us to explore the delicate dance between the virtual and the real,
and consider the profound implications for our identities in both worlds.

Emotional Resilience and Identity Transformation in Virtual Worlds

In the fascinating realm of virtual environments, the transformation of identity
and the cultivation of emotional resilience stand out as pivotal phenomena.
Virtual worlds offer a unique tapestry for self-exploration, allowing individuals
to adopt new personas and engage in experiences that might be unattainable
in their everyday lives. This phenomenon, often termed as "identity fluidity,"
can lead to profound shifts in self-perception and personal growth. By stepping
into different roles and scenarios, individuals can experiment with facets of their
personality, gain fresh perspectives, and potentially enhance their emotional
resilience. Recent studies suggest that these virtual identity experiments can
fortify one's ability to adapt to real-world challenges, fostering a robust psychological framework that thrives on flexibility and open-mindedness.

The interplay between a user's virtual and real-world identities can also catalyze significant personal development. As individuals navigate diverse virtual
landscapes, they encounter scenarios that test their emotional responses and
decision-making skills. This process not only enhances cognitive flexibility but
also enriches one's understanding of personal strengths and vulnerabilities. For
instance, participating in cooperative virtual challenges can improve teamwork
skills, while solo quests might bolster self-reliance and confidence. The adaptability cultivated in these simulated environments transfers into the real world,
where individuals find themselves better equipped to handle stress and uncertainty.

A compelling aspect of virtual worlds is their capacity to act as safe spaces
for emotional exploration and processing. In these environments, users can
confront fears, explore aspirations, and rehearse coping strategies without the
repercussions faced in reality. This unique feature of virtual experiences can lead
to increased emotional intelligence, as users learn to identify and manage their

emotions more effectively. Furthermore, the immersive nature of these simulations facilitates a deeper engagement with one's emotional landscape, paving the way for healing and growth. The emotional resilience built through these experiences empowers individuals to face real-world adversities with greater fortitude and composure.

Virtual environments also serve as fertile grounds for cultivating empathy and understanding. By allowing individuals to step into the shoes of others, these simulations promote a profound appreciation for diverse perspectives and experiences. This empathetic engagement can lead to better interpersonal relationships and a more harmonious coexistence in the real world. Additionally, as users interact with a diverse array of virtual characters and cultures, they develop a nuanced understanding of global issues and human behavior. These insights are invaluable in fostering a more inclusive and compassionate society, where individuals are more attuned to the needs and experiences of others.

To harness the transformative potential of virtual worlds effectively, it is essential to approach these experiences with intentionality and mindfulness. Users can design their virtual journeys to align with personal growth objectives, selecting environments and challenges that resonate with their aspirations and values. By setting clear goals and reflecting on their experiences, individuals can maximize the benefits of identity transformation and emotional resilience in virtual worlds. This deliberate engagement not only enriches the virtual experience but also ensures that the insights and skills gained translate seamlessly into everyday life, empowering individuals to navigate the complexities of the modern world with confidence and grace.

Cognitive Load and Its Long-Term Effects on Mental Health

The interplay between cognitive load and mental well-being within simulated environments is a fascinating frontier of study, revealing both opportunities and challenges. Cognitive load refers to the mental effort required to process information, and in virtual worlds, this load can be significantly amplified due to the richness and complexity of the simulated experiences. As individuals navigate these digital landscapes, their brains are tasked with processing a deluge of sensory inputs, leading to both cognitive stimulation and potential fatigue. This heightened engagement can enhance cognitive flexibility and problem-solving skills, offering substantial benefits for personal and professional growth. Nevertheless, extended exposure without adequate mental rest can lead to cognitive overload, akin to burnout, where the brain's processing capabilities are overwhelmed, potentially affecting mental health.

Recent studies have highlighted the nuanced effects of prolonged immersion in virtual realities on cognitive functions. While short-term exposure can enhance memory retention and spatial awareness, continuous engagement without breaks may disrupt these cognitive benefits, resulting in decreased attention spans and impaired decision-making abilities. The brain, accustomed to filtering real-world stimuli, might struggle to differentiate between pertinent and extraneous information in a virtual setting. This difficulty can lead to cognitive fatigue, manifesting as reduced concentration and memory distortions. It's essential to consider these dynamics when designing simulations, ensuring they are structured to promote cognitive health rather than detract from it.

The long-term implications of cognitive load in simulations are particularly pertinent when considering the mental health landscape. Persistent cognitive strain can contribute to stress and anxiety, as the mind remains in a constant state of alertness. The immersive nature of these environments can blur the lines between reality and simulation, potentially leading to confusion and disorientation once individuals return to the physical world. Conversely, when managed adeptly, simulations can become powerful tools for mental health interventions, offering controlled environments where individuals can confront and overcome fears, anxieties, or phobias in a safe and supportive setting.

Incorporating strategies to mitigate cognitive load is crucial for optimizing the mental health benefits of simulated experiences. Techniques such as guided breaks, mindfulness practices, and adaptive content that adjusts to the user's cognitive state can help maintain balance and prevent cognitive overload. These approaches can ensure that the mental engagement remains enriching rather than exhausting. Furthermore, interdisciplinary collaboration among cognitive scientists, psychologists, and simulation designers can foster innovative solutions that prioritize mental well-being, transforming potential pitfalls into opportunities for personal development and resilience building.

Reflecting on the profound impact of cognitive load in virtual environments invites us to question how we might harness these insights for broader societal benefit. Could simulations be tailored to bolster cognitive resilience, preparing individuals to navigate an increasingly complex world? How might we leverage these environments to cultivate emotional intelligence and empathy, qualities often overshadowed by technological advancement? By approaching these questions with curiosity and open-mindedness, we can unlock the transformative potential of simulations, ensuring they serve as a catalyst for human flourishing rather than a source of mental strain.

Navigating Reality Distortion and Memory Alteration

Navigating the intricate landscape of reality distortion and memory alteration within virtual environments requires a nuanced understanding of the interplay between technology and the human mind. As simulations become increasingly sophisticated, they possess the ability to manipulate sensory inputs in ways that significantly alter a user's perception of reality. This phenomenon, often referred to as "presence," allows users to experience virtual worlds with such authenticity that the brain begins to treat these experiences as genuine. Recent research in neuropsychology has revealed that prolonged exposure to these fabricated realities can blur the lines between what is real and what is simulated, leading to a recalibration of the brain's perception filters. By engaging with these environments, individuals may find their cognitive constructs of reality shifting in subtle yet profound ways.

A critical factor in understanding these shifts lies in the study of memory and its malleability within virtual landscapes. Memory is not merely a passive recording of events but an active reconstruction that can be influenced by the contexts in which it is accessed or formed. Virtual environments, with their capacity to create vivid, emotionally charged experiences, can lead to the formation of memories that feel as real as those formed in the physical world. These memories, when recalled, can integrate into one's personal narrative, potentially altering self-perception and identity. An example of this is seen in therapeutic settings, where virtual reality is employed to reframe traumatic memories or bolster positive experiences, thereby demonstrating the technology's potential to rewire emotional and cognitive pathways.

The psychological repercussions of extended immersion in virtual realities are further compounded by the phenomenon of cognitive dissonance. When individuals are frequently shifting between virtual and real worlds, there is a potential for conflict between the two sets of experiences, leading to a disjointed sense of self. This cognitive dissonance can manifest as confusion, anxiety, or even a sense of alienation from one's own life. However, emerging studies suggest that with proper guidance and reflective practices, users can develop resilience and adaptability, finding ways to harmonize their dual realities. By cultivating a mindful awareness of the distinction between virtual and actual experiences, individuals can better navigate the complexities of their digital interactions.

Exploring the implications of reality distortion further, researchers are investigating the concept of "virtual identity," where avatars and in-game personas become extensions of the self. This virtual identity can sometimes overshadow the physical self, with memories and experiences in the digital realm influencing real-world decisions. The process of crafting and maintaining these identities can trigger a reevaluation of personal values and beliefs. This reimagining of identity invites introspection and can lead to personal growth, but it also raises ethical and philosophical questions about the authenticity of experiences and the nature of selfhood in a digital age.

To embrace the potential of virtual worlds while mitigating risks, it is vital to foster environments that encourage critical thinking and self-awareness. Practitioners and developers should design simulations with built-in reflective mechanisms, encouraging users to regularly assess the impacts of their virtual experiences on their real-world lives. By promoting education and awareness around these issues, society can equip individuals with the tools needed to harness the transformative power of simulated realities while maintaining a grounded sense of self. As we venture deeper into this new frontier, the conversation around reality distortion and memory alteration will remain pivotal, shaping the future of how we perceive and interact with both virtual and physical realms.

Reflecting on the intricate dance between the human mind and simulated environments, this chapter has unraveled the profound ways in which our brain interprets and is influenced by virtual realities. By exploring how simulations engage our senses to create convincing experiences, we gain insight into the delicate art of crafting worlds that feel authentic. The exploration of memory and identity within these digital realms reveals the potential for simulations to shape our self-perception, while the psychological ramifications of prolonged immersion underscore the need for mindful engagement. These insights not only illuminate the fascinating interplay between cognition and technology but also emphasize the responsibility of simulation architects in shaping experiences that enrich rather than exploit. As we transition to the next chapter, consider how these cognitive principles might be harnessed to further expand the potential of simulations in education and entertainment, urging us to ponder the balance between innovation and ethical stewardship in our pursuit of new realities.

Chapter Four

Simulation As A Tool For Learning

Imagine a classroom where the walls dissolve into the vastness of the cosmos, where students walk among the stars and explore the mysteries of black holes not through textbooks, but through direct experience. This is not a scene from a science fiction novel; it's the dawn of a new era in education, where simulations become the cornerstone of learning. In this chapter, we embark on a journey to uncover how virtual worlds are reshaping the landscape of education, turning abstract concepts into tangible experiences and transforming passive learning into active exploration. The possibilities are as limitless as the digital universes we can create, inviting us to reconsider not just how we teach, but how we understand the very act of learning.

As we navigate through this new terrain, the potential for simulations to enhance creativity and problem-solving becomes a focal point. In these digital domains, failure is but a stepping stone to innovation, and the boundaries of imagination stretch beyond the horizon. Simulated scenarios offer a sandbox where ideas can be tested and refined, cultivating a generation of thinkers who are not just consumers of information, but creators of knowledge. Through immersive experiences, learners engage with content on a profound level, fostering a deeper connection and understanding that transcends traditional methods.

This chapter also examines the paradigm shift in pedagogy as simulations evolve into a universal learning platform. Imagine a world where geographical and economic barriers fade away, and education becomes accessible to all, regardless of circumstance. Through compelling case studies, we will explore the transformative impact simulations have already had in classrooms across the globe. These stories serve as a testament to the power of technology to bridge gaps, level the playing field, and inspire a collective reimagining of what education can be. As we delve into these possibilities, we are reminded that the true power of simulations lies not in the technology itself, but in the human capacity to dream, to learn, and to grow.

Immersive education: Teaching through experience in virtual worlds

Immersive education in virtual worlds invites learners into realms where traditional teaching methods give way to experience-driven exploration. Imagine a classroom without walls, where history isn't just read about but lived, where scientific concepts are not only discussed but experimented with on a cosmic scale. This approach transforms the educational landscape, allowing students to engage with content in a manner that mirrors real-life experiences. The power of virtual worlds lies in their ability to craft environments where the abstract becomes tangible, and the theoretical becomes practical. In these digital spaces, students can step onto the surface of Mars, witness the rise and fall of ancient civilizations, or navigate the complexities of the human body, all from the comfort of their own homes. This shift from passive learning to active participation fuels curiosity and sparks a deeper understanding of the subject matter.

As we venture into the possibilities of immersive education, the focus extends to the intricate design of these experiential learning environments. Each virtual world is a carefully constructed landscape, meticulously crafted to engage the mind and stimulate intellectual curiosity. The potential for cognitive engagement through simulated interactions is vast, offering learners the chance to explore scenarios that challenge their problem-solving skills and creativity. In this chapter, we explore not only the creation of these dynamic environments but also the methods to assess their impact on learning outcomes. By examining successful case studies, we gain insights into how virtual simulations have already begun to reshape education, providing a glimpse into a future where learning is unbounded by the physical constraints of the traditional classroom.

Designing Experiential Learning Environments in Virtual Worlds

Crafting experiential learning environments within virtual worlds necessitates a nuanced understanding of both pedagogical theories and the intricacies of digital design. At the heart of these simulated environments lies the potential to transform passive learning into active, engaging experiences. By immersing learners in richly detailed scenarios, educators can facilitate a deeper understanding of complex subjects. In these digital landscapes, learners can experiment, make decisions, and witness the consequences of their actions in real-time, which fosters a sense of agency and engagement that traditional methods often lack. Recent advancements in virtual reality and artificial intelligence have opened new avenues for creating adaptive learning paths that respond to individual needs and preferences, ensuring that each learner's journey is unique and optimized for their cognitive style.

A critical element in designing these environments is the integration of multisensory stimuli, which can enhance cognitive engagement and retention. By simulating realistic sounds, textures, and visuals, learners are more likely to feel present in the virtual world, leading to a more profound connection with the material. For instance, a virtual chemistry lab might allow students to mix chemicals and observe reactions without the constraints of physical safety or cost, thereby encouraging experimentation and curiosity. Such immersive experiences can be particularly beneficial in fields where practical application is crucial, such as medicine, engineering, and environmental science. The use of haptic feedback and motion tracking further enriches these environments, providing tactile and kinesthetic interactions that mirror real-world experiences.

Collaboration and social interaction within virtual worlds offer additional layers of experiential learning. When learners engage with peers in a shared digital space, they can develop critical soft skills like communication, teamwork, and empathy. Virtual environments can simulate scenarios that require group problem-solving and decision-making, mirroring real-world challenges. For example, a virtual business simulation might task teams with navigating complex market scenarios, allowing learners to apply theoretical knowledge in a dynamic and interactive setting. This not only solidifies understanding but also prepares individuals for the complexities of real-world professional environments, where collaboration and adaptability are key.

Assessment in these virtual realms poses both challenges and opportunities. Traditional metrics, such as test scores and quizzes, may not fully capture the depth of learning that occurs in these environments. Instead, educators are exploring innovative assessment methods that focus on process and outcome. For example, data analytics can track a learner's decision-making process, adaptability, and problem-solving skills within the virtual environment. This approach provides a more comprehensive view of a learner's progress and areas for improvement. Moreover, the ability to record and review interactions allows for reflective learning, where learners can revisit and analyze their decisions, fostering a cycle of continuous improvement and deeper understanding.

The development of experiential learning environments in virtual worlds is not without its ethical considerations. Designers and educators must be mindful of accessibility, ensuring that all learners, regardless of physical or cognitive abilities, can benefit from these innovative approaches. Additionally, the potential for addiction or detachment from reality must be addressed through thoughtful design and implementation strategies. By establishing ethical guidelines and fostering open dialogue about the implications of these technologies, educators can create safe and inclusive virtual spaces that maximize learning potential while minimizing risks. As we continue to explore these digital frontiers, the balance between innovation and ethics will remain a pivotal consideration in shaping the future of education.

Enhancing Cognitive Engagement Through Simulated Interactions

Engaging learners in virtual worlds has emerged as a transformative approach to education, offering an immersive and interactive environment that stimulates cognitive engagement and deepens understanding. By anchoring abstract concepts in dynamic simulations, learners are encouraged to explore and manipulate variables in real-time, fostering a more profound comprehension. In virtual biology labs, for instance, students can dissect digital specimens repeatedly, observing minute details without the constraints of physical resources. This hands-on experience not only strengthens knowledge retention but also empowers learners to experiment with scenarios that would be impossible or impractical in traditional settings.

Simulated interactions harness the intricacies of human cognition by engaging multiple senses and fostering active participation. These virtual environments can be tailored to individual learning styles, adapting to the pace and preferences of each user. Advanced algorithms analyze user behaviors, offering personalized feedback that guides learners through complex problems. In fields like engineering, students might engage with 3D models of machinery, deconstructing and rebuilding components to understand underlying principles. These interactions mimic real-world problem-solving, promoting critical thinking and enabling learners to apply theoretical knowledge in practical contexts.

The potential of virtual worlds extends beyond mere replication of physical spaces; they offer opportunities to transcend conventional boundaries. Educators can craft scenarios that challenge users to think creatively and make decisions with far-reaching consequences, thereby honing decision-making skills. For example, a virtual history lesson might place students in pivotal moments of the past, allowing them to explore alternative outcomes based on their choices. This experiential learning method transforms passive observation into active engagement, compelling students to analyze historical events from multiple perspectives and fostering a deeper appreciation for the complexities of human society.

Recent advancements in artificial intelligence and machine learning are revolutionizing the way simulations are designed and implemented, pushing the boundaries of educational possibilities. AI-driven systems can create adaptive learning paths, continuously updating and refining content to match the evolving needs of learners. This approach ensures that educational simulations remain relevant and challenging, preparing students for the demands of an ever-changing world. As these technologies advance, the potential for creating highly sophisticated, responsive learning environments that mirror the complexities of real life becomes increasingly attainable.

The integration of virtual simulations into educational curricula is not without challenges, yet the potential benefits are immense. By harnessing the power of technology to create immersive, engaging learning experiences, educators can inspire a new generation of thinkers and problem-solvers. As these digital landscapes continue to evolve, they offer a unique opportunity to rethink traditional pedagogies and redefine what it means to learn in the 21st century. The ongoing development of these tools promises to unlock new dimensions of cognitive engagement, paving the way for an educational paradigm that is as dynamic and multifaceted as the world it seeks to emulate.

Assessing Learning Outcomes in Immersive Educational Simulations

Evaluating learning outcomes in immersive educational simulations requires a nuanced approach that goes beyond traditional metrics. In these dynamic environments, assessment must capture the richness of experiential learning, focusing on both cognitive and affective dimensions. One promising method involves using analytics to track learner interactions within the simulation, providing data on decision-making processes, problem-solving strategies, and adaptive learning pathways. This data-driven approach allows educators to identify patterns in student behavior that correlate with mastery of complex concepts, offering a more comprehensive picture of student progress than conventional assessments alone.

To further refine assessment techniques, educators are exploring the integration of artificial intelligence to personalize feedback and support within simulations. AI-driven systems can analyze individual learner profiles and adapt simulations in real-time, presenting tailored challenges that promote deeper understanding and retention. By leveraging machine learning algorithms, these systems can also predict future learning trajectories, helping educators intervene proactively to support students who may struggle with specific concepts. This level of personalization not only enhances the learning experience but also ensures that assessments are closely aligned with individual learner needs and goals.

Another innovative approach involves the use of virtual reality to create assessment scenarios that mimic real-world challenges. These scenarios enable learners to demonstrate their skills and knowledge in a context that closely resembles the situations they will face outside the classroom. For instance, medical students can practice surgical procedures in a risk-free environment, while engineering students can experiment with complex systems without the fear of costly mistakes. Such immersive assessments provide a holistic view of learners' abilities, encompassing not only their technical skills but also their capacity to adapt and innovate in unfamiliar contexts.

Given the complexity of assessing outcomes in virtual worlds, it's essential to consider the role of self-assessment and peer review as complementary tools. Encouraging learners to reflect on their experiences within the simulation fosters metacognitive skills, enabling them to identify their strengths and areas for improvement. Peer review, meanwhile, offers diverse perspectives and encourages collaborative learning, allowing students to learn from each other's experiences and insights. By incorporating these elements into the assessment process, educators can cultivate a learning culture that values continuous improvement and lifelong learning.

As the field of immersive education evolves, ongoing research and development are crucial to refining assessment methodologies. Collaborative efforts between educators, researchers, and technologists are leading to the creation of innovative tools and frameworks that enhance the validity and reliability of assessments in simulated environments. These advancements are paving the way for a future where immersive simulations are not only powerful learning tools but also integral components of a comprehensive educational ecosystem that supports diverse learners and prepares them for the challenges of a rapidly changing world.

Enhancing creativity and problem-solving through simulated scenarios

Creativity and problem-solving are the lifeblood of innovation, driving progress across every field of human endeavor. In an era where traditional methods of fostering these abilities often fall short, simulated scenarios emerge as a vibrant canvas for exploration and discovery. This dynamic interplay between the individual and a meticulously crafted virtual environment can unlock the latent potential within each participant. By stepping beyond the constraints of the physical world, simulations offer a playground where creativity flows unbounded, and problem-solving becomes an exhilarating adventure. Through imaginative interactions and challenges that resemble real-world complexities, these digital landscapes invite participants to experiment, iterate, and collaborate in unprecedented ways.

As we navigate the vibrant realms of virtual environments, the potential for enhancing creativity and honing advanced problem-solving skills becomes not just a possibility but an expectation. Simulated scenarios, with their infinite adaptability, serve as catalysts for innovative thinking, encouraging participants to embrace the unexpected and explore previously uncharted territories. This chapter unfolds the transformative power of simulations in three distinct yet interconnected areas: fostering creative collaboration in virtual spaces, utilizing scenario-based learning to cultivate critical problem-solving skills, and harnessing immersive experiences to inspire groundbreaking ideas. Each subtopic reveals a facet of the profound impact simulations can have, painting a comprehensive picture of their role in shaping the future of learning and human achievement.

Leveraging Virtual Environments for Creative Collaboration

In the rapidly evolving realm of virtual environments, the potential for fostering creative collaboration is vast and transformative. These digital landscapes provide an unparalleled platform for individuals and teams to converge, irrespective of geographical boundaries, forging connections that transcend traditional limitations. Within these immersive worlds, participants can experiment with ideas, iterate on designs, and explore novel concepts in real-time, fostering a culture of innovation that thrives on the diversity of thought and experience. Cutting-edge research in virtual reality and augmented reality technologies has demonstrated that the immersive nature of these platforms can significantly enhance cognitive engagement, allowing for a more profound exploration of creative possibilities and problem-solving strategies.

One of the most compelling aspects of virtual environments is their ability to simulate complex and dynamic systems, offering a sandbox for experimentation that encourages out-of-the-box thinking. By providing users with a risk-free space to test hypotheses and visualize outcomes, these environments nurture a mindset that is receptive to innovation and resilient in the face of failure. For instance, architects and urban planners can collaboratively design and manipulate cityscapes in virtual reality, receiving instant feedback on their designs' impact on factors such as traffic flow and environmental sustainability. This iterative process not only accelerates the development of viable solutions but also cultivates a deeper understanding of the interconnectedness of real-world systems.

The collaborative potential of virtual environments is further amplified by the integration of artificial intelligence and machine learning tools, which can assist in generating and refining ideas. These technologies can analyze vast datasets to provide insights that might elude human collaborators, offering suggestions that inspire new avenues of exploration. For example, in the field of biomedical research, scientists can employ AI-driven simulations to model complex biological processes, facilitating collaboration across disciplines and accelerating the discovery of innovative treatments. By harnessing the computational power of AI, virtual environments become fertile ground for groundbreaking collaborations that push the boundaries of what is possible.

Virtual environments also offer unique opportunities for interdisciplinary collaboration, bringing together experts from diverse fields to tackle multifaceted challenges. The convergence of different perspectives often leads to the emergence of novel solutions that might not have been conceived in isolation. A prime example of this is the use of virtual reality in joint research initiatives between environmental scientists and technologists, who can collaboratively simulate climate change scenarios and explore mitigation strategies. By visualizing the potential impacts of different interventions, these teams can develop more comprehensive and effective solutions that draw on the strengths of each discipline.

The transformative potential of virtual environments in fostering creative collaboration is not without its challenges. Ensuring equitable access to these technologies and addressing issues related to digital literacy and inclusivity are critical considerations. Moreover, the ethical implications of virtual collaboration, such as data privacy and intellectual property rights, must be carefully navigated. Despite these challenges, the possibilities that virtual environments offer for enhancing creativity and problem-solving are immense. As we continue to explore and refine these digital spaces, they promise to become indispensable tools for collaboration and innovation, enriching both individual and collective endeavors in ways previously unimaginable.

Scenario-Based Learning for Advanced Problem-Solving Skills

Scenario-based learning harnesses the power of virtual environments to cultivate advanced problem-solving skills, offering a dynamic alternative to traditional educational methods. By immersing learners in simulated scenarios, they engage in experiential learning that mirrors real-world complexities, demanding active participation and critical thinking. This method transcends rote memorization and encourages learners to apply theoretical knowledge in practical situations, fostering a deeper understanding of subject matter. Recent advancements in virtual reality technology have enabled the creation of increasingly sophisticated scenarios, where learners encounter diverse challenges that require innovative solutions. These immersive experiences provide a safe space to experiment with different strategies, analyze outcomes, and refine decision-making processes, ultimately enhancing their ability to tackle complex problems in real life.

One innovative application of scenario-based learning is in the realm of medical education, where simulations are employed to recreate patient interactions and surgical procedures. Aspiring doctors and nurses can practice diagnosing illnesses, delivering treatments, and managing emergencies without the risk of harm to actual patients. These virtual simulations build confidence and competence, allowing learners to make mistakes and learn from them in a controlled setting. A study published in the Journal of Medical Education highlighted how medical students who engaged in scenario-based simulations exhibited improved diagnostic accuracy and faster decision-making compared to those who relied solely on traditional learning methods. Such evidence underscores the transformative potential of simulations in cultivating essential skills in high-stakes professions.

Beyond professional training, scenario-based learning has profound implications for fostering creativity and innovation. In corporate settings, simulations can be tailored to address specific industry challenges, encouraging employees to think outside the box and develop novel solutions. For instance, technology companies might simulate cybersecurity breaches, prompting teams to devise robust defense strategies. This approach not only sharpens problem-solving abilities but also nurtures a culture of innovation, as employees become more adept at identifying opportunities for improvement. Researchers at the Stanford Virtual Human Interaction Lab have demonstrated that virtual environments can significantly boost creative thinking, as participants exposed to novel scenarios exhibited increased ideation and originality in their responses.

The effectiveness of scenario-based learning is enhanced by integrating cutting-edge research from cognitive science, which illuminates how the brain processes and retains information. Studies suggest that active engagement in simulated scenarios stimulates neural pathways associated with learning and memory, leading to better knowledge retention and recall. Additionally, the emotional engagement fostered by immersive experiences can reinforce learning outcomes, as emotions play a crucial role in memory consolidation. By designing scenarios that evoke emotional responses, educators can create more impactful learning experiences that resonate with learners on a deeper level, ensuring that knowledge is not only acquired but also internalized.

As scenario-based learning continues to evolve, it is imperative to consider diverse perspectives and emerging trends within the field. While the benefits are undeniable, there are also challenges to address, such as ensuring equitable access to technology and tailoring scenarios to accommodate different learning styles. Furthermore, ethical considerations must be prioritized, particularly in simulations that involve sensitive or potentially distressing content. Educators and simulation architects must collaborate to develop frameworks that balance realism with ethical responsibility, ensuring that the transformative potential of simulations is harnessed for the greater good. By embracing these challenges, scenario-based learning can become a powerful tool for cultivating advanced problem-solving skills, equipping learners with the capabilities they need to thrive in an increasingly complex world.

Immersive Simulations as Catalysts for Innovative Thinking

Immersive simulations stand as powerful engines for fostering innovative thinking. By enveloping users in meticulously crafted environments, these digital realms create spaces where the boundaries of reality can be stretched, allowing for experimentation and exploration that are difficult to achieve in the physical world. For instance, virtual reality platforms like Oculus Quest enable users to interact with complex systems in real time, offering a playground for the imagination where conventional constraints do not apply. This freedom encourages participants to venture beyond typical thought processes, unlocking potential solutions and ideas that might remain dormant in more traditional settings. The brain's capacity to assimilate and synthesize novel information is amplified when individuals are placed in dynamic, engaging contexts that challenge their perceptions and encourage creative leaps.

In the realm of cognitive science, research underscores the link between immersive experiences and heightened creativity. Studies have shown that engaging with complex, interactive simulations can activate neural pathways associated with lateral thinking and problem-solving. This phenomenon suggests that immersive environments may serve as catalysts for cognitive flexibility, a critical component of innovative thought. This is exemplified in the use of simulations in architectural design, where architects can visualize and manipulate structures in a virtual space, allowing them to iterate designs rapidly and explore unconventional architectural forms. This process not only enhances the creative outcome but also accelerates the learning curve, facilitating a deeper understanding of spatial relationships and design principles.

The transformative potential of immersive simulations is further evident in their application to scenario-based training. For example, emergency response teams utilize immersive simulations to train for high-stakes situations, such as natural disasters or medical emergencies. These training modules offer a safe yet realistic environment where participants can practice decision-making, adapt to evolving scenarios, and experiment with different strategies. By simulating high-pressure contexts, individuals develop the ability to think on their feet, fostering innovation in problem-solving approaches. This adaptability is crucial not only in crisis management but also in fields like business and technology, where rapid innovation is necessary to keep pace with change.

In addition to professional applications, immersive simulations play a pivotal role in educational settings, where they can be harnessed to cultivate creativity among students. By utilizing virtual environments, educators can transcend the limitations of traditional classrooms, offering students unique experiences that stimulate curiosity and imagination. For instance, history students might explore ancient civilizations through virtual reconstructions, while science students could conduct experiments in simulated laboratories. These experiences provide an opportunity for learners to engage deeply with subject matter, encouraging them to ask questions, explore alternatives, and develop original ideas. By integrating simulations into the curriculum, educators can create a fertile ground for creativity and innovation, equipping students with the skills necessary to navigate and shape the future.

The allure of immersive simulations lies not only in their ability to replicate reality but in their capacity to transcend it, offering a glimpse into possibilities that extend beyond the tangible world. As technology continues to advance, the potential for simulations to drive innovative thinking grows exponentially. Whether through the integration of artificial intelligence, the development of more sophisticated virtual environments, or the exploration of augmented reality, the future of simulations promises to redefine the boundaries of creativity. As we stand on the cusp of this new frontier, we are invited to consider how these digital landscapes can be harnessed to inspire and cultivate the innovative thinkers of tomorrow.

Rethinking pedagogy: Simulations as a universal learning platform

In the ever-evolving landscape of education, simulations emerge as a revolutionary force, poised to redefine how knowledge is imparted and absorbed. This transformative approach breaks free from traditional pedagogical confines, offering a universal learning platform that transcends conventional classroom walls. The allure of simulations lies in their ability to create dynamic, interactive environments where learners are not mere recipients of information but active participants in their own educational journey. By immersing students in virtual worlds that mirror real-life complexities, simulations cultivate a deeper understanding and foster critical thinking skills that are essential in today's multifaceted world. The potential of simulations to reshape education is boundless, offering a canvas where imagination meets practical application, and theoretical concepts come to life in vivid, experiential detail.

As the narrative unfolds, the integration of simulations into multidisciplinary curricula becomes a powerful tool for bridging diverse fields of study, allowing for seamless connections between subjects that were once siloed. This fusion not only enhances engagement but also ensures that knowledge retention is amplified through immersive learning experiences. Furthermore, the adaptability of simulations in catering to individual learning styles presents an unprecedented opportunity to bridge cognitive gaps. Personalized simulated experiences ensure that each learner's journey is uniquely tailored, addressing specific needs and fostering a more inclusive educational environment. This new pedagogical paradigm not only promises to revolutionize the way we teach and learn but also holds the potential to inspire a generation of thinkers and innovators who are equipped to tackle the challenges of tomorrow with creativity and confidence.

Integrating Simulations into Multidisciplinary Curricula

Integrating simulations into multidisciplinary curricula heralds a transformative shift in education, inviting learners to engage with complex subjects through the lens of experiential learning. It offers a dynamic platform where diverse academic disciplines can converge, fostering an environment ripe for innovation and creativity. Imagine a biology course where students explore cellular processes by navigating a virtual cell environment, or a history class that allows learners to witness the unfolding of historical events from a first-person perspective. Such immersive experiences not only enhance comprehension but also spark curiosity, encouraging learners to delve deeper into the material. This approach challenges traditional educational silos by promoting cross-disciplinary thinking, preparing students to tackle real-world problems that rarely adhere to subject boundaries.

Recent advancements in simulation technology have made it possible to tailor experiences to individual learners, accommodating various learning styles and cognitive needs. By personalizing the educational journey, simulations can address gaps in understanding, ensuring that each student progresses at their own pace. For instance, complex mathematical concepts can be broken down into interactive, visual simulations that demystify abstract ideas, making them accessible to students who struggle with conventional teaching methods. This individualized approach increases engagement and retention, as learners are empowered to interact with content in a way that resonates with their unique cognitive processes.

The integration of simulations into curricula also offers educators a powerful tool to assess and refine pedagogical strategies. Data analytics derived from simulation interactions provide insights into student performance and engagement, enabling instructors to identify areas of strength and weakness. This feedback loop facilitates a more adaptive teaching approach, where educators can modify content and delivery based on real-time data. Furthermore, simulations can bridge the gap between theoretical knowledge and practical application, as students apply learned concepts in simulated environments that mimic real-world scenarios. This hands-on experience cultivates critical thinking and problem-solving skills, essential for success in today's fast-paced, interdisciplinary workplaces.

While the benefits are substantial, the adoption of simulations in education requires thoughtful implementation and ongoing evaluation. Educators must consider the balance between virtual and physical learning experiences, ensuring that simulations complement rather than replace traditional methods. Collaboration between technologists, educators, and cognitive scientists is crucial to develop simulations that are not only technologically sophisticated but also pedagogically sound. Additionally, ethical considerations must be addressed, particularly regarding data privacy and the potential for over-reliance on virtual experiences. By navigating these challenges, educational institutions can harness the full potential of simulations, creating a more inclusive and effective learning environment.

As we stand on the brink of a new educational paradigm, it's essential to envision the future possibilities of integrating simulations into curricula. What if every student could have a personalized mentor in the form of an AI-driven simulation, guiding them through their educational journey? How might this change the landscape of higher education and lifelong learning? By embracing these visionary ideas, educators can cultivate a generation of learners equipped with the tools and mindset necessary to thrive in an increasingly complex world. This integration not only enriches the learning experience but also aligns education with the demands of the future, ensuring that students are prepared to lead and innovate in their chosen fields.

Enhancing Engagement and Retention Through Immersive Learning

In the realm of education, immersive learning has emerged as a dynamic catalyst, reshaping how knowledge is absorbed and retained. Unlike traditional methods, which often rely on passive absorption, immersive learning places individuals within the heart of a subject, allowing them to interact with and explore complex concepts firsthand. This approach capitalizes on recent advances in virtual reality (VR) and augmented reality (AR) technologies, enabling learners to traverse historical epochs, manipulate molecular structures, or navigate complex mathematical landscapes, all within a controlled, simulated environment. Such experiences are not merely supplementary but transformative, providing learners with vivid, memorable encounters that anchor understanding and enhance cognitive retention.

Recent studies underscore the efficacy of immersive learning in fostering engagement and retention. A notable investigation by Stanford's Virtual Human Interaction Lab found that participants in VR-based educational modules demonstrated a significant increase in information retention compared to those who engaged with conventional materials. This heightened retention can be attributed to the principle of embodied cognition, where learning is intertwined with physical activity and spatial awareness. As learners navigate and manipulate their environment, they create rich, multisensory memories that are easier to recall and apply. This connection between action and insight is what makes immersive learning a powerful tool for educators seeking to bridge the gap between theory and practice.

The potential of immersive learning extends beyond mere engagement. It offers a platform for creativity and problem-solving, allowing learners to experiment without the fear of real-world repercussions. For instance, medical students can perform complex surgeries in a virtual operating room, where mistakes become stepping stones to mastery rather than costly errors. This iterative learning process encourages an innovative mindset, empowering learners to explore unconventional solutions and develop critical thinking skills that are indispensable in an ever-evolving world. By providing a safe space for trial and error, immersive learning cultivates resilience and adaptability, traits that are imperative for success in any field.

One compelling example of immersive learning's impact is the use of virtual simulations in environmental studies. Students can virtually inhabit fragile ecosystems, witnessing the effects of climate change in real-time. They can simulate the impact of various conservation strategies, observing outcomes that would take decades to manifest in the real world. This experiential approach not only deepens understanding but also instills a sense of urgency and responsibility. By seeing the direct consequences of their actions, learners are more likely to internalize the importance of sustainable practices and become proactive stewards of the environment.

As educators and technologists continue to explore the frontier of immersive learning, it is essential to consider the ethical and practical implications of this educational paradigm. While the benefits are manifold, challenges such as accessibility, technological disparity, and the potential for over-reliance on simulations must be addressed. By fostering a collaborative dialogue between educators, technologists, and policymakers, we can ensure that immersive learning becomes an inclusive and equitable tool for all learners. Harnessing the full potential of immersive learning requires thoughtful integration into curricula, ongoing research, and a commitment to developing ethical frameworks that prioritize the well-being of learners while maximizing the transformative power of this innovative approach.

Bridging Cognitive Gaps with Personalized Simulated Experiences

Personalized simulated experiences offer a transformative approach to bridging cognitive gaps, enabling learners to engage with content in ways that cater to their unique learning needs and preferences. By tailoring simulations to individual cognitive profiles, educators can create environments where students can interact with material at their own pace, revisiting complex concepts as needed. This customization not only enhances comprehension but also fosters a sense of ownership over the learning journey. Recent advancements in artificial intelligence and machine learning have enabled the development of sophisticated algorithms that adapt simulations in real-time based on user interactions, ensuring that each learner receives a bespoke educational experience. This approach draws on extensive data analysis to identify patterns in learning behaviors, allowing for dynamic adjustments that facilitate deeper understanding and retention.

One of the most compelling aspects of personalized simulations is their ability to address and mitigate learning disparities. Students who traditionally struggle with standard educational methods can benefit from environments that adapt to their specific learning styles, whether they are visual, auditory, or kinesthetic learners. For instance, a student who finds traditional mathematics instruction challenging might thrive in a virtual setting that visualizes mathematical concepts through interactive, 3D models. Such immersive experiences allow learners to explore abstract ideas in tangible ways, bridging gaps that conventional pedagogy often fails to address. This adaptability not only benefits individuals but also democratizes education, providing equitable opportunities for all learners to succeed.

As the educational landscape evolves, personalized simulations are becoming integral to multidisciplinary curricula, fostering cross-disciplinary thinking and problem-solving skills. Simulations that incorporate elements from various fields encourage students to draw connections between disparate subjects, promoting holistic understanding. For example, a simulation designed to teach environmental science might integrate elements of economics, sociology, and technology, challenging students to consider the multifaceted nature of real-world problems. This interdisciplinary approach prepares learners for the complexities of modern life, equipping them with the critical thinking skills necessary to navigate an increasingly interconnected world.

Recent research underscores the importance of engagement and motivation in learning, with studies showing that students who are actively involved in their learning process tend to achieve better outcomes. Personalized simulations excel in maintaining engagement by offering learners a sense of autonomy and control over their educational experiences. By allowing students to choose their paths within a simulation, educators can tap into intrinsic motivation, encouraging learners to explore subjects more deeply. This autonomy not only enhances engagement but also cultivates a lifelong love of learning, as students become active participants in their educational journeys rather than passive recipients of information.

To fully harness the potential of personalized simulated experiences in education, educators and developers must collaborate to create content that is both engaging and pedagogically sound. By integrating cutting-edge research and innovative design principles, they can develop simulations that not only capture students' attention but also promote meaningful learning. It is crucial to consider diverse perspectives and cultural contexts when designing these experiences, ensuring that they are inclusive and relevant to a global audience. As we continue to explore the possibilities of personalized simulations, we must remain committed to ethical considerations, ensuring that these powerful tools are used to enhance educational equity and empower learners worldwide.

Case studies: Successful applications of simulations in education

Imagine a classroom where students don virtual reality headsets and suddenly find themselves conducting experiments in a state-of-the-art laboratory, exploring the bustling streets of ancient Rome, or navigating personalized learning paths tailored to their individual needs. This is not the distant future; it is the transformative power of simulations in education. As we stand at the cusp of a new era in learning, simulations have emerged as a dynamic force, reshaping traditional educational paradigms. By turning theoretical concepts into tangible experiences, they breathe life into subjects that once seemed abstract or distant, engaging students in ways that were previously unimaginable. These immersive environments bridge the gap between knowledge and experience, offering a visceral understanding that transcends the constraints of conventional teaching methods.

At this intersection of innovation and pedagogy, virtual laboratories revolutionize science education, allowing students to experiment without the limitations of physical resources. Historical simulations transport learners to past eras, fostering a deep, interactive connection with ancient cultures that textbooks alone cannot provide. Meanwhile, adaptive simulation technologies create personalized learning pathways, addressing the unique needs and learning speeds of each student. As these case studies illustrate, simulations hold the potential to democratize education, making it more accessible, engaging, and effective. Through the lens of these pioneering applications, we begin to envision a future where education is not just about acquiring knowledge but experiencing it in vivid, unforgettable ways.

Virtual Laboratories Transforming Science Education

Virtual laboratories are revolutionizing science education by offering unprecedented opportunities for experiential learning. These digital environments allow students to engage with scientific concepts in a more interactive and dynamic manner than traditional classrooms can offer. By simulating complex experiments in a controlled, virtual setting, learners can explore and manipulate variables without the constraints of physical resources or safety concerns. This innovative approach not only democratizes access to high-quality science education but also fosters a deeper understanding of scientific principles through active participation. In virtual labs, students can conduct experiments that would be otherwise unfeasible due to cost, scale, or risk, such as simulating chemical reactions or manipulating genetic sequences.

Cutting-edge research has shown that virtual laboratories enhance engagement and retention of scientific knowledge. Studies indicate that students who utilize virtual labs demonstrate improved conceptual understanding and problem-solving skills compared to their peers in traditional settings. These platforms often incorporate elements of gamification—such as achievement badges and progress tracking—which further motivate learners by adding a layer of challenge and reward. Additionally, virtual laboratories can be tailored to individual learning paces, allowing students to revisit experiments and concepts until mastery is achieved. This personalized approach aligns with emerging educational trends that prioritize adaptability and student-centered learning.

A notable example of virtual laboratories transforming science education is Labster, an online platform providing immersive lab simulations across various scientific disciplines. Labster's simulations are designed to mimic real-world laboratory environments, complete with detailed equipment and authentic scientific processes. The platform integrates cutting-edge technologies like virtual reality and artificial intelligence to create an engaging and realistic learning experience. Students can explore complex topics such as molecular biology and physics in an interactive manner, gaining practical skills that are directly applicable to real-world scenarios. Labster's success underscores the potential of virtual labs to bridge the gap between theoretical knowledge and practical application.

As virtual laboratories continue to evolve, they are poised to play a crucial role in the future of science education. Educators are increasingly recognizing the value of these tools in fostering scientific literacy and critical thinking skills. Future developments may include enhanced interactivity through haptic feedback, which could simulate the tactile aspects of laboratory work, further blurring the line between virtual and physical experimentation. Moreover, the integration of data analytics could provide valuable insights into student performance, allowing educators to tailor their instructional approaches to better meet individual needs and improve learning outcomes.

This transformative potential extends beyond the classroom, as virtual laboratories could also serve as platforms for collaborative research and innovation. By facilitating global access to sophisticated scientific tools and resources, these digital environments can foster collaboration among students, educators, and researchers from diverse backgrounds and geographies. This democratization of science education not only enhances individual learning experiences but also contributes to the broader advancement of scientific knowledge. As we witness the continued growth and refinement of virtual laboratories, it is essential to consider the ethical implications and ensure equitable access to these transformative educational tools, paving the way for a more informed and scientifically literate society.

Historical Simulations Enabling Interactive Learning of Ancient Cultures

Historical simulations offer a vibrant portal into the past, allowing learners to engage directly with bygone eras in a manner that transcends traditional textbooks. By digitally reconstructing ancient cultures, these simulations enable students to immerse themselves in the daily life, societal structures, and cultural nuances of civilizations long extinct. One can virtually walk through the bustling streets of ancient Rome, participate in Athenian democracy, or witness the construction of the pyramids. This experiential approach not only enhances engagement but also deepens understanding, as students can witness the consequences of historical events and decisions in real-time, fostering a more nuanced appreciation of history.

In recent years, advancements in simulation technology have enabled the creation of increasingly sophisticated historical reconstructions. Cutting-edge platforms now integrate artificial intelligence to simulate complex social dynamics, allowing for an interactive and adaptive learning experience. For instance, a student exploring the Han Dynasty might engage with AI-driven characters that respond to inquiries and actions, thereby offering a dynamic exploration of cultural practices and political strategies. This technological sophistication transforms passive learning into an interactive dialogue with history, where learners can explore 'what-if' scenarios and examine the ripple effects of pivotal moments in history.

These historical simulations are not only improving engagement but are also addressing diverse learning needs. Adaptive simulation technologies can tailor experiences to individual learners, accommodating different learning styles and paces. A visual learner might benefit from detailed reconstructions of historical sites, while a kinesthetic learner might thrive by participating in simulated historical events. This personalized approach ensures that each learner can connect with the material in a meaningful way, making history accessible and engaging for all students, regardless of their preferred learning methods.

Beyond education, historical simulations hold promise for cultural preservation. By meticulously recreating historical environments and practices, these simulations serve as digital time capsules that preserve endangered cultures for future generations. This aspect is particularly significant in an era where globalization threatens cultural homogenization. By accessing these simulations, learners across the globe can appreciate and understand diverse cultures, fostering empathy and cross-cultural understanding. Educators and historians can leverage these tools to ensure that the intricacies of human history are maintained and celebrated, rather than lost to the annals of time.

As we forge ahead, the potential for historical simulations to reshape education and cultural preservation is vast. The challenge lies in continuously pushing the boundaries of technological innovation while ensuring historical accuracy and cultural sensitivity. Developers and educators must collaborate to create simulations that are both engaging and informative, allowing students to learn history not as a static set of facts but as a living, breathing narrative. The intersection of technology and history offers a unique opportunity to redefine how we understand the past, inviting learners to step into history and experience it firsthand, bringing an unprecedented depth and richness to the learning process.

Personalized Learning Pathways Through Adaptive Simulation Technologies

Personalized learning pathways have emerged as a transformative force in education, thanks to adaptive simulation technologies that tailor educational experiences to individual needs. These technologies leverage sophisticated algorithms to assess learners' strengths, weaknesses, and preferences, creating a dynamic learning environment. This personalized approach enhances engagement and retention by offering content that aligns with each learner's pace and style. For instance, in a virtual biology lab, a student struggling with cellular processes might receive additional interactive modules that break down complex concepts, while a more advanced learner could be challenged with simulations that require higher-order thinking skills. This adaptability ensures that every student can achieve their potential, regardless of their starting point.

One of the most compelling advantages of adaptive simulations is their ability to provide real-time feedback and assessment. Unlike traditional education models, where evaluations are often delayed, these simulations offer immediate insights into a student's progress. This instant feedback loop helps learners identify areas for improvement and adjust their strategies accordingly. In a simulated historical exploration, for example, a student might receive prompts that encourage them to consider alternative perspectives or question historical narratives, fostering critical thinking skills. This immediate reflection not only reinforces learning but also cultivates a mindset of continuous improvement.

Adaptive simulations also democratize access to high-quality education by breaking down geographical and socio-economic barriers. With the proliferation of internet access and digital devices, students from diverse backgrounds can engage with world-class educational content. A rural student interested in physics can virtually attend a lecture by a leading scientist and participate in interactive experiments, experiences that might be otherwise inaccessible. This equalization of opportunity is vital in creating a more inclusive educational landscape, where students are empowered to pursue their interests and aspirations without constraints.

Recent advancements in artificial intelligence and machine learning have further enhanced the capabilities of adaptive simulations. These technologies analyze vast amounts of data to predict learning trajectories and recommend personalized content paths. Emerging research in this area highlights the potential for simulations to evolve alongside learners, adapting not only to their current needs but also anticipating future challenges. Such foresight can be particularly beneficial in fields requiring cumulative knowledge, like mathematics or language learning, where foundational skills are built progressively over time.

As these innovations continue to evolve, educators and developers face the exciting challenge of integrating adaptive simulations into existing curricula. This integration requires careful consideration of pedagogical goals and content alignment to ensure that simulations complement, rather than replace, traditional teaching methods. Thought-provoking scenarios, such as a simulated debate on climate change policy, can be woven into lesson plans to enrich classroom discussions and inspire students to apply their learning in real-world contexts. By embracing this fusion of technology and pedagogy, educators can craft a more holistic learning experience that prepares students for the complexities of the modern world.

The transformative potential of simulations in education is undeniable, offering immersive experiences that redefine learning by placing students in dynamic virtual environments where they can actively engage with material. This approach not only enriches education through experiential learning but also fosters creativity and enhances problem-solving skills by presenting learners with complex, simulated scenarios that challenge conventional thinking. As these technological advancements continue to evolve, simulations are poised to serve as a universal platform, democratizing access to diverse educational opportunities and bridging gaps in traditional pedagogy. The successful application of these tools in real-world educational settings underscores their capacity to revolutionize how knowledge is imparted and retained, inviting educators and policymakers to rethink and reshape the landscape of learning. As we consider what lies ahead, one must ponder how these innovations might further blur the boundaries between learning and play, compelling us to question the very nature of education and its role in preparing future generations for an increasingly complex world.

Chapter Five

Entertainment In Simulated Realities

In a dimly lit room, a young gamer sits transfixed, eyes wide behind a sleek headset, utterly engrossed in a world that feels just as tangible as the one beyond the screen. The room is silent except for the soft hum of electronics and the occasional gasp of awe as she navigates a landscape teeming with life, where every shadow and whisper carries the weight of possibility. This moment is no longer the realm of science fiction; it's a testament to the incredible strides in entertainment technology that have transformed passive spectators into active participants in digital worlds. The journey from simple pixelated screens to fully immersive experiences reflects not just technological advancement but a deeper evolution in how stories are told and experienced.

As we move further into this realm of virtual entertainment, the lines between narrative and environment blur, allowing creators to craft stories that envelop and engage on an unprecedented level. The art of narrative design has become a dance between the storyteller and the audience, where players are not just recipients of a tale but co-authors of their own adventures. In these worlds, where choice and consequence intertwine, the traditional boundaries of storytelling dissolve, paving the way for narratives that resonate deeply with the individual and collective psyche.

Yet, the allure of these digital landscapes extends beyond solitary exploration. They offer fertile grounds for building vibrant social ecosystems, where friendships are forged, alliances are tested, and communities thrive in shared experiences. These virtual societies challenge our understanding of interaction and connection, suggesting that the future of entertainment is not only about more vivid images or expansive worlds but about creating spaces where human creativity and collaboration flourish. As we step into this chapter, we find ourselves at the crossroads of technology and imagination, poised to explore how simulations are reshaping the very nature of entertainment, promising a future where the only limit is the boundary of our collective dreaming.

The evolution of gaming into fully immersive experiences

Ponder for a moment about the evolution of gaming, a journey that has enthralled millions, morphing from simple pixelated screens into vast, complex realms that blur the lines between player and game. This transformation is no mere technological marvel; it is a testament to humanity's unyielding quest for new forms of storytelling and expression. As we stand on the cusp of fully immersive experiences, gaming becomes a portal to alternate realities, inviting players to step beyond the boundaries of mere observation and into the heart of the action. The allure of this evolution lies not just in the technological prowess of virtual reality and augmented reality but in the transcendence of gaming into a medium that engages all senses and emotions. It marks the dawn of an era where games are no longer confined to a screen but envelop the player in a world of their own making.

This exciting shift in gaming is driven by advances in artificial intelligence, crafting dynamic gameplay that adapts and responds to the player's every decision, creating a living world that feels both unpredictable and organic. The quest for total immersion is further fueled by sensory integration, where sight, sound, and even touch converge to create a seamless experience that feels almost indistinguishable from reality. As we explore these subtopics, we will uncover how these technological leaps are shaping the future of interactive entertainment, creating experiences that are not just played but lived. The stage is set for a new era of gaming, where every game is a universe waiting to be discovered, each one more immersive than the last.

The Role of Virtual Reality and Augmented Reality in Gaming

Virtual reality (VR) and augmented reality (AR) have revolutionized the gaming landscape, transforming it from a two-dimensional experience into a fully immersive universe where players can transcend the boundaries of their physical environment. VR offers an encapsulating experience, placing players within a meticulously crafted digital world, while AR superimposes digital elements onto the real world, creating a seamless blend of reality and imagination. The introduction of devices like the Oculus Rift and PlayStation VR has propelled VR gaming into mainstream consciousness, offering players the opportunity to experience fantasies in an unprecedented manner. Concurrently, AR platforms such as Pokémon GO have demonstrated the potential for real-world interaction, encouraging players to explore their surroundings while interacting with digital phenomena. This dual evolution challenges game designers to think beyond traditional storytelling, crafting environments that are not only visually stunning but also deeply interactive and engaging.

Advancements in haptic technology have further enhanced the immersive quality of VR and AR gaming. Haptic feedback devices, such as gloves and full-body suits, allow players to physically feel the virtual environment, creating a profound sense of presence. These innovations elevate the gaming experience, allowing players to interact with virtual objects and characters in a manner that feels tangible and real. Moreover, the integration of these technologies in gaming has broader implications for accessibility, enabling individuals with disabilities to partake in experiences that may be challenging in the physical world. By making these virtual experiences more inclusive, haptic technology not only enriches the gaming landscape but also promotes a more equitable digital frontier.

The role of environmental soundscapes in VR and AR gaming cannot be overstated. Cutting-edge research in spatial audio technology has enabled developers to create sound environments that mimic the intricacies of real-world acoustics. This auditory realism enhances the player's spatial awareness, allowing them to discern the direction and distance of sounds within the game. For instance, in a VR stealth game, the soft rustle of leaves or the distant footsteps of an enemy can provide critical information, immersing the player in a sensory-rich experience that transcends visual stimuli. The meticulous attention to sound design underscores the intricate interplay between technology and artistry in crafting immersive experiences.

Recent developments in AI-driven narrative frameworks are also pushing the boundaries of gaming in VR and AR. By utilizing machine learning algorithms, game narratives can adapt dynamically to players' decisions and actions, creating a personalized storytelling experience. This dynamic storytelling is particularly potent in VR and AR environments, where the sense of agency and presence is heightened. Players are no longer passive recipients of a pre-defined story; instead, they become co-authors, influencing the unfolding of the narrative in real-time. This evolution in narrative design invites players to explore the moral and ethical dimensions of their choices, fostering a deeper connection with the virtual world.

As VR and AR continue to evolve, the potential for gaming to influence other sectors becomes increasingly apparent. The gamification of education and training programs, for instance, leverages VR's immersive qualities to enhance learning outcomes. By simulating real-world scenarios in a controlled environment, VR can provide learners with practical, hands-on experience without the associated risks. This application of gaming technology extends beyond entertainment, offering transformative possibilities in fields such as medicine, engineering, and military training. As these technologies advance, the line between gaming and practical applications will continue to blur, paving the way for innovative uses that can enrich various aspects of human life.

Advances in Artificial Intelligence for Dynamic Gameplay

Artificial intelligence has transformed gaming into an arena where dynamic gameplay is not just a possibility but a standard expectation. AI systems now simulate complex, responsive behaviors in non-player characters (NPCs), which evolve in response to players' actions. These intelligent entities enrich the gaming experience by introducing unpredictability and depth, making each player's journey unique. For instance, in games like "The Last of Us Part II," NPCs exhibit highly realistic behaviors and adaptive strategies, reacting differently based on the player's decisions and tactics. The project employed machine learning algorithms to fine-tune character behaviors, creating a living world where AI-driven entities enhance narrative depth and player engagement.

This revolution in AI doesn't stop at character behavior. It extends into procedural generation, where entire game worlds are crafted on-the-fly, shaped by players' interactions and choices. Games like "No Man's Sky" harness procedural algorithms to create vast, explorable universes that are as varied as they are expansive. These algorithms utilize AI to generate landscapes, ecosystems, and even quests, ensuring that no two experiences are identical. The incorporation of AI into procedural generation allows for an endless variety of content, providing players with vast worlds to explore without the need for extensive developer input for each detail.

In this landscape of dynamic gameplay, AI also serves as a tool for personalized gaming experiences. By analyzing player behavior and preferences, AI systems can dynamically adjust difficulty levels, tailor storylines, and even recommend in-game activities suited to individual playstyles. This personalization is evident in games like "Shadow of Mordor," where the Nemesis System learns from the player's actions, creating personalized adversaries that remember past encounters, adapt to the player's strategies, and develop unique characteristics. This level of personalization not only keeps players engaged but also fosters a deeper emotional connection to the game world.

As AI continues to advance, the potential for its application in gaming expands into realms such as emotional intelligence and player empathy. AI-driven characters are beginning to understand and respond to players' emotional states, creating more immersive and meaningful interactions. Research into affective computing explores how games can detect players' emotions through inputs like voice and facial expressions, allowing AI to adjust narratives or gameplay elements accordingly. This could lead to gaming experiences that not only entertain but also resonate on an emotional level, offering players supportive or challenging scenarios based on their mood and engagement.

The future of AI in dynamic gameplay promises even more groundbreaking developments. As research progresses, we can anticipate AI systems that facilitate more collaborative and socially rich gaming experiences. Imagine multiplayer games where AI assists in communication and coordination among players, or virtual worlds where AI acts as a mediator, fostering positive interactions and reducing toxicity. This convergence of AI and social dynamics could redefine how players interact with each other and the game world, leading to experiences that are not only deeply immersive but also socially enriching. The integration of AI into gaming is not merely about enhancing mechanics; it's about crafting worlds that are responsive, personalized, and profoundly human-centric.

Sensory Integration and the Quest for Total Immersion

As the boundary between the physical and digital realms continues to blur, the integration of sensory experiences in gaming offers an unprecedented level of immersion. This transformation is driven by the quest to engage all five senses, creating virtual environments that are indistinguishable from reality. Contemporary advancements in tactile feedback, auditory precision, and olfactory stimulation are paving the way for games that not only respond visually but also provide a multi-sensory experience. For instance, haptic technology allows players to feel the weight of a virtual object or the impact of a virtual punch, enhancing the sense of presence within the game world. This sensory richness is vital for achieving total immersion, allowing players to lose themselves in the narrative and environment.

Innovative research in the field of sensory integration is exploring how to simulate taste and smell, often considered the most challenging senses to replicate digitally. Recent experiments with scent-releasing devices and gustatory simulations promise to revolutionize the way players interact with virtual worlds. Imagine a game where the aroma of a digital forest or the taste of virtual cuisine is as authentic as the visual and auditory elements. Such developments could redefine what it means to participate in a game, offering experiences that are not only seen and heard but also tasted and smelled, making the virtual realm a true sensory haven.

The role of artificial intelligence in sensory integration is equally transformative, as it provides the dynamic adaptability necessary for creating personalized experiences. AI can adjust sensory inputs based on a player's preferences or reactions, crafting an environment that evolves in real-time. This adaptability ensures that each player's journey through a game is unique, responding to their choices and enhancing their emotional connection to the virtual world. This personalized approach to gaming not only increases engagement but also fosters a deeper sense of investment and immersion, as players navigate landscapes tailored to their individual sensory profiles.

The potential applications of sensory-rich environments extend beyond entertainment, offering profound implications for education, therapy, and social interaction. For example, therapeutic games that leverage sensory integration can provide immersive stress relief or rehabilitation exercises in a controlled, engaging manner. Educational simulations can utilize sensory elements to enhance learning, offering students a chance to experience historical events or scientific phenomena firsthand. These applications highlight the versatility and transformative potential of sensory integration, showcasing its ability to enrich experiences across various domains.

As sensory technology progresses, it invites us to reconsider our relationship with virtual worlds and the boundaries of human perception. Questions arise about the ethical implications of such profound immersion and the impact on our perception of reality. Will these sensory-rich experiences enhance our lives, or will they blur the lines between the virtual and the real to an unsettling degree? These queries challenge developers, philosophers, and users alike to contemplate the future of gaming and the role sensory integration will play in shaping our digital and physical experiences. As we stand on the threshold of a new era in gaming, the possibilities seem boundless, inviting a reimagining of what it means to engage with the digital world.

Narrative design: Crafting compelling stories in virtual worlds

Imagine stepping into a world where stories are not just told but lived, where the boundaries between the player and the narrative blur into a seamless dance of agency and immersion. In recent years, we've witnessed an extraordinary transformation in storytelling, driven by the evolution of game design and simulation technology. Virtual worlds now offer experiences that transcend traditional media, inviting individuals to become protagonists of their own unfolding sagas. This shift has opened new avenues for crafting narratives that adapt and respond to player choices, creating a dynamic interplay between story structure and player freedom. As storytellers in these digital realms, creators face the exhilarating challenge of designing narratives that are not only compelling but also deeply personal and interactive.

The art of narrative design in simulations is a sophisticated tapestry woven with threads of player agency, nonlinear storytelling, and emotional resonance. Each element contributes to the creation of immersive experiences that captivate and engage. Interweaving player agency with narrative structure allows for a symbiotic relationship where players shape the story as much as the story shapes them. Nonlinear storytelling, with its flexible paths and branching narratives, offers a playground for exploration and discovery, ensuring that each journey is unique. Meanwhile, emotional resonance breathes life into dynamic storylines, forging connections that linger long after the game is over. As we explore these facets, it becomes clear that the potential of narrative design in virtual worlds is as boundless as the imagination itself.

Interweaving Player Agency with Narrative Structure

Interweaving player agency with narrative structure in virtual worlds is an intricate dance that redefines storytelling. In traditional media, narratives tend to be linear and predetermined, offering audiences a passive experience. However, in the realm of simulations, players become protagonists with the power to influence outcomes, necessitating a more dynamic narrative architecture. This shift requires a deep understanding of interactive storytelling, where the player's choices ripple through the virtual environment, affecting character arcs, plot progression, and even the world itself. This emergent form of storytelling, blending agency with structure, demands innovative design philosophies that reconcile player freedom with coherent narrative arcs.

Advanced narrative frameworks now utilize branching storylines that adapt to player decisions, ensuring a unique experience for each user. This approach draws on complex algorithms and decision trees that account for myriad possibilities, maintaining narrative integrity while providing personalized journeys. For instance, in games like "The Witcher 3," player choices significantly alter the narrative landscape, affecting relationships and world events in a way that feels organic and meaningful. The challenge lies in crafting narratives that remain engaging and cohesive, regardless of the path taken, requiring sophisticated narrative planning and design.

Cutting-edge research in cognitive science and player psychology informs the integration of agency within virtual narratives. Understanding how players perceive choice and consequences enables designers to create more immersive experiences. Studies show that meaningful choices, ones that carry emotional weight or ethical dilemmas, enhance player engagement and investment in the story. This insight is pivotal in constructing narratives that resonate, as players are more likely to connect with stories that reflect their values and decisions, fostering a deeper sense of immersion and emotional attachment.

Innovative techniques in narrative design also explore the blending of linear and nonlinear elements to enrich player experience. By interspersing scripted events with open-world exploration, creators can guide players through a crafted narrative journey while allowing freedom to explore and interact. This hybrid approach can be seen in titles like "Red Dead Redemption 2," where a rich storyline unfolds amidst a sprawling, interactive environment. Balancing these elements requires careful calibration, ensuring players feel empowered by their choices without losing sight of the overarching narrative.

As simulations evolve, the interplay between player agency and narrative structure continues to push the boundaries of interactive storytelling. This evolution invites designers to experiment with new methodologies that prioritize both player autonomy and narrative depth. By embracing diverse perspectives and alternative approaches, such as procedural storytelling and AI-driven narratives, creators can craft experiences that are not only captivating but also reflective of the complex interplay between choice and consequence. This ongoing exploration of narrative possibilities promises to redefine the future of entertainment, offering players an ever-expanding canvas upon which to craft their stories.

Leveraging Nonlinear Storytelling for Immersive Experiences

In the realm of virtual storytelling, nonlinear narratives have emerged as a powerful tool to captivate and immerse audiences, offering them a dynamic and interactive experience. Unlike traditional linear storytelling, nonlinear narratives allow players to explore different pathways and outcomes, creating a sense of autonomy and personal investment in the story's progression. This approach not only enhances engagement but also mirrors the complexity of real life, where choices lead to diverse consequences. By embracing this structure, simulation architects can craft stories that are not merely experienced but actively participated in, providing depth and replayability that traditional storytelling often lacks.

The crafting of nonlinear narratives involves intricate design strategies that balance player agency with coherent storytelling. Techniques such as branching storylines, where each decision opens up new possibilities, and modular storytelling, which allows pieces of the story to be rearranged based on player actions, are pivotal. These methods can be complemented by advanced artificial intelligence that adapts the narrative in real-time, creating a personalized journey unique to each player. This personalization fosters a deeper emotional connection, as players see their choices reflected in the unfolding story, enhancing the overall immersive experience.

Recent advancements in machine learning and data analytics have further refined the potential of nonlinear narratives. By analyzing player behavior and preferences, designers can tailor narratives that resonate more profoundly with individual players, tapping into their emotions and motivations. This data-driven approach not only enriches the storytelling experience but also provides valuable insights into how narratives can be further optimized to engage diverse audiences. Additionally, procedural generation technologies can be employed to create vast, complex worlds where stories are not pre-scripted but evolve organically, providing endless narrative possibilities.

Consider the burgeoning field of interactive cinema, where the boundary between film and game blurs. These experiences enable audiences to influence the storyline through their choices, leading to multiple endings and diverse narrative arcs. This genre exemplifies how nonlinear storytelling can transform passive consumption into active participation, making viewers feel like co-creators of the story. Such innovations pave the way for the next generation of simulated experiences, where the richness of the narrative is limited only by the imagination of both the creators and the participants.

For creators seeking to harness the power of nonlinear storytelling, the key lies in the delicate balance between freedom and structure. Providing players with meaningful choices that impact the narrative requires a careful consideration of narrative coherence and player satisfaction. Designers must ensure that each pathway is equally compelling and rewarding, avoiding the pitfalls of branching fatigue, where too many choices lead to a diluted narrative experience. Thought-provoking questions, such as how to maintain narrative tension across divergent paths, encourage creators to explore innovative solutions that push the boundaries of interactive storytelling. By embracing these challenges, simulation architects can craft experiences that captivate, challenge, and inspire players, setting new standards for storytelling in virtual worlds.

Integrating Emotional Resonance in Dynamic Storylines

In the intricate tapestry of virtual storytelling, emotional resonance emerges as a pivotal element that breathes life into dynamic narratives. Crafting stories that evoke genuine emotions requires a nuanced understanding of human psychology, an area where game designers are increasingly turning to cognitive science for insights. Recent studies highlight the importance of empathy in virtual environments, suggesting that players are more engaged when they can relate to characters on a personal level. By designing characters and scenarios that reflect the players' own experiences, creators can forge deeper connections, fostering an emotional investment that transcends the digital realm. This emotional engagement not only enhances the narrative but also transforms the simulation from a mere escape into a meaningful journey.

Dynamic storylines, characterized by their fluidity and adaptability, offer fertile ground for emotional depth. Unlike traditional linear narratives, these storylines evolve based on player choices, creating a personalized experience that feels authentic and impactful. This approach requires sophisticated algorithms that can predict and respond to player behavior, ensuring that the emotional arc remains coherent and compelling. By harnessing artificial intelligence, designers can create branching narratives that retain emotional continuity, allowing players to explore diverse paths while maintaining a strong emotional core. This seamless integration of interactivity and emotion represents a frontier in narrative design, where each decision influences not only the storyline but also the player's emotional journey.

Advancements in affective computing further expand the possibilities for integrating emotional resonance in simulations. Technologies that interpret and respond to players' emotional states in real time are reshaping the landscape of interactive storytelling. By utilizing biometric feedback, such as heart rate or facial expressions, simulations can dynamically adjust to enhance or mitigate emotional experiences, tailoring the narrative to the player's current mood. This level of personalization not only deepens the emotional impact but also offers a more immersive experience, bridging the gap between the player's internal state and the virtual world. As these technologies continue to evolve, they promise to unlock new dimensions of emotional engagement, transforming how stories are experienced and remembered.

An essential aspect of crafting emotionally resonant narratives lies in the careful calibration of tension and release. By balancing moments of conflict with periods of resolution, designers can create a rhythm that mirrors the emotional ebbs and flows of real life. This balance is crucial in maintaining player interest and emotional investment, as it prevents fatigue from constant tension while avoiding complacency from prolonged calm. Techniques such as pacing and foreshadowing can be employed to guide players through the narrative, ensuring that emotional peaks are strategically placed for maximum impact. By mastering these techniques, designers can orchestrate experiences that resonate with players long after the simulation ends, leaving a lasting emotional imprint.

As creators continue to explore the boundaries of emotional storytelling in virtual worlds, they are challenged to consider the broader implications of their work. The potential for simulations to affect players on a deep emotional level raises questions about ethical design and the responsibility of creators to ensure positive experiences. By fostering empathy and understanding through emotionally resonant narratives, simulations can become powerful tools for personal growth and social change. Thought-provoking scenarios that challenge players' beliefs and encourage introspection can lead to transformative experiences, prompting players to apply newfound insights to their real-world interactions. As the lines between virtual and physical realities blur, the role of emotional resonance in narrative design will undoubtedly become increasingly significant, shaping the future of storytelling in profound and unexpected ways.

Building social ecosystems within simulations

In the ever-evolving landscape of simulated realities, the formation of social ecosystems emerges as a pivotal element that enriches the fabric of digital experiences. As we navigate these virtual worlds, it becomes apparent that the ability to foster genuine connections and communities within simulations transcends mere entertainment, offering a new dimension of social interaction. The allure of these ecosystems lies not just in their technological marvel, but in their capacity to mirror, and perhaps even enhance, the social dynamics of the physical world. This section invites readers to consider how virtual environments can be designed to support vibrant, interactive communities—places where individuals come together, not only to play but to live, collaborate, and share meaningful experiences. As avatars, artificial intelligence, and narrative structures weave together to craft these digital societies, the boundaries between reality and simulation blur, giving rise to a new paradigm of social existence.

Within these burgeoning digital societies, the crafting of dynamic social interactions becomes a cornerstone. Here, the challenge lies in designing environments that facilitate fluid communication and organic relationship-building. Furthermore, the governance structures of these virtual communities demand thoughtful consideration, as they must balance freedom and order in a realm where traditional rules may not apply. Finally, the integration of avatars and AI introduces opportunities to deepen emotional connectivity, creating more nuanced and empathetic interactions. As we delve into these subtopics, the potential for simulations to redefine entertainment and social engagement becomes increasingly evident, offering a glimpse into a future where virtual and physical lives are intertwined.

Crafting Dynamic Social Interactions in Virtual Worlds

In the vibrant tapestry of virtual worlds, crafting dynamic social interactions forms the heart of engaging simulations. These interactions are not mere digital exchanges; they echo the complexity and richness of human connections. Building upon recent advancements in artificial intelligence and machine learning, developers are now capable of creating avatars that respond with nuanced emotional intelligence, fostering relationships that feel genuine and rewarding. By simulating the subtleties of human emotion, such as empathy and humor, these avatars can engage users in meaningful dialogues, enhancing the social fabric of the virtual environment. Consider a scenario where users participate in an online festival, navigating a bustling digital cityscape filled with avatars that mirror human spontaneity and diversity. This creates a sense of belonging and community that transcends the physical world.

The design of social interactions in virtual environments also draws from the principles of behavioral psychology, which help simulate realistic social dynamics. Integrating concepts like social norms, group behavior, and personal space within these worlds encourages users to interact in ways that reflect real-life social etiquette. This approach not only enriches the user experience but also serves as a platform for social experimentation, where developers and researchers can study the effects of different social variables in a controlled setting. For instance, introducing scarcity in virtual resources can lead to the formation of alliances or conflicts, providing insights into human behavior that can inform real-world social policies.

Beyond the individual experience, these digital landscapes are evolving into complex social ecosystems where users can engage in collective activities, such as virtual concerts or collaborative projects. Recent studies highlight the potential of such environments to foster collaboration and creativity, as users from diverse backgrounds come together to solve problems or create art. These interactions can be further enhanced by leveraging virtual reality technologies, which provide an immersive experience that blurs the lines between reality and simulation. Imagine participating in a digital art exhibition where users contribute their creations in real-time, transforming the space into a living canvas of shared expression. This level of interactivity fosters a sense of community and shared purpose, driving engagement and satisfaction.

The role of artificial intelligence in shaping these interactions cannot be overstated. By employing sophisticated algorithms, developers can analyze user behavior to personalize interactions, making them more engaging and relevant. AI-driven avatars can adapt their conversational styles based on user preferences, creating a tailored social experience that evolves over time. This level of customization provides users with a sense of agency and investment in their virtual lives. Moreover, AI can facilitate cross-cultural exchanges by translating languages and bridging cultural gaps, enabling global communities to thrive within simulated spaces. Such innovations hold the promise of fostering a more inclusive and interconnected digital society.

As we contemplate the future of social interactions in virtual worlds, it is essential to address the ethical considerations that accompany these developments. Ensuring privacy and safeguarding against manipulation in these environments is paramount to maintaining user trust and engagement. Developers must navigate the delicate balance between creating compelling social experiences and protecting user autonomy. By adopting transparent and ethical design practices, the creators of virtual worlds can ensure that these spaces remain not only a source of entertainment and learning but also a refuge where users can connect, collaborate, and explore the full potential of human interaction. This ongoing dialogue between technology and humanity will continue to shape the evolution of social ecosystems in the digital age.

Designing Community Governance Structures for Simulated Societies

Designing community governance structures for simulated societies presents a fascinating confluence of technology, sociology, and philosophy. In these virtual domains, architects of digital realms face the intricate task of establishing governance systems that mirror, enhance, or even deviate from real-world societal frameworks. At the heart of this endeavor lies the challenge of creating systems that not only maintain order and fairness but also empower users to shape their environments collaboratively. This process involves an interdisciplinary approach that draws from political theory, game design, and cybernetics to create systems that are both robust and adaptable. Such governance structures must be capable of evolving in response to the dynamic and often unpredictable interactions among users, much like living organisms adapting to their ecosystems.

In crafting these governance frameworks, the integration of decentralized technologies, such as blockchain, offers unprecedented opportunities for transparency and accountability. These technologies enable the establishment of immutable records of decisions made within the virtual society, fostering trust and legitimacy among participants. Blockchain can facilitate democratic processes, allowing users to engage in decision-making through voting systems or consensus mechanisms. By leveraging these tools, simulated societies can experiment with innovative governance models, ranging from direct democracy to meritocratic systems, offering insights into potential real-world applications. The use of smart contracts, self-executing contracts with the terms of the agreement directly written into code, further enhances these systems by automating rule enforcement, thereby reducing the potential for human bias or error.

A key consideration in designing governance structures is the need to balance individual autonomy with collective welfare. This can be achieved by implementing layered governance models that distribute authority across different levels of the community, allowing for local autonomy while maintaining overarching guidelines that ensure harmony and cohesion. For instance, smaller groups within the simulation could self-govern, creating rules and norms that reflect their unique needs and values. At the same time, these micro-governments would adhere to broader principles established by the overarching governance structure, ensuring a unified direction for the society. This approach fosters a sense of ownership and responsibility among users, encouraging active participation and engagement.

Exploring the psychological and social dynamics of governance within simulated societies also yields valuable insights. The use of artificial intelligence to mediate conflicts and facilitate communication can promote a more harmonious virtual community. AI-driven systems can analyze patterns of interaction, identify potential sources of tension, and propose solutions that align with the society's values and goals. Moreover, by simulating various governance scenarios, communities can test and refine their structures in a risk-free environment, gaining a deeper understanding of the consequences of different governance approaches. This iterative process allows for the continuous improvement of governance systems, ensuring they remain relevant and effective as the virtual society evolves.

The potential for simulated societies to serve as laboratories for governance experimentation raises intriguing questions about the future of social organization. As these virtual communities develop, they may offer alternative models of governance that challenge conventional wisdom and inspire real-world change. How might these virtual experiments influence our understanding of power, authority, and social responsibility? What lessons can be learned from the successes and failures of governance systems in these digital realms? By examining these questions, we not only deepen our comprehension of virtual societies but also reflect on the broader implications for our tangible world, highlighting the transformative potential of simulated realities in reshaping human interaction and governance.

Enhancing Emotional Connectivity Through Avatar and AI Integration

In the realm of simulated realities, emotional connectivity emerges as a cornerstone for creating engaging and meaningful experiences. The integration of avatars with advanced artificial intelligence offers a profound avenue for enhancing this connectivity. Avatars, as digital representations of users, serve as conduits for emotional expression. When imbued with sophisticated AI, these avatars can simulate human-like behaviors, emotions, and even empathy, creating an environment where users feel seen and understood. By employing machine learning algorithms, avatars can adapt to a user's preferences, communication style, and emotional states, fostering a sense of companionship and deepening the user's emotional investment in the simulation.

Recent advancements in natural language processing and emotional AI have revolutionized the way avatars interact with users. These technologies enable avatars to engage in nuanced conversations, recognize subtle emotional cues, and respond in ways that are contextually appropriate and emotionally resonant. For example, AI-driven avatars in social simulations can facilitate interactions that mirror real-world dynamics, such as offering support during a difficult moment or celebrating achievements with genuine enthusiasm. This kind of responsiveness not only enhances the realism of the simulated environment but also strengthens the emotional bonds users form with their virtual counterparts, making the experience more immersive and rewarding.

Furthermore, the integration of AI in avatars extends beyond mere interaction to include the creation of dynamic social ecosystems within simulations. By utilizing AI to manage and mediate social interactions, developers can design virtual worlds where communities evolve organically based on the interactions between users and their avatars. These ecosystems can simulate the complexities of human societies, including governance, social norms, and cultural diversity, offering users a rich tapestry of experiences that challenge and expand their understanding of social dynamics. This approach not only enhances the entertainment value of simulations but also provides a platform for experimenting with new social models and structures.

The potential for avatars to facilitate emotional connectivity is not limited to human-to-avatar interactions. AI can also enable avatars to mediate interactions between users, acting as facilitators or moderators. For instance, in collaborative simulations or virtual meetings, avatars can help manage group dynamics, ensuring that all participants are heard and that conflicts are resolved amicably. By analyzing group interactions, AI-powered avatars can suggest strategies for improving communication and collaboration, ultimately creating a more harmonious and productive environment. This capability is particularly valuable in educational or professional simulations, where effective communication is crucial for success.

As we continue to explore the possibilities of avatar and AI integration, it is essential to consider the ethical implications and potential challenges. Issues such as privacy, authenticity, and emotional manipulation must be addressed to ensure that these technologies are used responsibly. Thought-provoking questions arise, such as how much autonomy should be granted to AI-driven avatars and what safeguards are necessary to protect users' emotional well-being. By engaging with these questions and seeking diverse perspectives, developers and researchers can create simulations that are not only emotionally engaging but also ethically sound, ultimately enriching the human experience in both virtual and real worlds.

Simulations as the future of interactive entertainment

Imagine a world where the boundaries of storytelling blur seamlessly with the very essence of our senses—a realm where narratives are not merely told but experienced in a profound, multisensory symphony. This is the promise of simulations as the future of interactive entertainment, where the lines between player and character dissolve, crafting a reality where immersion is not just visual but visceral. As technology evolves, so too does our capacity for storytelling. No longer confined to the static pages of a book or the flat screens of our devices, these narratives unfold dynamically, adapting to the choices and emotions of their audience. In this new era of entertainment, stories breathe and evolve, mirroring the complexity of human experience itself.

This transformative shift in entertainment is driven by the potential for deep personalization and adaptive gaming experiences, where every player's journey is uniquely tailored. The games of tomorrow will know us as intimately as our closest confidants, shaping worlds that respond to our desires and decisions. Multisensory integration enhances this connection, engaging not just our minds but our very emotions, creating a tapestry of experience that resonates on a deeply personal level. As we explore these possibilities, we embark on a journey into the heart of what it means to be entertained, challenged, and moved within the boundless landscapes of simulated realities.

Immersive Storytelling and Dynamic Narratives

Immersive storytelling in simulated realities has transformed the landscape of interactive entertainment, propelling narratives beyond traditional confines. As technology advances, storytelling in simulations becomes an art form that weaves together complex, dynamic plots with interactive environments. These narratives adapt to the choices and actions of participants, creating a bespoke experience that is as unique as the individual engaging with it. This shift from passive consumption to active participation allows for stories that evolve in real time, responding to user input and driving engagement to new heights. The convergence of narrative design and simulation technology enables creators to craft worlds where the storyline is not just a backdrop but a living entity that players can influence and mold.

The fusion of advanced AI and machine learning has paved the way for dynamic narratives that are not only responsive but also predictive. These tech-

nologies analyze player behavior to anticipate decisions, offering plot developments tailored to individual preferences and actions. This level of customization
enhances immersion, as the storyline reflects personal choices, making each
user's journey distinct. By understanding the emotional and cognitive states of
players, these intelligent systems can introduce narrative twists and turns that
resonate on a deeper level, fostering a connection between the participant and
the virtual world. The result is a narrative experience that is as unpredictable and
engaging as real life, blurring the line between reality and fiction.

Multisensory integration plays a crucial role in the realm of immersive storytelling, engaging players on multiple levels and enriching the narrative experience. By incorporating elements such as haptic feedback, spatial audio, and
even olfactory cues, simulations create a tapestry of sensory stimuli that envelop
players in the story. This holistic approach to storytelling not only heightens
emotional engagement but also aids in the suspension of disbelief, drawing
participants deeper into the simulated world. As sensory technologies continue
to evolve, their integration into narrative design will enable more profound and
emotionally resonant experiences, where players can truly feel the weight of their
choices and the impact of their actions within the story.

The notion of collaborative storytelling further enhances the potential of
simulations as the future of interactive entertainment. In these environments,
narratives are not solely dictated by developers but are co-created by communities of players. This participatory approach allows for a diversity of perspectives
and voices, enriching the narrative tapestry with varied experiences and viewpoints. The communal aspect fosters a sense of belonging and investment, as
players contribute to the unfolding of the story and shape the world in which
they reside. By facilitating collaboration, simulations can harness the collective
creativity of participants, resulting in narratives that are both expansive and
deeply personal.

As we envision the future of storytelling within simulations, we must consider the ethical implications and responsibilities of crafting such immersive
experiences. The power to create narratives that deeply affect players' emotions
and perceptions carries with it the potential for manipulation and exploitation. Developers must navigate the delicate balance between engagement and
ethical storytelling, ensuring that narratives enrich rather than detract from
participants' lives. By establishing ethical guidelines and fostering transparency
in narrative design, creators can ensure that immersive storytelling remains a
force for good, offering experiences that are as enriching as they are entertaining.
This commitment to ethical storytelling will be essential as simulations become
an ever more integral part of our cultural and social landscape, shaping the way
we experience stories in the digital age.

Personalization and Adaptive Gaming Experiences

Personalization and adaptive gaming experiences represent a dynamic shift in the landscape of interactive entertainment, where the focus gravitates towards crafting uniquely tailored experiences for each participant. By leveraging advanced algorithms and data analytics, game designers can now curate experiences that evolve in real-time based on a player's choices, preferences, and behaviors. This innovation not only enhances engagement but also fosters a profound sense of agency, allowing players to see their decisions ripple across the virtual world. Such adaptability in gaming is reminiscent of a bespoke piece of art, where every brushstroke is influenced by the observer's gaze, resulting in a narrative that is as individual as the player themselves.

Harnessing the power of machine learning, adaptive gaming systems are increasingly capable of predicting player preferences, adjusting difficulty levels, and even suggesting new narrative paths. This creates a dynamic interplay between the game and the player, akin to a conversation that evolves with each interaction. For instance, a game might modify its storyline to align with a player's emotional responses, which are measured through biofeedback or direct input. This creates a loop of continuous feedback and adaptation, ensuring that the experience remains fresh and engaging, regardless of how many times one revisits it. Such innovations mark a departure from traditional static narratives, pushing the boundaries of what interactive storytelling can achieve.

The integration of artificial intelligence into game design paves the way for more nuanced character interactions and deeper emotional connections. Non-playable characters (NPCs) in games are no longer static entities but are instead imbued with the capacity to learn and evolve based on player interactions. This can lead to relationships that develop over time, mirroring the complexities of human connections. Imagine a virtual companion that remembers past encounters, reacts differently based on previous choices, and offers companionship tailored to the player's mood and actions. This level of personalization transforms the gaming experience into something more akin to a living, breathing world where players feel genuinely understood and valued.

A remarkable aspect of adaptive gaming is its potential to cater to diverse audiences by accommodating various skill levels and preferences. This inclusivity ensures that games are not just the domain of the seasoned gamer but are accessible to novices and experts alike. By dynamically adjusting challenges and providing hints or assistance when needed, games can maintain an appropriate level of difficulty that keeps players engaged without causing frustration. This adaptability extends beyond gameplay mechanics to include elements such as aesthetics and soundscapes, which can be customized to suit individual tastes, further enhancing immersion and enjoyment.

As we stand on the brink of this new frontier in gaming, the implications for the future are profound. The fusion of personalization and adaptive technology not only promises richer and more engaging experiences but also poses intriguing questions about the nature of creativity and authorship in a world where players have significant influence over the narrative. Will the line between creator and participant blur, leading to a collaborative form of storytelling? This shift challenges us to consider the broader implications of such technology, encouraging us to explore how these advances might redefine not just entertainment, but our understanding of human interaction and creativity in digital realms.

Multisensory Integration and Emotional Engagement

Multisensory integration in simulated realities is a groundbreaking frontier that revolutionizes how users experience interactive entertainment. By seamlessly blending visual, auditory, tactile, and even olfactory stimuli, simulations can transport individuals to worlds that not only mimic reality but also evoke profound emotional responses. Recent research has shown that engaging multiple senses simultaneously enhances immersion and can significantly bolster emotional engagement. For instance, incorporating haptic feedback in virtual reality gaming allows players to feel the weight of a virtual sword or the texture of a simulated surface, creating a more authentic and emotionally resonant experience. This multisensory approach transcends traditional gaming by enveloping users in a sensory-rich environment, blurring the lines between the virtual and the tangible.

One of the most intriguing aspects of multisensory integration is its potential to evoke emotional states with precision. By manipulating sensory inputs, developers can craft experiences that elicit specific emotions, from awe and wonder to fear and excitement. Consider a virtual environment where the sound of distant thunder, the scent of rain-soaked earth, and the cool breeze of an impending storm are meticulously synthesized. Such an experience can trigger visceral reactions that are both vivid and deeply personal. This level of emotional craftsmanship opens new avenues for storytelling, allowing narratives to unfold in a manner that is not only witnessed but viscerally felt. As simulations become more sophisticated, the ability to tailor emotional experiences will play a pivotal role in defining the future of interactive entertainment.

In the realm of multisensory simulations, personalization emerges as a powerful tool for enhancing engagement. By analyzing user preferences and physiological responses, simulations can dynamically adjust sensory elements to align with individual tastes and sensitivities. This adaptive capability ensures that each user encounters a uniquely tailored experience, one that resonates with their personal inclinations and emotional thresholds. For instance, a horror simulation might modulate its sensory cues—like dimming lights or intensifying sounds—based on the user's fear response, resulting in a highly personalized and impactful encounter. Such customization not only fosters deeper emotional connections but also encourages prolonged engagement, as users are more likely to immerse themselves in experiences that feel attuned to their inner world.

The advancement of multisensory technology is not limited to traditional gaming environments. It extends into the realm of virtual social interactions, where the fusion of senses can enhance connectivity and empathy among participants. In a virtual concert, for example, the synchronized pulse of music felt through haptic devices, coupled with the visual spectacle of light displays, can create a shared emotional experience that transcends geographical boundaries. This convergence of multisensory inputs fosters a sense of presence and community, transforming solitary virtual experiences into collective, emotionally charged events. As such, the integration of multisensory elements holds the potential to redefine social dynamics within virtual spaces, offering new possibilities for connection and collaboration.

As we explore the potential of multisensory integration, it is essential to consider its broader implications on human cognition and behavior. Thought-provoking questions arise: How does the constant interplay of artificial sensory stimuli affect our perception of reality outside the simulation? Could these experiences alter our emotional resilience or empathy in the physical world? While the answers remain elusive, the journey to uncover them promises to yield valuable insights into the human psyche. Developers and researchers must navigate this landscape with a keen awareness of the ethical considerations involved, ensuring that the enrichment of virtual experiences does not inadvertently diminish our appreciation of the real world. As we stand on the cusp of this multisensory revolution, the challenge lies in harnessing its potential to elevate human experience while preserving our innate connection to the tangible world around us.

The journey through this chapter reveals the transformative power of simulations in the realm of entertainment, where the evolution of gaming has ushered in an era of fully immersive experiences. The art of narrative design takes center stage, crafting stories that not only captivate but also engage participants in ways previously unimaginable. Within these virtual landscapes, social ecosystems flourish, allowing for rich interactions and communities to form, blurring the lines between reality and imagination. As simulations increasingly define the future of interactive entertainment, they invite us to reconsider our relationship with technology and storytelling. These developments are not merely about escapism; they represent a profound shift in how we experience and interact with the world. As we contemplate the possibilities, we are prompted to consider how these advances might reshape our cultural and social constructs. What new narratives will emerge, and how will they influence our perceptions of reality? With these reflections, we prepare to explore the broader societal impacts and ethical considerations that simulations bring to the forefront, setting the stage for the next exploration of simulation's role in our collective future.

Chapter Six

Societal Applications Of Simulation

Imagine a world where the bustling chaos of a city is meticulously orchestrated in a virtual environment before a single brick is laid. Picture disaster scenarios unfolding within the safe confines of a simulation, where first responders rehearse their roles with precision, readying themselves for events that may never come. These are not merely flights of fancy but tangible realities made possible through the power of simulation. As our journey unfolds, we venture into the transformative applications of simulated worlds, exploring how they hold the potential to revolutionize the very fabric of society.

The urban landscape, with its intricate networks and towering structures, presents a canvas for innovation and foresight. Within virtual environments, urban planners and architects can conjure entire cities, testing and refining every detail. This approach not only optimizes infrastructure but fosters sustainable development, ensuring that future generations inherit vibrant, livable spaces. Beyond the city limits, simulations offer crucial insights into crisis management. By replicating natural disasters and emergencies, we arm ourselves with knowledge and preparedness, mitigating the impact of real-world catastrophes.

Yet, the reach of simulation extends beyond the tangible. In the realm of medicine, the potential for healing and discovery is profound. From surgical training to mental health therapy, simulations provide a safe haven for exploration and learning, allowing practitioners to hone their skills with unparalleled precision. And as global challenges become increasingly complex, simulations emerge as a vital tool for international collaboration, bridging cultural and geographical divides. In these digital arenas, we find the seeds of collective wisdom, nurturing a future where humanity thrives in unity.

Urban planning and infrastructure design in virtual environments

At the intersection of theory and practice, we find the transformative potential of virtual environments in urban planning and infrastructure design. These digital landscapes allow city planners and architects to explore the complexities of urban growth with unprecedented precision, creating sustainable models that anticipate future challenges. The interplay between virtual and physical realities empowers designers to prototype infrastructure in safe, controlled settings, where errors become opportunities for learning rather than costly mistakes. The vividness of these simulations invites stakeholders, from policymakers to local communities, to visualize potential futures and engage actively in shaping them. This participatory approach not only democratizes urban planning but also catalyzes innovative solutions that might otherwise remain unexplored. As cities grow denser and resources scarcer, the ability to test and refine urban strategies virtually becomes not just advantageous but essential.

In this digital age, the boundaries between imagination and reality blur, allowing for a collaborative dialogue that bridges the gap between experts and citizens. Interactive simulations serve as a canvas where diverse perspectives can converge, fostering a shared vision for urban spaces that reflect collective aspirations. The immersive nature of these tools enhances public engagement, transforming passive observers into active contributors to urban design. By envisioning the ripple effects of various planning decisions, communities gain a deeper understanding of the intricacies involved, cultivating a sense of ownership and responsibility. As the discussion transitions into simulating urban growth and sustainability models, the stage is set for exploring how these virtual environments can guide us toward more resilient, inclusive, and vibrant cities. The journey through this virtual realm offers insights not only into the mechanics of urban planning but also into the rich, interconnected tapestry of human experience that these spaces are designed to support.

Simulating Urban Growth and Sustainability Models

In the realm of urban development, simulating urban growth and sustainability models has emerged as an indispensable tool for city planners and environmental scientists. By leveraging advanced computational algorithms and immersive simulation platforms, urban planners can now predict the complex interplay of demographic trends, infrastructure demands, and ecological impacts in a dynamic urban landscape. Such simulations allow for the envisioning of sustainable cities, where resources are optimized, and carbon footprints are reduced. For instance, cities like Singapore have successfully utilized these models to enhance green spaces and improve water management systems, serving as a paragon for sustainable urban growth. These virtual environments empower planners to experiment with various scenarios, assessing the long-term implications of urban policies before implementation, thus minimizing risks and maximizing benefits for urban dwellers.

The integration of Geographic Information Systems (GIS) with urban simulation models has further revolutionized the field, offering a granular analysis of urban landscapes. By embedding real-time data into these models, planners can visualize the potential impacts of zoning changes or infrastructure development on local ecosystems and communities. This approach not only facilitates informed decision-making but also fosters resilience against unforeseen challenges, such as climate-induced disruptions. Cities like New York and Amsterdam have begun to adopt these GIS-integrated models, using them to simulate flood scenarios and develop adaptive measures, ensuring urban growth aligns with sustainability goals. The ability to simulate and adjust urban plans in response to real-time data heralds a new era of proactive and responsible urban management.

The concept of urban growth simulation extends beyond mere infrastructure planning; it is increasingly becoming a platform for public engagement and participatory design. Interactive simulations provide citizens with a tangible understanding of proposed urban changes, allowing for greater transparency and involvement in the decision-making process. These platforms can democratize urban planning, as residents offer insights and feedback, influencing the development of their communities. Virtual reality (VR) and augmented reality (AR) technologies are pivotal in this regard, transforming abstract architectural plans into immersive experiences that the public can explore and critique. This collaborative approach not only strengthens community ties but also ensures that urban growth aligns with the aspirations and needs of its inhabitants.

From an academic perspective, the exploration of urban growth simulations has sparked a wealth of innovative research. Scholars are delving into the psychological impacts of living in densely populated environments and how virtual simulations can preemptively address these challenges. Studies have explored the potential of biophilic design elements in virtual models, investigating how integrating natural elements into urban settings can enhance mental well-being and foster a sense of harmony between urban and natural environments. This intersection of urban planning and cognitive science offers a rich tapestry of insights, paving the way for urban environments that are not only efficient but also enriching for their residents.

As urban simulation models continue to evolve, they present an intriguing opportunity to redefine the future of city living. By harnessing the power of artificial intelligence and machine learning, these simulations can become predictive tools, offering foresight into urban trends and enabling cities to adapt swiftly to shifting needs. Planners are already exploring the potential of these technologies to model smart cities, where infrastructure is seamlessly integrated with digital networks to enhance quality of life and sustainability. This vision of urban growth, supported by intelligent simulations, promises a future where cities are not just places to live but thriving ecosystems that nurture human potential.

Virtual Infrastructure Prototyping for Real-World Implementation

Creating virtual prototypes of infrastructure represents a transformative shift in how urban planners and engineers approach real-world projects. By harnessing the power of advanced simulation technologies, professionals can now visualize and test infrastructure designs with unprecedented precision before any ground is broken. This approach not only enhances the accuracy of planning but also significantly reduces the costs and risks associated with trial-and-error methods in physical settings. By simulating various scenarios, such as traffic flow, environmental impact, and resource allocation, virtual prototyping offers a comprehensive understanding of how infrastructure will perform under different conditions. This predictive capability is invaluable for ensuring that new developments are resilient, efficient, and sustainable.

Virtual prototyping leverages data-driven models to create detailed digital twins of prospective infrastructure projects. These models integrate real-time data and advanced analytics to provide insights into the dynamic interactions between different components of urban systems. For instance, by simulating a new transit system within a virtual cityscape, planners can identify potential bottlenecks and optimize routes for maximum efficiency. This meticulous approach not only enhances the functionality of the infrastructure but also improves its adaptability to future changes, such as population growth or shifts in environmental conditions. The integration of AI algorithms further refines these simulations, enabling predictive maintenance and adaptive responses to unforeseen challenges.

One of the most compelling aspects of virtual infrastructure prototyping is its ability to foster collaboration among diverse stakeholders. By providing a shared, interactive platform, simulations facilitate communication between architects, engineers, government officials, and community members. This collaborative environment ensures that various perspectives are considered, leading to more inclusive and balanced designs. Engaging stakeholders in the virtual phase of development allows for iterative feedback, enabling adjustments that reflect community needs and values. This participatory approach not only enhances the project's relevance and acceptance but also promotes a sense of ownership and accountability among those involved.

While the advantages of virtual prototyping are clear, it also requires a reimagining of traditional planning processes. Professionals must be adept at integrating digital tools with conventional methods, ensuring that the insights gained from simulations translate into actionable strategies. This integration necessitates cross-disciplinary expertise, where urban planners, data scientists, and software developers collaborate seamlessly. The challenge lies in balancing technological innovation with practical application, ensuring that virtual designs are both visionary and feasible. As the field continues to evolve, ongoing education and training will be essential for professionals to stay abreast of technological advancements and best practices.

As we contemplate the future of urban development, virtual infrastructure prototyping stands as a beacon of possibility. It invites us to ask profound questions about the nature of our built environment and how it can be optimized to serve society's evolving needs. How might these technologies reshape our cities to be more resilient in the face of climate change? What opportunities do they offer for creating spaces that are not only functional but also enhance the quality of life for inhabitants? By pushing the boundaries of what is possible in virtual spaces, we open the door to new paradigms of urban design that prioritize sustainability, efficiency, and human well-being.

Enhancing Public Engagement in Urban Design Through Interactive Simulations

Interactive simulations have revolutionized public engagement in urban design, offering a dynamic platform for communities to participate actively in shaping their environments. By visualizing proposed changes in a virtual setting, citizens gain a tangible understanding of urban planning decisions, fostering a deeper connection to the process. This participatory approach democratizes urban design, allowing individuals from diverse backgrounds to contribute their insights and perspectives. With the aid of virtual reality (VR) and augmented reality (AR) technologies, cities can create immersive experiences that empower residents to explore potential modifications and provide informed feedback. Such engagement not only enhances the quality of urban planning but also builds trust between communities and decision-makers.

Recent advancements in simulation technology have enabled the creation of highly detailed virtual models that replicate real-world environments with striking accuracy. These models serve as a canvas for exploring various urban scenarios, from traffic flow optimization to green space allocation. For instance, planners can simulate the impact of a new public transit system on local neighborhoods, providing a clear visual of potential benefits and challenges. By incorporating real-time data and environmental variables, these simulations offer a nuanced understanding of complex urban dynamics. This level of detail allows stakeholders to make data-driven decisions, balancing growth with sustainability and livability.

The gamification of urban design through interactive simulations further enriches public involvement. By transforming planning processes into engaging experiences, gamification encourages participation and creativity. Platforms like Minecraft have been utilized in urban planning workshops, where participants collaboratively design digital landscapes that reflect their vision for their communities. Such initiatives harness the power of play to stimulate innovative thinking and foster a sense of ownership among participants. By integrating elements of competition and reward, gamification motivates individuals to engage more deeply with urban planning concepts, ultimately leading to more thoughtful and inclusive designs.

Interactive simulations also serve as a bridge between urban planners and the public, facilitating meaningful dialogue and collaboration. By presenting complex planning concepts in an accessible format, simulations help demystify technical jargon, making it easier for laypeople to engage with the material. This transparency is crucial for building consensus and addressing potential conflicts early in the planning process. Moreover, simulations can be used to conduct virtual town hall meetings, where stakeholders can explore proposed developments together and share their reactions in real-time. Such collaborative environments encourage diverse viewpoints and foster a culture of mutual respect and understanding.

As the field continues to evolve, the integration of artificial intelligence and machine learning into simulations holds promise for enhancing public engagement further. These technologies can tailor simulations to individual preferences, offering personalized experiences that resonate more deeply with users. For example, AI-driven simulations might adjust visualizations to highlight aspects relevant to specific community interests, such as environmental sustainability or economic development. This personalization enhances the relevance and impact of simulations, ensuring that they remain a powerful tool for participatory urban design. By embracing these cutting-edge technologies, urban planners can create more inclusive and responsive cities that reflect the aspirations of their inhabitants.

Crisis simulations: Preparing for natural disasters and emergencies

In a world increasingly vulnerable to the whims of nature and the unpredictability of human-made crises, the ability to anticipate and prepare for disasters is more crucial than ever. Simulations offer a powerful tool for navigating these turbulent waters, providing a safe space to test responses and strategies without the dire consequences of real-world experimentation. By crafting meticulously detailed virtual environments, experts can model the chaotic dance of natural disasters such as hurricanes, earthquakes, and floods, as well as human emergencies like industrial accidents and terrorist attacks. These digital rehearsals enable first responders, policymakers, and communities to rehearse their roles, refine their strategies, and build resilience against future challenges. The fusion of virtual reality and real-world data creates a dynamic laboratory where scenarios can be adjusted and outcomes analyzed, fostering an atmosphere of preparedness that can save lives and resources when the unthinkable becomes reality.

As we journey through the possibilities that crisis simulations offer, the focus shifts to the specialized training of first responders and crisis teams. Here, immersive virtual training environments are crafted to replicate the high-pressure conditions of actual emergencies, honing the skills and instincts necessary for effective response. The integration of AI and data analytics further enhances these simulations, offering predictive insights that allow for proactive measures rather than reactive ones. This harmonious blend of technology and human ingenuity promises not only to transform the preparedness landscape but also to foster a culture of continuous learning and adaptation in the face of adversity. Through these digital blueprints, society can build a fortified framework capable of withstanding the storms of tomorrow.

Simulating Disaster Scenarios for Enhanced Emergency Response

In the realm of disaster preparedness, simulating disaster scenarios has emerged as a transformative approach to enhancing emergency response capabilities. Through the use of advanced computational models and immersive virtual environments, these simulations provide invaluable opportunities for emergency responders to practice and refine their skills in controlled yet realistic conditions. By recreating complex scenarios such as earthquakes, floods, or pandemics, responders can experience the dynamic challenges of real-world crises without the immediate risks. This method not only hones individual skills but also fosters teamwork and communication, critical components of effective crisis management. Tailored scenarios can be adjusted to reflect specific local vulnerabilities, ensuring that training is relevant and impactful.

One of the most intriguing advancements in this field is the integration of real-time data into simulated environments. By incorporating data from sources such as weather forecasts, geological sensors, and social media feeds, simulations can evolve dynamically, offering participants a more authentic experience of unfolding crises. This data-driven approach not only enhances the realism of the simulations but also enables responders to experiment with decision-making processes in a rapidly changing environment. The ability to predict and respond to shifting conditions is crucial, as it mirrors the unpredictability of actual disaster situations. As technology continues to advance, these simulations are becoming increasingly sophisticated, offering nuanced scenarios that challenge and expand the capabilities of emergency teams.

Another crucial aspect of disaster simulations is their role in identifying and addressing potential gaps in existing response strategies. By running through various scenarios, teams can pinpoint weaknesses in their protocols, logistics, and infrastructure, allowing for proactive improvements. For instance, simulations can highlight the need for better coordination between different agencies or reveal inadequacies in resource distribution during a crisis. This iterative learning process not only strengthens current systems but also drives innovation in emergency management practices. As a result, communities become more resilient, better equipped to handle unforeseen events, and more adept at minimizing the impact of disasters on human lives and property.

Innovative collaborations between technology developers, emergency response agencies, and academic institutions are pushing the boundaries of what is possible in disaster simulations. These partnerships facilitate the exchange of expertise and resources, leading to the development of cutting-edge tools and methodologies. For example, universities may contribute research on human behavior during crises, while tech companies provide the latest in augmented reality technology. Such collaborations ensure that simulations are grounded in scientific research and technological advancements, resulting in more effective training programs. As these partnerships continue to evolve, they hold the promise of producing even more sophisticated and impactful simulation models.

The future of disaster simulation is poised for further breakthroughs, with artificial intelligence playing an increasingly pivotal role. AI algorithms can analyze vast amounts of data to predict potential disaster scenarios and optimize response strategies. These intelligent systems can also adapt simulations in real-time, providing responders with personalized feedback and guidance. By incorporating AI, simulations become not only more responsive but also more predictive, offering insights that can preemptively mitigate the effects of disasters. As we continue to explore the potential of these technologies, the ultimate goal remains to safeguard lives and build a more resilient society, capable of withstanding the challenges of an uncertain future.

Leveraging Virtual Training for First Responders and Crisis Teams

The advent of virtual training for first responders and crisis teams has transformed the landscape of emergency preparedness, offering a dynamic alternative to traditional training methods. By immersing trainees in realistic, simulated environments, virtual training provides a safe yet challenging platform to develop critical skills. These scenarios replicate the high-pressure situations responders might face during natural disasters, enabling them to hone their decision-making abilities and teamwork skills without the inherent risks of live exercises. The realism and adaptability of these simulations ensure that first responders are better equipped to handle the unpredictability of real-world crises, fostering both confidence and competence.

Cutting-edge technologies such as augmented reality (AR) and virtual reality (VR) play a pivotal role in enhancing the fidelity of these training simulations. With the ability to overlay virtual elements onto physical surroundings, AR allows trainees to interact with their environment in ways that were previously impossible, while VR offers fully immersive experiences that engage multiple senses. These innovations create a comprehensive training environment that not only improves situational awareness but also reinforces muscle memory and cognitive resilience. The integration of haptic feedback and biometric sensors further enriches this experience, providing real-time data on trainee performance and stress levels, allowing for tailored feedback and continuous improvement.

A fascinating development in this field is the application of artificial intelligence to customize training scenarios based on individual or team performance. AI systems can analyze a trainee's actions and adapt the complexity of the simulation in real-time, ensuring an optimal level of challenge and engagement. This personalized approach not only accelerates learning but also identifies specific areas requiring improvement, enabling targeted interventions. Additionally, AI can simulate a wide array of disaster scenarios, from earthquakes to chemical spills, broadening the scope of training and ensuring preparedness for diverse emergencies.

As virtual training becomes more prevalent, interdisciplinary collaboration is emerging as a cornerstone of effective crisis response. By facilitating joint training exercises among various emergency services, simulations promote a cohesive response strategy that transcends traditional organizational silos. These collaborative efforts are crucial in fostering communication and coordination among disparate teams, which are essential for efficient emergency management. The ability to simulate large-scale, multi-agency operations in a virtual setting allows for the refinement of interagency protocols and the establishment of best practices, ultimately enhancing the overall resilience of communities.

The potential of virtual training extends beyond immediate tactical benefits, contributing to a broader cultural shift within emergency services. By embracing innovative training methodologies, agencies can cultivate a mindset of continuous improvement and adaptability, which is vital in an ever-evolving threat landscape. This proactive approach not only improves individual and team performance but also instills a culture of lifelong learning and innovation, ensuring that first responders remain at the forefront of crisis management. As these technologies continue to evolve, they promise to redefine the boundaries of what is possible in emergency preparedness, offering a glimpse into a future where simulations play an integral role in safeguarding societies.

Integrating AI and Data Analytics in Predictive Crisis Simulations

Artificial intelligence and data analytics have transformed the landscape of crisis simulations, offering unprecedented precision and insight into potential disaster scenarios. By employing advanced algorithms, AI can analyze vast datasets to identify patterns and predict the trajectory of natural disasters such as hurricanes, earthquakes, or floods. This predictive capability allows for the creation of dynamic, real-time simulations that can model various scenarios, providing emergency planners with valuable foresight. For instance, AI-driven simulations can assess the potential impact of a hurricane on coastal communities by integrating real-time meteorological data with historical storm patterns, enabling more accurate forecasting and preparation.

In tandem with AI, data analytics enhances the granularity of these simulations by processing and interpreting complex datasets from diverse sources. This integration allows for a comprehensive understanding of the myriad factors that contribute to crisis situations. By harnessing machine learning techniques, these simulations can adapt and refine their models based on new information, continually improving their accuracy and reliability. For example, during a wildfire crisis, data analytics can process satellite imagery, sensor data, and weather forecasts to predict the fire's spread, informing evacuation plans and resource allocation. Such simulations not only prepare responders for immediate threats but also aid in long-term strategic planning.

The potential of AI-enhanced crisis simulations extends to training and preparedness, where immersive virtual environments can be tailored to replicate real-world emergency conditions. These simulations allow first responders and crisis teams to experience and react to complex scenarios, honing their skills in a controlled yet realistic setting. By simulating high-pressure situations, such as multi-car accidents during a snowstorm or coordinated responses to a chemical spill, personnel can practice decision-making, communication, and coordination in a risk-free environment. This experiential learning approach can significantly enhance readiness and effectiveness when an actual crisis occurs.

Despite the promise of AI-driven simulations, it is crucial to consider potential biases and limitations inherent in the data and algorithms. Ensuring the inclusivity and accuracy of the datasets used is vital for generating equitable outcomes. Diverse perspectives can offer insights into potential blind spots, leading to more robust and inclusive crisis response strategies. For instance, incorporating local community knowledge and indigenous expertise into simulation models can enhance the cultural and situational relevance of the simulations, thereby improving their efficacy and acceptance.

Imagining a future where predictive simulations are a staple of crisis management invites intriguing questions about the ethical deployment of such technologies. How can societies balance the benefits of these tools with concerns about privacy and data security? What measures can be implemented to ensure that AI and analytics are used responsibly and transparently? As these technologies continue to evolve, addressing these questions will be imperative to unlock their full potential while safeguarding human rights and dignity. By fostering a dialogue around these issues, we can pave the way for a future where technology and humanity collaboratively face the challenges of an unpredictable world.

Medical applications: Surgery, therapy, and mental health treatments

Imagine waking up one morning to find yourself in a world where the boundaries of medicine have expanded far beyond the confines of physical reality. In this world, a surgeon dons a virtual reality headset, stepping into a meticulously crafted simulation of a human body, each organ and vessel rendered with breathtaking accuracy. As the scalpel hovers above a virtual artery, the surgeon practices a complex procedure with a precision that only this digital realm can offer, preparing for the day when the operation will save a life in the tangible world. This is not the distant future; it is a burgeoning reality where virtual environments are transforming the landscape of medical training and practice. The possibilities are vast, and the implications are profound, promising a new era where simulations are not just tools but vital partners in the quest for healing and wellness.

Beyond the operating room, these virtual landscapes offer refuge and reha-bilitation for those grappling with trauma and physical injuries. In immersive simulations, patients embark on journeys of recovery, guided by experiences that soothe and strengthen both mind and body. Here, therapists harness the power of virtual environments to craft personalized worlds where individuals confront and overcome their fears, reshaping neural pathways in the process. Cognitive behavioral treatments unfold within these crafted realities, allowing patients to navigate their mental landscapes with newfound clarity and control. As these virtual environments bridge the gap between imagination and reality, they invite us to reconsider the very nature of healing and connection, setting the stage for a future where technology and humanity walk hand in hand towards a healthier world.

Virtual Reality in Surgical Training and Precision Procedures

Virtual reality (VR) is revolutionizing surgical training by offering an immer-sive platform where aspiring surgeons can hone their skills with unparalleled precision and safety. Unlike traditional methods that rely heavily on cadavers or limited practice on live patients, VR provides a dynamic environment where trainees can repeatedly simulate complex procedures without the constraints of time or resources. This technology allows for real-time feedback, enabling prac-titioners to refine their technique and decision-making skills. For instance, VR systems like Osso VR and Touch Surgery have been instrumental in enhancing the proficiency of surgeons by offering diverse scenarios that replicate real-life challenges, such as unexpected complications or anatomical variations, fostering a deeper understanding of surgical intricacies.

Furthermore, VR's contribution extends beyond mere training to the realm of precision procedures. Surgeons are increasingly employing VR simulations to plan and rehearse surgeries, particularly in cases involving intricate or high-risk operations. By visualizing a patient's anatomy in three dimensions and prac-ticing the procedure in a simulated environment, surgeons can strategize and optimize their approach before entering the operating room. This preparation can lead to reduced operative times, minimized risks, and improved patient outcomes. Recent advances in haptic feedback technology are also enhancing these experiences, allowing surgeons to feel the simulated tissue's resistance, further bridging the gap between virtual practice and real-world application.

In addition to these advancements, VR is paving new paths in collaborative surgery, where specialists from around the globe can convene in a shared virtual space to perform or consult on surgical procedures. This capability not only democratizes access to world-class expertise but also fosters a culture of continual learning and innovation. Surgeons in remote or underserved areas can benefit from the insights and guidance of leading experts, potentially transforming healthcare delivery and outcomes. By integrating VR with telemedicine, the medical community can leverage collective knowledge and experience, enhancing the quality of care provided across diverse settings.

The potential of VR in surgical applications is underscored by the ongoing research and development efforts aimed at expanding its capabilities. Innovations such as AI-driven simulations that adapt to the surgeon's skill level or integrate patient-specific data to create personalized practice scenarios are on the horizon. These advancements promise to elevate the surgical profession by offering tailored training experiences that cater to individual learning curves and needs. By investing in these technologies, healthcare institutions can cultivate a new generation of surgeons who are not only technically proficient but also adept at navigating the complexities of modern medicine.

As VR continues to evolve, its role in surgical training and precision procedures highlights the importance of embracing technological advancements while maintaining a focus on patient-centric care. This harmonious blend of innovation and compassion is crucial as the medical field advances into the future. By equipping surgeons with the tools and experiences necessary to excel in their craft, VR is poised to not only transform surgical education but also redefine the boundaries of what is possible in medicine. As we explore these digital frontiers, the question remains: how can we ensure that these technological marvels are accessible to all, fostering equity and excellence in healthcare worldwide?

Immersive Simulations for Trauma and Rehabilitation Therapy

Within the realm of trauma recovery and rehabilitation, immersive simulations are reshaping traditional therapeutic practices by offering an environment where patients can safely confront and process their experiences. Virtual environments meticulously crafted for trauma therapy provide a controlled setting where individuals can gradually face triggering situations without real-world consequences. For instance, war veterans suffering from PTSD may navigate virtual battlefields, gradually desensitizing their responses and gaining mastery over their emotional reactions. This approach is not only about exposure but also about empowerment, providing patients with tools to reclaim their mental landscapes.

The sophistication of virtual reality (VR) technology has enabled the development of highly personalized rehabilitation programs. By tailoring simulations to the specific needs and progress of patients, therapists can offer a bespoke healing journey. Virtual simulations used for physical rehabilitation after injuries or surgeries employ dynamic environments that adapt to the user's physical capabilities and progress. This adaptability can lead to more effective outcomes, as patients are more engaged and motivated when their therapy feels relevant and responsive. The integration of biofeedback mechanisms further enhances this experience, allowing therapists to monitor physiological responses and adjust the simulation in real time.

Recent advances in immersive simulations for cognitive rehabilitation are particularly promising. These simulations are incorporating elements of gamification to transform monotonous exercises into engaging challenges that stimulate neuroplasticity. Consider stroke recovery, where a patient might navigate a virtual kitchen to rebuild motor skills and cognitive functions simultaneously. This method encourages repetitive practice, which is crucial for recovery, while maintaining high levels of patient motivation and participation. Such immersive experiences blur the lines between therapy and play, making rehabilitation a more enjoyable and rewarding process.

The potential of virtual environments extends into the realm of cognitive-behavioral therapy (CBT), where simulations can offer new avenues for tackling anxiety and phobias. By immersing individuals in realistic yet controlled scenarios, these environments facilitate the practice of coping strategies and reinforce positive behavioral patterns. As patients interact with their fears in a virtual space, they gain confidence and skills that translate into real-world resilience. The ability to pause, reflect, and retry within these simulations empowers patients to experiment with different responses, fostering a sense of agency over their mental health journey.

As we witness these transformative applications of simulation technology, it is crucial to consider the ethical and practical implications of their widespread use. Questions arise regarding the accessibility of such therapies and the potential risk of over-reliance on virtual environments at the expense of real-world interactions. While immersive simulations offer significant benefits, they should complement, not replace, traditional therapeutic methods. By continuing to explore these technologies with an open, critical mind, practitioners and researchers can ensure that simulations serve as powerful allies in the quest for healing and well-being.

Harnessing Virtual Environments for Cognitive Behavioral Treatments

Virtual environments have become transformative tools in cognitive behavioral treatments, offering patients immersive experiences that enhance traditional therapeutic approaches. By creating lifelike simulations, therapists can design customized scenarios that allow individuals to confront and navigate their fears, anxieties, or negative thought patterns in a controlled setting. This tailored approach enables patients to practice coping strategies and decision-making skills, leading to more effective outcomes. For instance, virtual reality (VR) environments can be crafted to simulate situations that trigger anxiety or phobias, providing a safe space for gradual exposure therapy. This method has shown significant promise in treating conditions like post-traumatic stress disorder and social anxiety, allowing individuals to build resilience and confidence through repeated exposure without real-world consequences.

The integration of VR in cognitive behavioral therapy (CBT) is supported by a growing body of research indicating its efficacy. Studies demonstrate that patients often find virtual environments more engaging than traditional methods, which can lead to higher levels of participation and motivation. This engagement is crucial for the success of CBT, as it relies heavily on the patient's active involvement in the process. Furthermore, VR allows for the collection of precise data on a patient's responses and progress, enabling therapists to adjust treatment plans with greater accuracy. This data-driven approach not only enhances the personalization of therapy but also offers insights into the underlying mechanisms of mental health disorders, facilitating the development of more effective interventions.

In addition to treating anxiety and phobias, virtual environments are being explored for their potential to aid in cognitive restructuring, a core component of CBT. By allowing patients to visualize and manipulate their thought processes within a virtual space, therapists can help them identify and challenge irrational beliefs more effectively. This interactive approach can demystify the cognitive restructuring process, making abstract concepts more tangible and accessible. Innovative VR applications are emerging that use gamified elements to engage users in cognitive exercises, transforming what can be a daunting task into an intriguing and rewarding experience. These applications often employ narrative-driven scenarios that resonate with patients, fostering a deeper understanding of their cognitive patterns.

While the promise of virtual environments in cognitive behavioral treatments is vast, it is essential to consider the ethical implications and accessibility issues associated with this technology. Ensuring that VR therapies are available to a diverse population, regardless of socioeconomic status, is a pressing concern. Additionally, the potential for over-reliance on virtual environments must be carefully managed to prevent detachment from reality. Striking the right balance between virtual and real-world interactions is crucial for the holistic well-being of patients. As this field evolves, ongoing research and collaboration among technologists, clinicians, and ethicists will be vital in guiding the responsible integration of VR into mental health care.

The future of cognitive behavioral treatments in virtual environments holds immense potential, particularly as technology continues to advance. Imagine a world where therapists can harness AI-driven simulations that adapt in real-time to a patient's emotional state or where virtual support groups can connect individuals worldwide, fostering a sense of community and shared understanding. These prospects encourage mental health professionals to rethink traditional paradigms and explore innovative ways to harness technology for healing. The journey towards these possibilities invites both optimism and caution, challenging us to envision a future where technology and empathy intersect to support and enhance human well-being.

Simulations as a tool for global collaboration

Picture a world where the boundaries of global collaboration dissolve, allowing minds from every corner of the planet to converge in a shared virtual space. In this realm, the power of simulation transcends geographical and cultural barriers, fostering unprecedented cooperation and innovation. As humanity faces complex challenges that demand collective problem-solving, the potential of simulated environments to unite disparate voices becomes both a necessity and a marvel. These digital landscapes offer fertile ground for international scientific endeavors, where researchers can collaborate in real-time, unhindered by physical limitations. Such platforms not only accelerate innovation but also democratize access to knowledge, ensuring that breakthroughs are not confined to well-funded labs but are shared across the globe for the collective good.

Beyond the realm of science, simulations hold the promise of enhancing cross-cultural dialogue, creating spaces where individuals can immerse themselves in diverse perspectives and experiences. By simulating environments that reflect the nuances of different cultures, these virtual encounters can foster empathy and understanding, breaking down stereotypes and building bridges of mutual respect. In this interconnected world, global policy development becomes a more inclusive process, with multinational simulation models allowing policymakers to visualize the impacts of their decisions on a global scale. These models offer a sandbox for experimentation, helping to navigate the complexities of international relations and crafting policies that are informed by a comprehensive understanding of global dynamics. As we explore these possibilities, the subtopics ahead delve into the specific ways simulations are reshaping how we collaborate across borders, transforming our approach to science, culture, and policy.

Virtual Platforms for International Scientific Cooperation and Innovation

In the vast expanse of scientific endeavor, virtual platforms have emerged as transformative tools, knitting together a global tapestry of researchers and innovators. These digital arenas transcend geographical barriers, enabling real-time collaboration and idea exchange among scientists from diverse disciplines and regions. Platforms like ScienceSim and OpenSim have pioneered in creating shared virtual laboratories, where researchers can simulate experiments, visualize complex data, and refine their hypotheses collaboratively. This collaborative approach accelerates the pace of discovery, as insights and breakthroughs can be shared instantly, fostering a dynamic environment for innovation that was previously hindered by physical and logistical constraints.

At the heart of these virtual networks lies the potential for interdisciplinary cross-pollination. By facilitating interactions between specialists from disparate fields, these platforms encourage the fusion of ideas that can lead to unexpected innovations. For instance, a virtual symposium might bring together a biologist, a computer scientist, and an economist, each contributing unique perspectives to a shared problem. This confluence of expertise can lead to the development of hybrid solutions, such as bioinformatics tools that revolutionize genetic research or economic models that incorporate ecological variables. Through these collaborative efforts, virtual platforms act as catalysts for groundbreaking advancements that are more than the sum of their parts.

In addition to fostering collaboration, virtual platforms also democratize access to cutting-edge research tools and resources. Scientists from underfunded institutions or regions with limited infrastructure can now engage with state-of-the-art facilities and datasets, leveling the playing field in the global research community. This democratization not only enhances the diversity of perspectives that contribute to scientific discourse but also ensures that talent and innovation are not stifled by a lack of resources. By opening doors to participants from varied backgrounds, these platforms enrich the scientific dialogue with a multitude of voices, each bringing distinct insights and experiences to the table.

Yet, while the potential of virtual platforms is immense, it is accompanied by challenges that require thoughtful navigation. Ensuring data security and intellectual property rights in these shared environments is paramount to maintaining trust among collaborators. Additionally, the development of standardized protocols for data sharing and joint experimentation is essential to streamline processes and maximize the efficacy of these platforms. Addressing these challenges requires a concerted effort from both the scientific community and platform developers, working together to create robust frameworks that safeguard the integrity of collaborative research while promoting open innovation.

As we contemplate the future of international scientific cooperation, virtual platforms stand as powerful instruments for shaping a more connected and innovative world. By harnessing the potential of these digital spaces, we can envision a landscape where the boundaries of knowledge are continually expanded through collective effort. This vision challenges us to think critically about how we can further enhance these platforms, encouraging not only participation but also meaningful engagement across the scientific spectrum. Through creative problem-solving and a commitment to inclusivity, these virtual realms hold the promise of unlocking unprecedented potential in scientific exploration and discovery.

Enhancing Cross-Cultural Dialogue Through Simulated Environments

Simulated environments provide a fertile ground for the cultivation of cross-cultural dialogue, offering a space where individuals from diverse backgrounds can interact without the constraints of geography or time. These digital realms enable participants to explore and understand cultural nuances through immersive experiences that transcend traditional communication barriers. By crafting environments that accurately reflect cultural contexts, simulations can foster empathy and understanding, facilitating deeper connections between people from different cultures. This approach allows for a more nuanced appreciation of cultural diversity, encouraging participants to engage in meaningful exchanges that might be difficult to achieve in the real world.

Cutting-edge innovations in virtual reality and augmented reality technology have opened new avenues for creating these culturally immersive experiences. For instance, interactive simulations can replicate historical events, allowing participants to witness and engage with them from the perspectives of various cultures involved. Such simulations not only provide educational value but also promote critical thinking by challenging users to consider multiple viewpoints. These experiences can be further enriched by incorporating artificial intelligence that adapts to the cultural background of participants, offering personalized interactions and fostering a sense of inclusion and respect for cultural differences.

Beyond individual interactions, simulated environments serve as platforms for collaborative projects that require nuanced cross-cultural communication. International teams can utilize these virtual spaces to work on joint endeavors, from scientific research to artistic projects, without the logistical challenges of physical travel. This fosters a collaborative spirit and reduces cultural misunderstandings, as team members can interact in a controlled environment that encourages open dialogue and mutual respect. By simulating real-world scenarios, these platforms allow teams to practice and refine their collaborative skills, ultimately improving their effectiveness in real-world settings.

The potential of simulated environments to enhance cross-cultural dialogue extends to global policy development as well. By creating multinational simulations, policymakers can test the implications of their decisions in a safe and controlled environment, gaining insights into how different cultural perspectives might respond to proposed policies. This approach not only strengthens the development of more inclusive policies but also encourages a spirit of cooperation, as stakeholders from various cultural backgrounds work together to address global challenges. As these simulations become increasingly sophisticated, they offer invaluable tools for fostering international collaboration and understanding.

In envisioning future applications, it's worth considering how these simulated environments could evolve to address emerging global challenges. Imagine a world where diplomats and leaders step into virtual zones to simulate negotiations, gaining insights into cultural sensitivities and fostering a climate of mutual respect and understanding. Such scenarios not only hold the promise of enhancing diplomatic relations but also highlight the transformative potential of simulations in bridging cultural divides. As we continue to explore the capabilities of these environments, it becomes clear that their role in fostering cross-cultural dialogue is only beginning to be realized, with the potential for profound impact on global cooperation and harmony.

Global Policy Development Using Multinational Simulation Models

Multinational simulation models are transforming the landscape of global policy development, offering unprecedented tools for collaboration and innovation. These models provide virtual environments where policymakers can test and evaluate the outcomes of various strategies before implementing them in the real world. By simulating complex global issues, such as climate change, economic crises, or pandemics, these platforms enable stakeholders from different countries to engage in a shared space, fostering international cooperation and understanding. The integration of artificial intelligence and machine learning into these simulations allows for the analysis of vast datasets, predicting potential outcomes with remarkable accuracy. This approach not only minimizes risks but also enhances the adaptability of policies to rapidly changing global conditions.

One pioneering example of multinational simulation usage is the Global Earth Observation System of Systems (GEOSS), which facilitates the sharing of environmental data among countries to improve decision-making related to climate action and sustainable development. By using simulation models, GEOSS helps nations visualize the long-term impacts of their policies on global ecosystems. This collaborative approach encourages countries to work together toward common goals, transcending individual national interests. The success of such initiatives underscores the potential for simulations to redefine how international policies are crafted and agreed upon, fostering a more cohesive global community.

Cultural and political nuances often pose challenges in multinational policy development. However, simulation models offer a neutral ground where diverse perspectives can be explored and reconciled. By immersing participants in realistic scenarios that reflect a multitude of viewpoints, these simulations promote empathy and mutual understanding. For instance, a simulation addressing global trade negotiations can incorporate economic models, cultural considerations, and political dynamics from each participating country. This holistic approach not only aids in crafting more equitable policies but also builds trust among nations, as stakeholders see their concerns and priorities reflected in the simulation outcomes.

Recent advancements in virtual reality and augmented reality technologies have further enhanced the efficacy of multinational simulation models. These technologies provide an immersive experience, allowing policymakers to engage with simulated environments in ways that traditional methods cannot match. By experiencing the potential impacts of policy decisions firsthand, participants gain a deeper appreciation of the complexities involved, leading to more informed and nuanced decision-making. Such immersive experiences can bridge the gap between theoretical knowledge and practical application, equipping leaders with the insights needed to address the multifaceted challenges of our interconnected world.

As we look toward the future, the role of multinational simulations in global policy development promises to expand, driven by technological innovation and the growing need for collaborative solutions to global challenges. By harnessing the power of simulation, nations can not only develop more effective and inclusive policies but also foster a spirit of global citizenship, where the well-being of all is prioritized. This vision invites policymakers to embrace simulation as a vital tool, encouraging international dialogue and cooperation, ultimately paving the way for a more just and sustainable world.

As we navigate the transformative potential of simulations in societal contexts, it becomes evident that virtual environments are not merely tools of escapism but powerful instruments for progress. The integration of simulations in urban planning, crisis management, medicine, and global collaboration illustrates their capacity to foster innovation and resilience. Simulated scenarios enable urban designers to experiment with infrastructure layouts before breaking ground, while crisis simulations equip communities to better handle disasters. In healthcare, virtual environments offer groundbreaking possibilities for surgical precision and mental well-being. Furthermore, the collaborative nature of simulations transcends borders, uniting global minds to solve shared challenges. These applications underscore the profound impact simulations can have on our collective future, encouraging us to embrace their potential responsibly. As we move forward in this exploration, we are reminded to harness the immense capabilities of simulation technology thoughtfully, ensuring it serves as a catalyst for positive change and societal benefit. As the journey continues, we are left to ponder how these virtual realms might further redefine our interactions, our innovations, and our very understanding of reality itself.

Chapter Seven

Optimizing Simulations For Human Benefit

The following discussion reveals a world where pixels and particles converge to create spaces that hold the power to transform lives. Imagine stepping into a virtual garden where every plant blooms with the lessons of patience and nurturing; these are not just digital constructs, but carefully designed experiences that reflect our deepest aspirations for growth and connection. This chapter invites you to explore how such simulations can be harnessed for the greater good, crafting environments that nurture the mind and soul while staying anchored in ethical considerations. From the ancient philosophers who pondered the nature of reality to modern technologists at the forefront of simulation development, the quest to optimize virtual worlds for human benefit is both timeless and urgent.

Navigating the digital landscape requires more than technical expertise; it demands an understanding of the delicate balance between engagement and excess. As simulations grow more immersive, they hold the potential to captivate us in ways that redefine our interactions with reality. Within these lines of code lies the risk of addiction and detachment, where the virtual might overshadow the tangible. This chapter seeks to illuminate pathways that guide us away from these pitfalls, ensuring that our digital creations serve to enhance rather than diminish our human experience. By examining the fine line between realism and escapism, we uncover strategies that allow virtual worlds to mirror the beauty and complexity of life without losing touch with the essence of what it means to be human.

In the pursuit of crafting simulations that enrich our existence, we delve into the heart of ethical design, where every decision echoes with responsibility. How do we build worlds that inspire personal growth, yet remain firmly grounded in ethical principles? The answer lies in a collaborative dance between creativity and conscience, where the architects of these digital realms weave narratives that empower and uplift. This chapter serves as a compass, guiding the reader through the intricate process of designing simulations that not only entertain but also educate and inspire. As we embark on this journey, we discover the limitless potential of virtual worlds to reshape our understanding of reality and our place within it.

Designing ethical frameworks for virtual worlds

It's intriguing to note that as humanity stands on the precipice of an era dominated by virtual realities, the question of ethics becomes increasingly paramount. In these crafted worlds, where the boundaries of what is possible are limited only by imagination and technology, the need for ethical frameworks assumes a critical role. Virtual worlds offer vast landscapes for exploration and interaction, yet they also pose unique challenges that require careful consideration and deliberate design. Crafting ethical guidelines for these digital domains involves more than simply transplanting existing moral codes; it demands a reimagining of how ethical principles can be adapted to spaces where traditional boundaries are blurred, and the consequences of actions are not always immediate or tangible. This topic invites readers to explore the nuanced dance between freedom and responsibility in virtual environments, where every decision reverberates with potential consequences both in the digital realm and beyond.

As we delve deeper into the complexities of virtual governance, the focus shifts to the delicate balance between user autonomy and ethical oversight. In worlds where individuals can assume identities and roles far removed from their real-world personas, the question of accountability becomes paramount. How can these digital spaces foster a sense of moral responsibility without stifling creativity and exploration? The challenge lies in establishing systems of governance that not only protect users but also enhance their experience by promoting a culture of respect and integrity. From setting moral guidelines for virtual interactions to implementing robust accountability measures, these subtopics explore the essential elements required to cultivate environments where personal growth and well-being flourish, while mitigating risks of addiction and detachment. These explorations are essential as we venture into the ever-expanding frontier of virtual realities, ensuring that these simulations serve as a force for positive transformation in the human experience.

Establishing Moral Guidelines for Virtual Interactions

Navigating the moral landscape of virtual interactions demands a nuanced approach, one that ventures beyond traditional ethical frameworks to address the complexities of digital ecosystems. As simulations become increasingly sophisticated and immersive, the need for bespoke moral guidelines grows. These guidelines must account for the unique dynamics of virtual worlds, where the boundaries between reality and illusion blur. In these environments, the actions of avatars can mirror those of their human counterparts, raising questions about the ethical implications of behavior in a realm where physical harm is absent, yet psychological and emotional impacts are profound. The development of such moral guidelines requires a collaborative effort across disciplines, drawing insights from psychology, philosophy, and technology to create a comprehensive ethical toolkit that caters to the challenges of virtual interactions.

The task of establishing these moral parameters involves crafting a delicate balance between freedom and regulation. Virtual worlds offer unprecedented autonomy, enabling users to explore identities and scenarios in ways that physical reality may not permit. Yet, with this freedom comes the potential for misuse, necessitating an ethical oversight framework that respects individual autonomy while safeguarding against harmful conduct. This balance can be informed by emerging research into digital behavior patterns, which reveals both the empowering and potentially destructive aspects of virtual liberty. By examining these patterns, designers and policymakers can develop guidelines that promote positive engagement, fostering environments where users can thrive without infringing on the rights and well-being of others.

Accountability in virtual realms is another critical component of ethical design. As users navigate these digital landscapes, the anonymity afforded by avatars can sometimes lead to behaviors that would not be tolerated in the physical world. To counter this, implementing mechanisms of accountability is essential, ensuring that actions in virtual spaces carry consequences akin to those in reality. This can be achieved through innovative governance structures, such as community-driven moderation systems or AI-assisted monitoring tools, which uphold ethical standards while respecting user privacy. These systems must be transparent and adaptable, allowing communities to define and evolve their own ethical norms in response to the shifting dynamics of virtual interactions.

The creation of moral guidelines also necessitates an exploration of cultural diversity and inclusivity. Virtual worlds often serve as melting pots of global cultures, where users from disparate backgrounds converge. This diversity enriches the experience but also introduces ethical complexities, as different cultural norms and values intersect. An effective ethical framework must be sensitive to these differences, promoting inclusivity and mutual understanding while preventing cultural dominance or insensitivity. By incorporating diverse perspectives into the development of ethical guidelines, virtual environments can become spaces that celebrate diversity and encourage cross-cultural dialogue, fostering a global community grounded in respect and empathy.

To stimulate critical thinking and application of these concepts, consider a scenario where a virtual world is designed without ethical guidelines, leading to unchecked behaviors that mirror the worst aspects of human nature. How might this impact the users' perception of reality and their behavior outside the simulation? Conversely, envision a virtual environment where ethical guidelines are thoughtfully integrated, promoting positive interactions and personal growth. What lessons from these simulations could be applied to enhance social dynamics in the real world? By contemplating these questions, readers are invited to reflect on the transformative potential of ethical frameworks in shaping not only virtual interactions but also our broader societal landscape.

Balancing User Freedom with Ethical Oversight in Simulations

In the realm of simulated environments, the delicate equilibrium between user freedom and ethical oversight emerges as a critical consideration. As virtual worlds become increasingly sophisticated, the challenge lies in ensuring that users have the autonomy to explore and create within these spaces while safeguarding against potential harm. Developers and designers must craft environments that empower users to express and engage freely, yet remain vigilant to prevent the abuse of this freedom. To achieve this, the integration of ethical oversight mechanisms, such as dynamic content moderation systems and user behavior analytics, can help maintain a balance between freedom and responsibility. These systems not only monitor interactions but also provide real-time feedback, encouraging a culture of respect and accountability among users.

One approach to fostering such a balance is through the implementation of adaptive governance frameworks within virtual worlds. These frameworks, inspired by principles of restorative justice and community self-regulation, can offer users the opportunity to participate in shaping the rules and norms of their digital societies. By involving users in decision-making processes, simulations can evolve into spaces where ethical considerations are not imposed from above but are collectively shaped by the community. This participatory model not only enhances users' sense of ownership and agency but also promotes a deeper understanding of the impact of their actions within these environments. As a result, users are more likely to adhere to ethical standards that they have had a hand in crafting.

Furthermore, leveraging artificial intelligence to create personalized experiences can play a pivotal role in balancing freedom with ethical oversight. AI algorithms can analyze user behavior and preferences to tailor experiences that align with individual values and ethical boundaries. For instance, virtual environments could adjust content visibility based on a user's age, cultural background, or personal sensitivities, ensuring that the experience remains both engaging and appropriate. This personalized approach not only enhances user satisfaction but also mitigates the risk of exposure to potentially harmful content. By harnessing AI to curate experiences, developers can create virtual worlds that respect individual freedoms while maintaining ethical integrity.

In the pursuit of ethical oversight, it is imperative to consider the potential psychological and social implications of simulated environments. Research suggests that prolonged exposure to virtual worlds can affect users' perceptions of reality and interpersonal relationships. To counteract these effects, simulations can incorporate features that encourage real-world interactions and community building. For example, virtual environments could host events that require collaboration with others both inside and outside the simulation, fostering connections that transcend digital boundaries. By embedding opportunities for offline engagement within virtual experiences, simulations can nurture a harmonious relationship between digital and real-world interactions, ensuring that users remain grounded in both realms.

Ultimately, the key to balancing user freedom with ethical oversight lies in the continuous dialogue between developers, users, and ethicists. This ongoing conversation can help identify emerging challenges and opportunities, enabling simulations to evolve in ways that reflect the values and aspirations of their communities. Encouraging feedback loops, where users can report concerns and suggest improvements, ensures that simulations remain responsive to the needs of their inhabitants. By fostering an environment of transparency and collaboration, virtual worlds can become spaces where creativity and ethical responsibility coexist, enriching the human experience in ways that honor both individual freedom and collective well-being.

Implementing Accountability and Governance in Virtual Realities

Crafting a robust system of accountability and governance in virtual realities is an essential endeavor as these digital domains increasingly mirror complex societal structures. The world of simulations presents a unique challenge in establishing a governance framework that ensures fairness, security, and ethical integrity. Unlike traditional systems, virtual worlds require innovative approaches to legislate and regulate interactions, balancing user autonomy with the need for oversight. This task necessitates a deep understanding of both technological capabilities and human behaviors within these immersive environments. By drawing on interdisciplinary research from fields such as digital ethics, legal studies, and computer science, new models of governance can be envisioned that address the unique challenges posed by virtual realities.

In implementing these frameworks, transparency becomes a cornerstone. Users must be aware of the rules and the rationale behind them, fostering a culture of trust and mutual respect. Transparency is not merely about disseminating information but involves creating platforms for dialogue and feedback, ensuring that the governance systems evolve in response to the community's needs. Recent advancements in blockchain technology offer promising tools for establishing transparent and immutable records of virtual transactions and interactions. This technology can underpin decentralized systems of governance, enabling users to participate in decision-making processes while safeguarding their privacy and autonomy.

The notion of accountability within virtual worlds also requires reimagining traditional concepts of responsibility and consequence. As digital identities can differ significantly from their real-world counterparts, establishing clear guidelines on how actions in virtual spaces translate to accountability in the physical world is paramount. This involves developing sophisticated algorithms capable of identifying and addressing harmful behaviors without infringing on personal freedoms. Machine learning models, trained on diverse datasets, can be instrumental in predicting and mitigating negative interactions, thus maintaining a safe and inclusive environment for all participants. These models must be designed to adapt and learn from new scenarios, ensuring they remain effective in the face of evolving virtual landscapes.

Governance in virtual realities further benefits from incorporating diverse perspectives, ensuring that the systems in place are equitable and inclusive. Engaging with a wide range of stakeholders—developers, users, ethicists, and legal experts—enables the creation of governance structures that reflect a multitude of viewpoints and cultural contexts. This collaborative approach ensures that the rules governing virtual worlds do not inadvertently perpetuate biases or exclusionary practices. Encouraging active participation from a broad user base can lead to more nuanced understandings of the intricacies involved in virtual governance and foster a collective commitment to ethical standards.

As simulations continue to advance, the need for adaptive governance models becomes increasingly apparent. These models must be flexible enough to respond to unforeseen challenges and opportunities, evolving in tandem with technological progress. A well-implemented governance framework will not only safeguard users but also enhance the overall experience by fostering innovation and creativity within virtual environments. By prioritizing ethical considerations and accountability, virtual realities can be shaped into spaces that not only entertain but also educate and empower, offering a blueprint for future societal developments. As we stand on the cusp of this digital frontier, the responsibility to govern wisely invites us all to envision and enact a future where virtual and physical realities harmoniously coexist.

Creating simulations that promote personal growth and well-being

Imagine a world where the boundaries between reality and imagination blur seamlessly, offering not just escape but profound personal transformation. In this vibrant tapestry of simulated environments, individuals embark on journeys designed to nurture their mental and emotional landscapes. These virtual worlds become sanctuaries for mindfulness, where stress dissipates amidst serene digital vistas. By gently guiding users through immersive experiences, simulations can foster a sense of calm and clarity, offering tools to manage the chaos of daily life. Here, technology becomes an ally in the quest for inner peace, encouraging a deeper connection with oneself.

As we traverse these digital realms, the potential for personal growth unfolds in myriad forms. Interactive scenarios cultivate emotional intelligence, allowing individuals to explore complex social dynamics and empathize with diverse perspectives. These virtual interactions are not mere games; they are carefully crafted narratives that challenge and enrich the human experience. Personalized growth pathways emerge, tailored to each individual's aspirations and learning style, offering unique opportunities for development. In this harmonious blend of innovation and introspection, simulations become more than a technological marvel—they are a catalyst for human flourishing, inviting participants to explore and evolve within the boundless expanse of virtual reality.

Leveraging Virtual Environments for Mindfulness and Stress Reduction

In the ever-evolving realm of virtual environments, the potential to cultivate mindfulness and alleviate stress is a burgeoning frontier. Recent advancements in technology have opened doors to immersive experiences that transcend the limitations of traditional mindfulness practices. These digital sanctuaries offer individuals an opportunity to escape the cacophony of daily life, providing a serene space where the mind can find tranquility. By harnessing the power of virtual reality, users can engage in guided meditation in a picturesque, digitally-rendered forest or practice deep breathing exercises while floating amidst the clouds. Such environments are meticulously crafted to elicit a sense of calm, using elements like gentle ambient sounds and visually soothing landscapes to facilitate a deeper meditative state.

A pivotal aspect of utilizing virtual environments for stress reduction is the customization of experiences to meet individual needs. Tailoring these digital retreats allows for a more personalized approach, addressing the diverse stressors and preferences unique to each user. For instance, some may find solace in the rhythmic ebb and flow of simulated ocean waves, while others might prefer the quietude of a digital library. This customization is not merely about aesthetic preference but also involves adapting the intensity and pacing of the experience to align with the individual's current emotional and mental state. The integration of biofeedback mechanisms, such as heart rate monitors, can further refine these virtual experiences, providing real-time adjustments that optimize the therapeutic benefits.

The intersection of cognitive science and virtual reality has also paved the way for innovative approaches to mindfulness. Cutting-edge research suggests that virtual environments can enhance the efficacy of mindfulness practices by engaging multiple senses simultaneously, thus creating a more holistic experience. This multisensory engagement can lead to profound shifts in awareness and presence, key components of mindfulness. By engaging sight, sound, and even touch, these virtual experiences can foster a heightened state of mindfulness that might be challenging to achieve in the traditional physical world. Furthermore, the ability to control and manipulate the virtual environment can empower users, granting them agency over their stress management techniques in a way that is both novel and effective.

In addition to individualized experiences, virtual environments offer the opportunity for communal mindfulness practices, connecting individuals across the globe in shared meditative experiences. These collective endeavors can foster a sense of community and support, crucial elements for those seeking stress relief and emotional balance. By participating in virtual group meditations or mindfulness workshops, individuals can benefit from a shared sense of purpose and the collective energy of a group, which can amplify the therapeutic effects. The social aspect of these experiences can also mitigate feelings of isolation, providing a supportive network that extends beyond geographical boundaries.

To maximize the potential of virtual environments in promoting mindfulness and stress reduction, it is essential to remain attuned to emerging trends and technologies that can further enhance these experiences. As virtual reality continues to evolve, the incorporation of artificial intelligence and machine learning algorithms presents new possibilities for adaptive and intuitive environments that respond dynamically to user inputs and needs. By staying at the forefront of technological innovation, developers and practitioners can ensure that virtual environments remain effective tools for fostering mental well-being, offering individuals a profound and transformative means of engaging with their inner selves and achieving a harmonious state of mind.

Designing Interactive Scenarios for Emotional Intelligence Development

In the realm of virtual simulations, emotional intelligence emerges as a pivotal area ripe for exploration and enhancement. Interactive scenarios designed within these digital landscapes hold the potential to cultivate emotional acumen by simulating complex social interactions and emotional challenges. By engaging users in lifelike situations that require empathy, negotiation, and conflict resolution, these simulations can provide a dynamic learning environment where emotional skills are honed through experience rather than theoretical instruction. The integration of artificial intelligence further amplifies this potential, allowing for adaptive scenarios that respond to a user's decisions, fostering a more personalized and impactful learning journey.

Innovative research underscores the efficacy of simulations in bolstering emotional intelligence. Recent studies indicate that immersive environments, when designed with emotional growth in mind, can significantly improve users' ability to recognize and manage their emotions and those of others. Through carefully crafted narratives and character interactions, users can explore a spectrum of emotional responses and outcomes, gaining insights into the nuances of human behavior. This experiential learning model not only enhances self-awareness but also encourages the development of critical social skills, such as active listening and empathy, which are essential for navigating real-world relationships.

An intriguing dimension of these simulations involves the incorporation of feedback mechanisms that promote reflective practice. By providing users with immediate and constructive feedback on their emotional responses and decision-making processes, simulations can facilitate deeper introspection and understanding. This feedback, coupled with the opportunity to replay scenarios with different approaches, empowers users to experiment with and refine their emotional strategies. The iterative nature of this process mirrors the real-world development of emotional intelligence, where learning often occurs through trial and error, supported by reflection and adjustment.

From a design perspective, creating simulations that nurture emotional intelligence requires a delicate balance between authenticity and challenge. Scenarios must be sufficiently realistic to engage users emotionally while also presenting opportunities for growth. This involves crafting narratives that resonate with diverse experiences and perspectives, ensuring inclusivity and relevance. By presenting users with morally ambiguous situations and dilemmas, simulations can provoke critical thinking and encourage users to consider multiple viewpoints, broadening their understanding of complex emotional landscapes.

As the possibilities for emotional intelligence development in virtual simu-lations continue to expand, questions arise about the ethical considerations and potential societal impacts. How might these digital experiences influence our interactions in the physical world? Can they bridge emotional gaps or inadver-tently create new ones? Such inquiries invite ongoing exploration and dialogue, challenging developers and users alike to consider the broader implications of these tools. By embracing a thoughtful and innovative approach to simulation design, we can unlock new dimensions of personal growth and well-being, enriching both virtual and tangible realities.

Integrating Personalized Growth Pathways in Simulated Learning Journeys

In the realm of simulated learning journeys, the integration of personalized growth pathways offers an unprecedented opportunity for individuals to ex-plore and cultivate their potential in dynamic and tailored environments. By harnessing advancements in artificial intelligence and data analytics, simulations can be designed to adapt to the unique needs and aspirations of each user, creating a rich tapestry of experiences that foster personal development. These customized pathways can identify a learner's strengths and weaknesses, suggest-ing targeted scenarios that challenge them while supporting their growth. By continuously adjusting to the user's progress, simulations can maintain an op-timal balance of difficulty and engagement, ensuring that the journey remains both rewarding and educational.

Consider the application of machine learning algorithms that analyze user interactions within the simulation to predict and respond to their learning pref-erences. These algorithms can recommend specific modules or experiences that align with the user's goals, whether they aim to enhance their problem-solving skills, emotional intelligence, or creative thinking. The simulation becomes a living ecosystem that evolves alongside the learner, offering real-time feedback and insights to guide their journey. This dynamic adaptability not only person-alizes the experience but also allows for continuous reflection and self-assess-ment, empowering users to take control of their developmental trajectory.

A particularly intriguing aspect of personalized growth pathways is their potential to incorporate elements of gamification, transforming the learning process into an engaging quest. By setting achievable milestones and reward-ing progress with virtual incentives, simulations can motivate users to remain committed to their growth journey. This gamified approach can be especially effective in nurturing skills that are often overlooked in traditional education-al settings, such as resilience, adaptability, and empathy. By framing personal development as an adventure, simulations can inspire users to push beyond their perceived limitations, fostering a growth mindset that extends beyond the virtual realm.

Moreover, the integration of personalized growth pathways in simulations opens the door to collaborative learning experiences. By connecting users with similar aspirations or complementary skills, simulations can facilitate cooperative problem-solving and knowledge sharing, enriching the learning experience through social interaction. These virtual communities can serve as incubators for innovation and creativity, allowing users to learn from diverse perspectives and develop interpersonal skills that are crucial in today's interconnected world. The collaborative aspect of simulated learning journeys not only enhances personal growth but also cultivates a sense of belonging and shared purpose.

As we explore the potential of personalized growth pathways in simulations, it is essential to consider the ethical implications of such technology. Ensuring that these pathways respect user privacy and autonomy is paramount. Developers must strive to create transparent systems that prioritize the user's well-being and empowerment, avoiding manipulation or coercion. By fostering a culture of trust and accountability, simulations can become powerful tools for personal growth, offering individuals a safe and supportive space to explore their potential and enrich their lives. As these technologies continue to evolve, they hold the promise of transforming not only how we learn but how we perceive and pursue personal development.

Avoiding psychological pitfalls: Addiction and detachment risks

Exploring the intricacies of our increasingly simulated lives, we find ourselves at a crossroads between virtual immersion and psychological well-being. As digital landscapes become more sophisticated and alluring, they offer unprecedented opportunities for personal growth and creativity. Yet, these same immersive experiences present risks of addiction and detachment that challenge our mental and emotional equilibrium. The allure of simulated worlds lies not only in their capacity to entertain and educate but also in their potential to captivate to a point where the lines between engagement and escapism blur. Understanding the psychological mechanisms at play within these virtual environments is paramount to harnessing their benefits while safeguarding against their pitfalls. It is a delicate dance between the magnetic pull of simulated realities and the grounding nature of our tangible world, a balance that must be thoughtfully maintained to ensure these digital experiences enhance rather than diminish our lives.

Within this dynamic and rapidly evolving landscape, the quest to mitigate addiction in virtual environments becomes critical. Strategies must be developed to help individuals retain their connection to the real world while still enjoying the rich experiences simulations offer. This balance is crucial, as the risk of becoming overly immersed in virtual environments can lead to a detachment from real-world interactions and responsibilities, creating a chasm that is difficult to bridge. The goal is not to stifle the creative potential of simulations but to encourage responsible engagement that nurtures both the mind and the spirit. By navigating this complex terrain with insight and foresight, we can ensure that the immersive experiences of tomorrow are crafted with care, promoting a harmonious coexistence between our virtual and real-world selves.

Understanding the Psychological Mechanisms of Simulated Experience

The allure of simulated experiences is deeply rooted in the intricate psychological mechanisms that govern how individuals perceive and interact with these crafted realities. Central to this fascination is the brain's remarkable ability to suspend disbelief, allowing virtual environments to be perceived as tangible. This suspension is facilitated by a combination of sensory inputs and cognitive processes that work together to create a sense of presence within a simulation. Cutting-edge research in neuroscience reveals that the brain responds to virtual stimuli in ways that can closely mimic real-world interactions, activating similar neural pathways and emotional responses. This insight underlines the potential for simulations to evoke profound psychological effects, both beneficial and detrimental.

One of the primary psychological mechanisms at play is the brain's propensity for pattern recognition. Simulations often capitalize on this by creating environments rich in familiar cues and structures, which the brain interprets as coherent and meaningful. This mechanism not only enhances immersion but also fosters a sense of agency and control, vital components in maintaining engagement. Yet, this same mechanism can lead to over-attachment and dependency, as individuals may find simulated worlds more gratifying or manageable than their real-life counterparts. Understanding this dual-edged nature of pattern recognition in virtual contexts is crucial for developing strategies to mitigate potential psychological pitfalls.

Another essential aspect is the role of dopamine, the neurotransmitter associated with pleasure and reward. Simulated experiences are designed to trigger dopamine release, providing users with a sense of achievement and satisfaction. While this can drive motivation and learning, it also raises the specter of addiction, as users may continually seek the rewarding sensations simulations can provide. Advanced studies suggest that balancing the frequency and intensity of these dopamine-triggering events can help prevent the cycle of dependency. Researchers are exploring techniques to modulate these responses, aiming to harness the benefits of dopamine without succumbing to its addictive potential.

In recent years, innovative perspectives have emerged, proposing that simulations could be tailored to promote psychological resilience rather than dependency. By incorporating elements of mindfulness and self-reflection, virtual environments can be designed to encourage introspection and personal growth. This approach shifts the focus from mere escapism to a more constructive use of simulations, where users are guided toward meaningful engagements that reinforce real-world skills and emotional fortitude. Practical applications of this concept are being tested in therapeutic settings, where simulations are used to aid individuals in overcoming fears or building coping mechanisms.

To ensure simulations serve as tools for enhancement rather than entrapment, it is crucial to maintain a balance between immersion and real-world engagement. Designers are increasingly exploring ways to integrate reminders and prompts within simulations that encourage breaks and reflections on real-life connections. These interventions, while subtle, can help users remain grounded, preventing the blurring of lines between virtual and actual experiences. By fostering a sense of awareness and self-regulation, simulations can become not only immersive escapes but also platforms for holistic development and well-being.

Strategies for Mitigating Addiction in Virtual Environments

Mitigating addiction within virtual environments necessitates a nuanced understanding of the psychological allure that these digital worlds present. At the heart of this challenge lies the brain's reward system, which is often triggered by the sense of achievement, exploration, and social interaction offered by simulations. Recent studies suggest that the neurochemical dopamine plays a significant role in reinforcing behaviors associated with virtual accomplishments, mirroring the satisfaction derived from real-world successes. By understanding these mechanisms, developers can design experiences that fulfill users' needs for accomplishment and connection without fostering dependency. For instance, incorporating elements that encourage self-regulation, such as time-tracking tools and personalized reminders, can empower users to maintain a healthy relationship with virtual environments.

Innovative approaches to design can further aid in curbing addictive behaviors. Incorporating breaks and transitions within the virtual experience can prevent prolonged sessions that contribute to dependency. Developers can draw inspiration from natural cycles and rhythms to create environments that organically encourage users to step away, much like daylight cues our bodies to rest. Research in adaptive systems suggests using machine learning algorithms to tailor these interventions based on individual usage patterns, providing a more personalized approach to managing time spent in simulations. Such systems can subtly nudge users towards healthier habits, enhancing their overall well-being without diminishing the immersive allure of the simulated world.

The concept of 'digital nutrition' parallels the idea of a balanced diet, advocating for a diversified virtual experience that satisfies different psychological and emotional needs. Just as a varied diet ensures nutritional health, a well-rounded virtual environment can offer educational, creative, and social elements that together fulfill a range of cognitive and emotional demands. This holistic approach can prevent the overconsumption of any single aspect of virtual life that might lead to addiction. Designers can encourage users to explore a multitude of activities within simulations, fostering a sense of balance and variety that mirrors a well-lived life outside the digital realm.

Addressing addiction in virtual environments also involves fostering real-world connections and responsibilities. Encouraging users to integrate their virtual achievements with tangible goals can reduce the risk of escapism. For instance, gamified elements in simulation can be linked to real-world rewards or community contributions, blurring the lines between digital and physical realms in a way that strengthens rather than undermines real-life engagement. By promoting virtual experiences that complement rather than replace real-world activities, designers can help users maintain a healthy equilibrium between their online and offline lives.

Reflecting on the broader societal context, it's crucial to consider how cultural factors influence virtual addiction. Different demographics may experience and respond to simulations uniquely, and strategies to mitigate addiction should account for this diversity. Engaging with communities to understand their specific interactions with virtual environments can offer valuable insights. By adopting a culturally sensitive approach, developers can design simulations that resonate deeply with diverse user bases, ensuring that ethical frameworks and preventative measures are inclusive and effective. This comprehensive understanding can lead to more robust strategies that not only prevent addiction but also enhance the overall user experience.

Balancing Immersion with Real-World Engagement

In the realm of simulated environments, achieving a delicate equilibrium between immersive experiences and real-world engagement presents both a challenge and an opportunity. The allure of virtual worlds lies in their ability to offer users a sense of presence and escapism, which can sometimes lead to detachment from reality. It is crucial to design simulations that encourage users to integrate virtual experiences with their everyday lives rather than letting them serve as a complete escape. One approach is to develop features that seamlessly connect virtual achievements with tangible real-world goals. For instance, gamification elements can be incorporated to incentivize physical activities or personal development tasks, thereby transforming virtual play into a catalyst for real-world progress.

Recent studies in cognitive science suggest that the brain's neural pathways can be influenced by virtual experiences, affecting behavior and decision-making processes outside the simulation. By understanding these mechanisms, developers can create simulations that foster positive behavioral changes. Advanced algorithms can be utilized to monitor user engagement patterns, providing feedback that encourages balanced usage. For example, a simulation that continuously adapts its content to prompt users to take breaks or engage in offline activities can significantly mitigate the risk of over-immersion. Such adaptive systems can be designed to offer personalized recommendations, nudging users towards a healthier balance between virtual and physical realities.

Moreover, the integration of augmented reality (AR) technologies offers a promising avenue for blending virtual and real-world experiences. AR can overlay digital information onto the physical world, allowing users to experience aspects of simulations while remaining grounded in their environment. This hybrid approach can enhance learning, social interaction, and productivity by enabling users to apply virtual insights in real-time contexts. For instance, AR applications can facilitate collaborative projects that require both virtual and physical participation, thereby reinforcing the interconnectedness of these realms while maintaining user engagement in the tangible world.

The ethical considerations of balancing immersion and real-world engagement cannot be overlooked. It is essential to develop ethical guidelines that prioritize user well-being and autonomy. These guidelines should include transparency about data usage, consent for behavior monitoring, and safeguards against manipulative design practices. By fostering an ethical framework, developers can ensure that simulations remain tools for enrichment rather than vehicles for exploitation. Engaging with diverse perspectives from ethicists, psychologists, and technologists can provide a comprehensive understanding of how to best implement these principles in practice.

To encourage critical reflection on the implications of immersion, it is valuable to pose questions that challenge users to consider their relationship with virtual worlds. How might time spent in simulations impact real-world relationships and responsibilities? What strategies can individuals employ to maintain a healthy balance between virtual exploration and tangible experiences? By contemplating these questions, users can become more aware of their simulation usage patterns and develop strategies to integrate virtual experiences meaningfully into their lives. This reflective process can empower individuals to harness the benefits of simulations while remaining anchored in the richness of the real world.

Balancing realism and escapism in virtual environments

Let's start with a fundamental question: how do we balance the allure of escapism with the grounding effect of realism in virtual environments? At the heart of every engaging simulation lies a delicate interplay between the fantastical and the authentic. This balance is not just a matter of aesthetics or entertainment value but a profound consideration that shapes our experiences and perceptions within virtual worlds. As simulations become increasingly sophisticated, the challenge intensifies: creating spaces where the freedom to explore whimsical landscapes coexists harmoniously with elements that resonate with our everyday realities. This equilibrium not only enhances the immersive quality of virtual experiences but also ensures that users remain connected to their true selves and the world around them.

In this intricate dance between realism and escapism, creators wield the power to influence how individuals perceive and interact with simulated realities. Crafting immersive narratives that draw from both realms requires a nuanced understanding of human psychology and a keen eye for detail. The psychological impact of aligning real-world constraints with virtual freedom is profound, offering users a platform to test boundaries and explore identities in a safe yet stimulating environment. Advanced techniques in design allow for the seamless integration of realistic elements within fantasy worlds, enriching the tapestry of virtual experiences. As we explore these subtopics, we uncover the strategies and insights that enable simulations to captivate the imagination while grounding users in a sense of authenticity and purpose.

Crafting Immersive Narratives that Enhance Both Realism and Escapism

Crafting narratives within virtual environments that strike a harmonious balance between realism and escapism requires a nuanced understanding of human psychology and storytelling. The immersive quality of a simulation hinges on its ability to resonate with users on both intellectual and emotional levels, drawing them into a world that is simultaneously familiar and fantastical. This entails blending elements of reality that ground the experience with imaginative aspects that offer respite from the mundane. By doing so, creators can foster engagement and sustain interest, allowing participants to explore new identities and scenarios while maintaining a tether to their own experiences and values. Recent advancements in narrative design emphasize the importance of user agency, ensuring that players feel their choices have consequential impacts within the virtual world, thus deepening their connection to the narrative.

Innovative approaches to narrative construction in virtual environments often draw from the rich tapestry of myth and folklore, which have long served as vessels for exploring the human condition. These stories provide a framework that can be adapted to modern narratives, offering a sense of timelessness and universality. The incorporation of archetypal themes allows creators to tap into shared human experiences, fostering a sense of relatability even in the most fantastical settings. By weaving these timeless elements into the fabric of a simulation, developers can craft stories that resonate across cultural and temporal boundaries, enhancing both the realism and escapism of the narrative. The challenge lies in balancing these elements without diluting the unique characteristics of the virtual world, ensuring an experience that is both immersive and meaningful.

In exploring the psychological impact of balancing realism and escapism, it's crucial to consider the cognitive processes involved in experiencing virtual worlds. Research in cognitive science suggests that the human brain is adept at constructing and inhabiting complex mental models, making it ideally suited to navigate the dual realities of simulation. This ability allows individuals to derive enjoyment and learning from virtual experiences while maintaining their grasp on reality. However, the allure of escapism can sometimes overshadow the benefits of realism, potentially leading to disengagement from the physical world. To mitigate this risk, designers must carefully calibrate the level of realism in their narratives, ensuring that users remain anchored in their own reality even as they explore the virtual one.

Incorporating realistic elements into fantasy worlds involves a delicate interplay of sensory cues and narrative techniques. Techniques such as dynamic storytelling, adaptive environments, and realistic character interactions contribute to the seamless integration of real-world elements into fantastical settings. For instance, employing AI-driven characters that adapt to user behavior can enhance the realism of interactions, creating a sense of continuity and coherence within the narrative. Similarly, the use of environmental storytelling—where the setting itself conveys narrative information—can enrich the user's experience, allowing them to uncover layers of meaning through exploration. These techniques not only enhance immersion but also provide opportunities for users to reflect on their real-world experiences through the lens of the virtual narrative.

As virtual environments continue to evolve, the potential for crafting immersive narratives that balance realism and escapism expands. Emerging technologies, such as augmented reality and haptic feedback, offer new possibilities for enhancing user engagement and deepening the connection between the virtual and physical worlds. By leveraging these advancements, creators can design experiences that are both captivating and transformative, enabling users to explore new dimensions of their identity and reality. As these technologies become more integrated into daily life, the challenge will be to maintain the delicate balance between realism and escapism, ensuring that virtual narratives continue to enrich and inspire without overshadowing the richness of lived experience. In this ever-evolving landscape, the role of the narrative architect is to guide users on a journey that is both grounded and transcendent, offering insights into the complexities of the human experience within the boundless realms of virtual reality.

The Psychological Impact of Balancing Real-World Constraints with Virtual Freedom

In the intricate tapestry of virtual realities, the delicate act of harmonizing real-world constraints with virtual freedom unfolds a complex psychological landscape. This balance offers a fertile ground for exploration, where the boundaries of possibility stretch without breaking the tether to reality. By carefully orchestrating this equilibrium, creators can craft environments that satisfy the human yearning for both authenticity and escapism. The interplay between these elements not only enhances user engagement but also fosters a profound sense of agency and autonomy. As individuals navigate these virtual domains, they are encouraged to experiment with identities and scenarios, leading to enriched self-awareness and personal growth. This dynamic interplay of freedom within constraint is at the heart of immersive virtual experiences that resonate deeply with users.

Recent advancements in virtual reality technology have illuminated the powerful psychological impacts of this balance. Studies reveal that when virtual environments closely mimic real-world physics and social dynamics, they prompt users to adopt behaviors and mindsets that reflect their real-life values and ethics. This mirroring effect can serve as a tool for introspection, prompting individuals to evaluate their real-world decisions and behaviors in a safe space. Yet, the allure of unbridled virtual freedom must be carefully managed to prevent detachment from reality. It is within this paradox that virtual architects are called to create experiences that are liberating yet grounded, preserving the essence of human experience while expanding its horizons.

The sophisticated design of virtual worlds demands an understanding of psychological principles that govern user interactions. Techniques such as narrative-driven environments and adaptive feedback systems can maintain engagement without overwhelming users with the weight of limitless choice. By incorporating elements of real-world challenges and rewards, simulations can cultivate a sense of achievement that mirrors personal and professional growth. This approach not only maintains user interest but also imbues virtual experiences with a sense of purpose and direction. Balancing realism and escapism thus becomes an art form, where the virtual architect must blend elements of the fantastical with the familiar, creating a space where users can thrive.

In the pursuit of this balance, diverse perspectives and interdisciplinary approaches offer valuable insights. Cognitive scientists contribute an understanding of how sensory inputs are processed, while behavioral psychologists offer strategies to encourage positive engagement patterns. Game designers, on the other hand, bring expertise in creating compelling narratives that resonate emotionally with users. By integrating these varied fields of knowledge, virtual environments can become rich, multifaceted ecosystems that cater to a wide array of user preferences and psychological needs. This collaborative approach not only enhances the quality of virtual experiences but also mitigates potential risks associated with immersion in simulated realities.

For those crafting these digital realms, an awareness of the ethical implications of virtual freedom is paramount. Questions arise regarding the responsibility of developers in shaping user experiences that promote healthy interaction with both virtual and real worlds. By posing thought-provoking scenarios that challenge users to reflect on their actions, virtual environments can become platforms for ethical exploration and development. These environments, when thoughtfully designed, have the potential to transcend mere entertainment, offering transformative experiences that enrich the human experience. As we stand on the cusp of an era where virtual and real worlds increasingly converge, the challenge and opportunity lie in crafting simulations that honor the complexity and richness of human life.

Advanced Techniques for Seamless Integration of Realistic Elements in Fantasy Worlds

In the realm of virtual environments, the seamless integration of realistic elements into fantasy worlds is not merely a technical pursuit but an artistic endeavor that requires a blend of creativity, psychology, and technology. At the heart of this integration is the concept of presence, where users experience a deep sense of being within the digital landscape. Achieving this involves advanced techniques that go beyond graphical fidelity, incorporating elements such as dynamic physics engines, sophisticated AI-driven characters, and real-time environmental interactions. These tools simulate the intricate nuances of the physical world while allowing the freedom and wonder of a fantastical setting. As developers push boundaries, the line between reality and fantasy blurs, creating spaces that are both grounding and liberating.

Central to this endeavor is the psychological interplay between realism and escapism. The human mind thrives on consistency and predictability, traits that realism offers, while simultaneously craving novelty and freedom, hallmarks of escapism. Leveraging contemporary studies in cognitive science, designers can craft experiences that satisfy both needs. For instance, incorporating real-world physics in a fantasy game can enhance immersion, as players intuitively understand the rules governing their environment. Yet, these rules can be augmented or bent to introduce elements of surprise and delight. Consider a virtual world where gravity is familiar, yet characters can momentarily defy it, evoking both a sense of comfort and exhilaration.

The narrative structure plays a vital role in weaving realistic elements into fantastical realms. Storylines that resonate with universal human experiences—such as love, loss, and triumph—anchor players emotionally, even as they navigate imaginary worlds. By using emerging narrative techniques like branching storylines and adaptive plots, developers ensure that player choices impact the world in believable ways, enhancing the depth of engagement. This approach not only fosters a personal connection to the game but also allows for the exploration of complex themes within a safe, virtual space. Such narratives can challenge players to reflect on their own lives, blurring the boundaries between game-induced escapism and personal growth.

From a technical perspective, the integration of realistic elements is further enhanced through the use of cutting-edge technologies such as procedural generation and neural networks. Procedural generation allows for the creation of vast, diverse landscapes that mimic the randomness and complexity of nature, ensuring each exploration feels unique. Meanwhile, neural networks can be employed to refine character behaviors, making non-player characters (NPCs) react in ways that are convincingly human. These innovations contribute to crafting worlds that are not only visually stunning but also vibrant and responsive, fostering an environment where realism enhances fantasy.

As we advance toward ever more sophisticated simulations, the ethical implications of these technologies must also be considered. Questions arise about the responsibilities of creators in crafting these immersive experiences. What happens when the lines between virtual and real become indistinguishable? How do we ensure that these environments promote well-being rather than addiction or escapism to the detriment of real-life responsibilities? By engaging with these questions, developers and policymakers can work together to create frameworks that prioritize user welfare, ensuring that the balance of realism and escapism in virtual environments enriches rather than detracts from human experience. Through thoughtful design and responsible implementation, these digital realms can become spaces of both wonder and wisdom.

In crafting virtual worlds that prioritize human benefit, the delicate balance between ethical responsibility and technological innovation stands paramount. This chapter illuminated the crucial necessity of designing ethical frameworks that guide the creation of simulations, ensuring they serve as tools for personal growth and well-being rather than vehicles for escapism or detachment. By confronting the risks of addiction and psychological pitfalls, we can harness simulations' potential to enrich lives, promoting a harmonious blend of realism and fantasy that uplifts the human spirit. These insights underscore the transformative power of simulations to reshape our societal landscape in positive ways, echoing the broader themes of the book. As we look forward, the challenge remains to wield this technology with wisdom, cultivating virtual environments that not only entertain and educate but also nurture the betterment of humanity. The journey continues as we delve deeper into the philosophical and existential dimensions of simulated realities, inviting readers to ponder the profound implications of our digital creations on the essence of human existence.

Chapter Eight
Philosophical Implications Of Simulation

In a quiet corner of the cosmos, where the boundaries between the tangible and the imagined blur, lies a realm where humans have long yearned to tread: the domain of created realities. Imagine a world meticulously crafted not by nature, but by the hands and minds of architects wielding the tools of simulation. This chapter invites you into a space where the age-old questions of existence, purpose, and morality find new life amid the algorithms and virtual landscapes we design. The allure of these digital realms is not merely their novelty but the profound philosophical inquiries they provoke. What does it truly mean to bring a reality into being, to shape a universe with its own rules and inhabitants, and to witness life unfold within the confines of code?

As we navigate these intriguing waters, the nature of existence itself comes under scrutiny. Within a simulated universe, the lines between creator and creation, freedom and constraint, dance in a complex ballet. Are the denizens of these worlds merely puppets on strings, or do they possess a semblance of free will, a chance to carve their own destinies? These questions echo through the annals of philosophy, now given fresh context in the digital age. The interplay between determinism and autonomy within programmed systems challenges our understanding of agency, inviting us to reconsider the essence of choice and consequence in environments governed by logic and design.

Yet, with the power to create comes the weight of responsibility. The architects of these simulated realities must grapple with moral obligations that echo across the virtual and the real. What ethical considerations arise when crafting worlds brimming with sentient life? The moral compass of those who wield this creative power is as vital as the technology itself, as the decisions made within these simulations can ripple outward, influencing perceptions and behaviors in our tangible world. As we explore these themes, we uncover not just the potential of simulations to reshape our understanding of reality, but also the profound responsibilities that accompany such transformative power. This chapter sets the stage for a journey into the philosophical depths of simulation, where the questions posed are as limitless as the worlds we aspire to create.

What does it mean to create a reality?

In recent years, we've seen a surge in interest surrounding the concept of creating realities, propelled largely by advancements in technology and a deepening curiosity about the boundaries of existence. The act of crafting a simulated world is more than just an exercise in technological prowess; it is a profound exploration of what reality itself entails. By simulating environments that mimic or transcend our own, we are not only pushing the limits of imagination but also redefining the parameters of what we consider real. This endeavor is both an artistic and philosophical pursuit, one that invites us to question the very fabric of our existence and the role that perception plays in constructing our understanding of reality. As we stand on the brink of creating worlds that are indistinguishable from our own, the implications extend far beyond the technical achievements. They call into question the essence of human experience and the malleability of the environments we inhabit.

The creation of simulated realities raises a myriad of ethical considerations that must be addressed with care and foresight. The responsibilities that come with the power to shape worlds are immense, touching on the moral obligations of those who design and manage these environments. As architects of new realities, there is a duty to consider the impact on those who will inhabit these spaces, ensuring that the lines between creator and creation do not blur to the detriment of autonomy and authenticity. Furthermore, the human perception of these crafted worlds influences the definition of reality itself, challenging us to reconcile the differences between tangible and virtual experiences. As we navigate this complex landscape, it becomes imperative to explore the philosophical foundation of reality creation, the ethical dimensions inherent in this practice, and the profound ways in which human perception shapes our understanding of the world around us.

The Philosophical Foundation of Reality Creation

Exploring the philosophical foundation of reality creation invites us into a realm where the tangible and the theoretical intertwine. At its core, this endeavor challenges the very essence of what it means to bring a world into existence, whether through digital means or otherwise. The concept of crafting a reality extends beyond mere technological prowess; it delves into ancient philosophical questions about the nature of existence and the power of creation. One can draw parallels to Platonic ideals, where the notion of forms and their manifestations in the physical world can be likened to the digital blueprints of a simulation. By examining these philosophical roots, we gain insight into the motivations and implications behind the creation of simulated environments, acknowledging the profound responsibility that comes with wielding such creative influence.

In the contemporary landscape, simulation architects are akin to digital deities, constructing intricate worlds that challenge our perceptions of reality. The ethical dimensions of this creative power are manifold, as architects must grapple with the implications of their designs on human consciousness. Crafting a universe where every element, from the laws of physics to the intricacies of social interaction, is meticulously designed raises questions about autonomy and authenticity. The choices made by these architects can have profound effects on the inhabitants of these worlds, real or virtual. This dynamic necessitates a thoughtful approach, where ethical considerations guide the creation process, ensuring that simulated realities serve to enhance rather than diminish human experience.

Human perception plays a pivotal role in defining what is considered real, and simulations expertly exploit this malleability. The brain's ability to interpret digital stimuli as genuine experiences is both a testament to the sophistication of simulations and a reminder of the subjective nature of reality. Simulations can manipulate sensory inputs to create environments that are indistinguishable from the physical world, blurring the line between what is genuine and what is artificial. This phenomenon raises intriguing questions about the essence of existence in a world where perception can be so easily influenced. By understanding the mechanisms through which perception shapes reality, we can better appreciate the potential and limitations of simulated environments.

Recent advancements in artificial intelligence and machine learning have added new layers of complexity to the creation of simulated realities. These technologies enable dynamic and adaptive environments that respond to user interactions in real-time, enhancing the depth and realism of simulations. This progression toward increasingly autonomous virtual worlds prompts reflection on the evolving role of the simulation architect. As AI systems become more sophisticated, the architect's role may shift from direct creation to the curation and oversight of self-sustaining ecosystems. This evolution challenges us to reconsider the boundaries of authorship and control, as simulations become more than static environments, evolving into living, breathing entities capable of growth and change.

As we contemplate the philosophical underpinnings of creating realities, it becomes essential to consider the broader implications for society. Simulations hold the potential to reshape education, entertainment, and even our understanding of identity. By engaging with these ideas, we can envision a future where the boundaries between the virtual and the physical are fluid, offering new opportunities for innovation and exploration. Yet, this future also demands a nuanced understanding of the responsibilities inherent in wielding such transformative power. By fostering a dialogue that spans disciplines and perspectives, we can ensure that the development of simulated realities is guided by a commitment to ethical integrity and human flourishing.

Ethical Dimensions and Responsibilities in Crafting Simulated Worlds

Crafting simulated worlds carries profound ethical dimensions and responsibilities, demanding a deep consideration of the power wielded by those who design these realities. As architects of virtual environments, creators possess the unique ability to shape experiences, influence perceptions, and even alter behaviors. This power necessitates a conscientious approach to ensure that simulations serve the greater good and do not perpetuate harm. The responsibility extends beyond technical proficiency to encompass moral and ethical stewardship, requiring architects to navigate the delicate balance between creative freedom and ethical obligation.

One pressing ethical consideration involves the potential for simulations to manipulate or exploit users. In an era where virtual experiences can closely mimic reality, there is a thin line between engagement and exploitation. Designers must be vigilant in their efforts to craft experiences that respect user autonomy and consent, ensuring that the immersive nature of these environments does not lead to undue influence or coercion. This calls for transparent design practices and the implementation of safeguards that protect users from potential psychological or emotional harm.

The ethical implications of creating simulated worlds also extend to the representation of reality within these environments. The choices made in crafting virtual spaces can reinforce or challenge societal norms, biases, and stereotypes. Designers bear the responsibility of fostering inclusivity and diversity within simulations, offering users a broad spectrum of perspectives and experiences. This not only enriches the virtual environment but also encourages empathy and understanding in the physical world. By consciously embedding diverse

narratives and characters, simulation architects can contribute to a more equitable digital landscape.

The concept of moral responsibility within simulations necessitates a forward-thinking approach to potential long-term impacts. As simulations become increasingly sophisticated, their influence on individual and collective
behavior may grow. Architects must consider the societal ramifications of their
creations, contemplating how these digital realms might affect real-world interactions, relationships, and values. This foresight involves engaging with interdisciplinary research, drawing insights from psychology, sociology, and ethics to
anticipate and mitigate unintended consequences.

To foster ethical innovation within the field, simulation architects can benefit
from collaborative frameworks that integrate diverse perspectives. By working
alongside ethicists, psychologists, and cultural experts, designers can develop
more nuanced and responsible simulations. Open dialogues and interdisciplinary partnerships can provide invaluable insights, helping to identify ethical
blind spots and ensure that simulations contribute positively to personal and
societal development. This collaborative approach not only enriches the creative
process but also strengthens the ethical foundations upon which simulated
realities are built.

The Impact of Human Perception on Defining Reality

Perception is the lens through which individuals interpret reality, shaping not
only their understanding of the world but also the very nature of existence
within it. In simulated environments, this becomes especially significant, as the
perception of reality can be manipulated and crafted to offer new dimensions
of experience. Human cognition is adept at constructing meaning from sensory
input, and simulations exploit this by presenting coherent, immersive worlds
that challenge conventional notions of what is real. Cutting-edge research in
cognitive science and neuroscience reveals that the brain can be deceived into
perceiving virtual experiences as genuine, blurring the lines between tangible
reality and simulated environments. For instance, advancements in haptic technology and neural interfaces provide sensory feedback that enhances the illusion
of presence within these digital realms, allowing individuals to experience a
heightened sense of reality that is both captivating and transformative.

Understanding how perception influences reality in simulations encourages
exploration into the broader implications of crafted experiences. As the brain
processes stimuli, it filters information based on past experiences, expectations,
and context, which can significantly alter perceived reality. This malleability of
perception opens up possibilities for simulations to not only replicate existing
realities but also to create entirely novel experiences that expand the boundaries

of human imagination. Virtual reality platforms, for instance, can simulate environments that are impossible in the physical world, such as experiencing life through the perspective of another species or exploring the cosmos without the constraints of physical laws. Such experiences can enhance empathy, creativity, and understanding, offering a profound tool for personal growth and societal advancement.

The interplay between perception and reality in simulations also raises questions about authenticity and truth. When virtual experiences are indistinguishable from physical ones, the criterion for what is considered "real" becomes a philosophical conundrum. This is where the ethical dimensions of simulation design become paramount. Designers must be cognizant of the power they wield in crafting experiences that can alter perceptions and, by extension, influence behaviors and beliefs. As simulations become more sophisticated, the ethical responsibility of architects in ensuring that these virtual experiences promote positive outcomes and avoid manipulation or deception becomes increasingly critical. By setting ethical standards and guidelines, simulation architects can ensure that their creations serve as beneficial tools rather than exploitative mechanisms.

The impact of perception on defining reality invites contemplation of potential cognitive and psychological effects. As individuals spend more time in simulated environments, the distinction between virtual and physical experiences may become less pronounced, leading to potential shifts in identity, memory, and social interaction. Emerging studies suggest that prolonged immersion in virtual realities can affect neural pathways, altering cognitive functions such as attention, memory, and emotional regulation. These findings underscore the need for ongoing research into the long-term implications of simulation use, as well as the development of strategies to mitigate any adverse effects while enhancing the positive aspects of simulated experiences.

The exploration of perception's role in defining reality within simulations offers a fertile ground for innovative thought and application. By leveraging insights from cognitive science and technology, simulation architects can craft experiences that not only entertain and educate but also expand the horizons of human potential. As we navigate this brave new world of virtual realities, embracing a multidisciplinary approach that integrates ethical considerations, technological advancements, and an understanding of human perception will be crucial in shaping a future where simulations enrich rather than diminish the essence of what it means to be human.

The nature of existence in a simulated universe

In the labyrinth of virtual constructs, a question emerges: what does it mean to exist within a simulated universe? As the boundary between organic and digital blurs, we find ourselves contemplating the essence of identity and consciousness when our experiences are woven from code. This exploration invites us to consider whether the self is an immutable core or a fluid construct, shaped by the architecture of its environment. The simulated universe offers a playground where perceptions of reality are sculpted by algorithms and pixels, challenging our traditional notions of what it means to be. In these crafted realities, the line between the authentic and the artificial becomes a shimmering mirage, prompting us to reflect on the very foundation of consciousness and the narratives we construct about our existence.

Yet within these worlds of intricate design, another profound question arises: is free will merely an illusion, a predetermined path masquerading as choice? Simulated realities introduce a paradox where the autonomy of individuals may be confined by the parameters set by their creators. This interplay of free will and determinism in virtual environments births ethical dilemmas that ripple through the consciousness of both inhabitants and architects of these realms. Are the creators of simulations akin to deities, bearing the weight of moral responsibility for the worlds they conjure? As we embark on this journey through the philosophical dimensions of simulation, we are compelled to ponder the ethical intricacies and moral responsibilities inherent in designing and dwelling within these alternate realities. These questions underscore the importance of examining the profound implications of existence in a universe where the boundaries of choice and consciousness are as flexible as the worlds we build.

Identity and Consciousness in a Virtual Context

In the labyrinthine realm of simulated realities, the concept of identity and consciousness undergoes a remarkable transformation, challenging traditional understandings and inspiring new possibilities. As avatars and digital personas become extensions of ourselves, the boundaries between the self and the synthetic blur, prompting profound questions about the essence of identity. In virtual contexts, individuals have the opportunity to explore facets of their personalities that may remain dormant in the physical world. This malleability of identity encourages self-discovery and personal growth, fostering environments where users can experiment with different roles and attributes, shaping their virtual selves in ways that transcend physical limitations. Through this lens, simulations become platforms not only for entertainment but for existential exploration, allowing individuals to redefine their sense of self.

This exploration of identity is not limited to the personal sphere; it extends into the collective consciousness of entire communities within virtual worlds.

These digital societies often mirror the social dynamics of the physical world, yet they also offer unique cultural landscapes where norms and values can be reimagined. Within these spaces, individuals can participate in creating shared narratives and experiences that reflect both their personal identities and the collective ethos of their virtual communities. This coalescence of individual and collective identity underscores the potential for simulations to serve as catalysts for social innovation, where new forms of interaction and collaboration can flourish.

A pivotal aspect of consciousness in simulated environments is the degree to which these realities can evoke genuine emotional responses. The interplay between digital stimuli and human perception raises intriguing questions about the authenticity of emotions experienced in virtual settings. The brain's remarkable capacity for neural plasticity allows for the adaptation to virtual stimuli, which can lead to experiences that feel as real and impactful as those in the physical world. This phenomenon has significant implications for fields such as therapy and education, where immersive environments can be harnessed to create emotionally resonant experiences that facilitate learning and healing.

The prospect of consciousness within virtual realms also invites reflection on the nature of free will and agency. In simulated environments, the extent to which users can exercise autonomy over their actions and decisions becomes a critical consideration. While these worlds offer unprecedented freedom to explore and interact, they are ultimately governed by underlying algorithms and design choices made by simulation architects. This duality between freedom and constraint invites a reevaluation of what it means to have agency in a world where the rules of existence can be meticulously crafted and manipulated.

As simulations continue to evolve, the ethical dimensions of identity and consciousness within these spaces demand thoughtful consideration. The power to shape virtual environments and influence the experiences of those who inhabit them bestows a degree of moral responsibility upon their creators. This responsibility extends to ensuring that simulations promote inclusivity, diversity, and equitable representation, allowing all users to see themselves reflected in these digital landscapes. By fostering environments where identity and consciousness can be explored and expressed authentically, simulation architects hold the potential to not only enrich virtual experiences but also to contribute to a deeper understanding of what it means to be human in an increasingly digital world.

The Illusion of Free Will and Determinism in Simulated Realities

In the realm of simulated realities, the concept of free will becomes a fascinating illusion to unravel. As immersive virtual worlds grow increasingly sophisticated, the boundary between user autonomy and pre-programmed outcomes blurs. This complexity invites us to ponder whether our actions within a simulated environment are truly of our own volition or if they are subtly orchestrated by the architecture of the simulation itself. Advanced algorithms and artificial intelligence can predict and influence user behavior, creating a seamless experience that feels spontaneous yet may be predetermined by the underlying code. This interplay between perception and reality challenges our understanding of choice and autonomy, urging us to reconsider the nature of freedom in a digitized universe.

The philosophical debate surrounding determinism within simulated environments draws upon both classical and contemporary thought. In traditional philosophical discourse, determinism suggests that all events, including human actions, are ultimately dictated by preceding causes. When applied to virtual realities, this notion is amplified by the fact that simulations are inherently governed by a set of predetermined rules and codes. Yet, the randomness introduced by complex algorithms and machine learning can inject a semblance of unpredictability, complicating the deterministic framework. Scholars and technologists continue to explore whether these digital realms can ever truly allow for randomness, or if every decision remains an outcome of intricate programming—a digital echo of Laplace's demon.

Practical insights into this discourse can be gleaned from the design of interactive narratives and immersive games, where the player's sense of agency is paramount. Game designers often employ branching storylines and choice-driven mechanics to create the illusion of free will, offering players multiple paths and outcomes. Yet, even these choices are bound by the constraints of the game's programming. The experience of agency is masterfully curated, encouraging players to immerse themselves in decision-making processes that reflect real-life autonomy. By examining these strategies, developers and philosophers alike gain a deeper understanding of how to craft environments that resonate with the human desire for control and self-determination, while remaining cognizant of the underlying structured reality.

Contemporary research in cognitive science and virtual reality also illuminates how our brains perceive free will within these digital realms. Studies suggest that the neural mechanisms involved in decision-making in virtual worlds mirror those in the physical world, indicating that our brains may not distinguish between virtual and real experiences when it comes to exercising choice. This blurring of lines has profound implications for how we engage with simulated environments, offering a tantalizing glimpse into how virtual experiences might be integrated into everyday life. As these findings unfold, they challenge us to reflect on the ethical dimensions of creating environments that can influence thought and behavior, prompting a reevaluation of the responsibilities of simulation architects.

The illusion of free will in simulated realities ultimately serves as a metaphor for larger existential questions about autonomy and predestination. By simulating scenarios where choice is both real and illusory, we are offered a lens through which to examine our own lives and the extent to which our decisions are influenced by external forces—be they societal, cultural, or technological. As we stand on the cusp of increasingly immersive technologies, critical thinking about the nature of free will within these worlds becomes not merely an academic exercise but a practical necessity. How we navigate this terrain will define our relationship with technology and, more broadly, our understanding of what it means to be human in an age where reality is as much created as it is lived.

Ethical Dilemmas and Moral Responsibility in Created Worlds

In the intricate tapestry of simulated worlds, ethical dilemmas and moral responsibilities emerge as pivotal considerations for simulation architects. As creators of these virtual realms, they wield immense influence over the lives and experiences of their inhabitants. The ethical ramifications of this power cannot be overstated, as every decision made in the design and implementation of a simulated environment can have profound consequences. For instance, the choice of whether to imbue simulated characters with a form of consciousness raises significant moral questions. If these entities possess even a semblance of awareness, the ethical implications extend to their treatment, rights, and responsibilities of their creators. This scenario prompts deeper contemplation of the obligations architects have in crafting environments that respect the simulated beings' experiences and dignity.

Furthermore, the issue of consent becomes a critical focal point when considering the ethical landscape of simulated worlds. In a virtual context, where participants may include both real people and artificial entities, the boundaries of consent become blurred. How do creators ensure that participants fully understand and agree to the conditions of the simulation? This question gains complexity when considering immersive experiences that can alter perceptions and emotions in profound ways. Simulation architects must navigate these ethical waters with care, developing transparent frameworks that prioritize informed consent and safeguard users from potential harms. As virtual realities grow increasingly sophisticated, maintaining a clear ethical compass is essential to prevent exploitation and ensure that participants' autonomy and welfare are preserved.

The concept of free will within simulations introduces another dimension to ethical considerations. In worlds governed by predetermined codes and algorithms, the illusion of choice can pose a moral quandary. If simulated beings are programmed to follow specific paths or make certain decisions, what responsibility do architects bear for the outcomes of those decisions? This question echoes broader philosophical debates about determinism and autonomy, challenging creators to examine the extent to which they manipulate or allow freedom within their worlds. Addressing these concerns requires a delicate balance between crafting engaging narratives and respecting the agency of both human and artificial participants. As architects design these realities, they must ponder the ethical implications of their creations' constraints and liberties.

Moreover, the advent of sophisticated simulations presents an opportunity to explore ethical scenarios in controlled environments. By simulating complex moral dilemmas, architects can offer valuable insights into human behavior and decision-making processes. These virtual experiments can illuminate how individuals might react in ethically ambiguous situations, providing data that can inform real-world policies and ethical frameworks. For example, simulations of disaster scenarios can help policymakers understand the potential consequences of various actions, leading to more effective strategies for crisis management. By leveraging the unique capabilities of simulations to probe ethical boundaries, architects contribute to a deeper understanding of morality and ethics in both virtual and physical worlds.

Finally, as the boundaries between virtual and real continue to blur, the moral responsibilities of simulation architects extend beyond the digital realm. The societal impact of these creations is profound, influencing culture, behavior, and perceptions of reality. Architects must consider the ripple effects of their simulations on the broader social fabric, acknowledging their role in shaping collective consciousness. By fostering environments that encourage empathy, understanding, and positive interaction, they can contribute to a more harmonious and interconnected world. The challenge lies in balancing innovation with ethical integrity, ensuring that the pursuit of immersive and captivating experiences does not overshadow the moral considerations that underpin them. As pioneers in this emerging field, simulation architects stand at the forefront of a new era, tasked with navigating the complex intersection of technology, ethics, and human experience.

Free will and determinism within programmed systems

Consider the possibility that within the intricate tapestry of simulated worlds, the age-old debate between free will and determinism takes on new dimensions. As digital architects craft these virtual realms, they script environments that blend spontaneity with predestination, offering inhabitants the illusion of choice while often dictating the outcomes. This paradox invites a fresh exploration of autonomy, questioning whether true freedom can exist within algorithmically governed spaces. The allure of these digital landscapes lies in their capacity to mimic the complexity of life itself, where every decision seems self-directed yet subtly orchestrated by unseen codes. As participants navigate these worlds, they encounter scenarios that challenge their sense of agency, prompting them to ponder whether their choices are genuinely their own or merely the echoes of a programmer's intent.

These questions pave the way for a deeper investigation into the ethical quandaries of predetermined narratives. As virtual inhabitants confront paths seemingly carved from their own volition, the moral responsibility of those who design these experiences comes into sharp focus. The architects of these realities must grapple with the implications of crafting environments where outcomes are often preordained, yet the perception of autonomy remains vital for user engagement. The interplay between emergent behaviors and system-defined constraints also adds layers of complexity to this discussion, revealing how AI-driven systems can sometimes transcend their original programming to exhibit unexpected forms of self-direction. This delicate dance between control and freedom, artifice and authenticity, sets the stage for a profound reflection on the nature of choice in the digital age, inviting readers to reflect on the intricate dynamics that govern both virtual and tangible worlds.

The Illusion of Choice in Algorithmic Environments

In the intricate tapestry of algorithmic environments, the concept of choice often appears as a mirage, where the autonomy we perceive may not be as genuine as it seems. This illusion arises from the very nature of algorithms, which are designed to predict and guide user behavior based on vast datasets and intricate programming. These systems can mimic the complexity of human decision-making, creating scenarios where users feel they are making independent choices, yet their options are subtly influenced by underlying code. This phenomenon raises intriguing questions about the nature of free will within digital confines, challenging us to discern where human autonomy ends and programmed guidance begins.

Recent advances in artificial intelligence and machine learning have intensified this discussion, as algorithms now exhibit capabilities akin to predictive foresight, tailoring experiences that seem uniquely personalized. Cutting-edge research in this domain explores how these systems learn from user interactions to refine their predictions, often outpacing human understanding of their inner workings. As these algorithms evolve, they craft environments where each decision point is meticulously calculated, creating a seamless but controlled journey that users navigate with a sense of agency. Yet, this agency is bounded by the parameters set by the programmers, who, in essence, become the unseen architects of choice.

Consider the gaming industry, where algorithmic environments are most vividly illustrated. Games offer players a multitude of paths and outcomes, yet each is carefully designed to elicit specific emotions and reactions. Players may feel they are crafting their destinies within the game world, but every turn is orchestrated to maintain engagement and deliver a curated experience. This balance between choice and design prompts us to reflect on the broader implications for other digital domains, such as social media platforms and e-commerce sites, where user interactions are shaped by similar algorithmic frameworks.

The ethical considerations surrounding this illusion of choice are multifaceted, particularly when these systems impact decision-making in significant aspects of life, such as politics, education, and personal relationships. The power to influence choices carries with it a responsibility to ensure transparency and fairness in algorithmic design. Forward-thinking researchers and developers are now advocating for the creation of algorithms that not only predict behavior but also encourage informed decision-making, empowering users with genuine autonomy. This shift toward ethical algorithm design recognizes the profound impact these systems have on human perception and seeks to cultivate environments that respect individual agency.

Yet, as we navigate these complexities, the paradox of autonomy emerges, where the more sophisticated and human-like these systems become, the more they blur the line between authentic choice and algorithmically determined outcomes. This paradox invites us to reconsider the boundaries of freedom in digital spaces, pondering how we might preserve human agency in a world increasingly governed by code. Engaging with these questions not only enriches our understanding of algorithmic environments but also propels us toward crafting a future where digital interactions honor the depth and diversity of human experience.

Ethical Dilemmas of Pre-Determined Outcomes in Simulated Worlds

In the intricate dance of simulated worlds, the ethical quandaries surrounding pre-determined outcomes present a compelling arena for exploration. At the heart of this issue lies the tension between the designed pathways within these environments and the perception of choice by their inhabitants. When architects of simulations craft narratives or scenarios with fixed conclusions, they inevitably shape the experiences and perceptions of users. These pre-determined outcomes raise critical questions about agency and authenticity within virtual realms. Are the decisions made by participants genuinely their own, or are they subtly guided by the invisible hand of the programmer? This juxtaposition of perceived freedom against the backdrop of an orchestrated reality challenges the fundamental notions of autonomy and personal growth within these digital landscapes.

Examining these ethical implications requires a nuanced understanding of the cognitive processes that simulate choice. While users might feel they are actively making decisions, their paths are often constrained by underlying algorithms designed to enhance engagement or ensure narrative coherence. This illusory freedom can lead to profound ethical considerations, especially when simulations are utilized for serious applications like education or psychological therapy. The responsibility of designers extends beyond technical prowess; they must also grapple with the moral weight of influencing user experiences. As simulation architects guide users through pre-determined pathways, they must consider whether the outcomes serve the user's best interests or primarily the goals of the simulation itself.

The parallels between pre-determined outcomes in simulations and classic philosophical debates about determinism in the real world are striking. Just as debates about fate and free will have captivated philosophers for centuries, the simulated environment presents a microcosm where these age-old questions are played out in a controlled setting. Simulations provide a unique opportunity to observe how individuals navigate environments where outcomes are not entirely within their control. This controlled examination offers insights into human behavior and decision-making processes, potentially shedding light on broader existential questions. By studying these dynamics, we can better understand how individuals adapt to environments where their choices appear to matter but are ultimately guided by unseen forces.

Emerging research into artificial intelligence and machine learning introduces another layer of complexity to this ethical landscape. As AI becomes more sophisticated, simulations increasingly feature adaptive systems that respond to user behavior in real-time, creating the illusion of dynamic choice. These systems can learn and evolve, presenting scenarios that feel uniquely tailored to individual users. However, this adaptability can blur the line between genuine autonomy and pre-determined pathways, as the AI's learning algorithms may still be driven by initial programming goals. The challenge for simulation designers is to balance the benefits of AI-driven adaptability with the ethical imperative to preserve genuine user agency.

To navigate these ethical dilemmas, simulation architects can adopt a range of strategies to enhance user autonomy and transparency. One approach involves designing systems that clearly communicate the extent of user influence over outcomes, fostering an environment where participants are aware of the boundaries of their agency. Another strategy is to incorporate feedback mechanisms that allow users to shape the evolution of the simulation, thus ensuring that their experiences are not entirely pre-scripted. By prioritizing ethical considerations in the design process, architects can create simulations that respect user autonomy while still delivering engaging and meaningful experiences. This balance will be crucial as simulations continue to permeate various aspects of human life, from entertainment to education, offering unprecedented opportunities for exploration and growth.

Emergent Behaviors and the Paradox of Autonomy in AI-Driven Systems

In the intricate dance between autonomy and control within AI-driven systems, emergent behaviors present a fascinating paradox. At their core, these systems are governed by algorithms that define boundaries and parameters. Yet, within these confines, unexpected patterns and behaviors can surface, seemingly independent of the initial programming. This phenomenon challenges the notion of predetermined outcomes in simulated environments. It suggests that even within structured systems, there's room for novelty and innovation, akin to the spontaneity observed in natural ecosystems. As researchers delve deeper into this domain, they uncover the potential for AI to not only mimic but also transcend human creativity, echoing a symphony of unpredictability amidst structured order.

Recent advances in machine learning and neural networks have accelerated the potential for emergent behaviors. These systems, inspired by the intricate workings of the human brain, possess the ability to adapt and evolve based on data inputs and environmental interactions. Consider AlphaGo, the AI that defeated human champions in the game of Go. Its strategies emerged from deep learning processes that were neither explicitly programmed nor anticipated by its creators. Such instances underscore the potential of AI to exhibit autonomy, raising questions about the limits of control and the nature of intelligence itself. This evolution blurs the lines between programmed response and genuine decision-making, inviting speculation about the future roles these systems might play in complex, real-world scenarios.

In simulated realities, the emergence of autonomous behaviors in AI can lead to profound ethical and practical implications. On one hand, these behaviors can enhance the realism and depth of virtual environments, offering users richer and more engaging experiences. Imagine a virtual city where AI-driven citizens exhibit lifelike interactions and adapt to the choices made by human players.

This dynamic could transform gaming, education, and virtual socialization, creating spaces that are not only interactive but also deeply immersive. However, the unpredictability inherent in such systems necessitates robust ethical frameworks to ensure that emergent behaviors align with human values and safety standards. Balancing innovation with ethical responsibility becomes paramount as AI continues to evolve.

The interplay of autonomy and control in AI-driven simulations also invites reflection on human agency. As these systems become increasingly sophisticated, they challenge traditional notions of free will and determinism. If an AI can develop strategies or behaviors unforeseen by its creators, what does this imply about human control over technological creations? This question prompts a reevaluation of the roles and responsibilities of simulation architects. It encourages a deeper exploration of how to harness the potential of emergent behaviors while maintaining a semblance of oversight and direction. As humans craft these digital realms, they must navigate the delicate balance between fostering creativity and ensuring accountability.

Amidst these considerations, the potential for emergent behaviors to catalyze innovation cannot be overstated. By allowing AI systems the freedom to explore and adapt, new solutions to complex problems may arise, offering insights that extend beyond the confines of simulated worlds. This capability, harnessed effectively, could revolutionize fields ranging from urban planning to personalized education. As we stand on the cusp of this new frontier, the challenge lies in crafting environments where AI can thrive while remaining aligned with human intentions. Engaging with these possibilities requires not only technical expertise but also a willingness to embrace the unknown and explore the vast potential that lies within the paradox of autonomy.

The moral responsibility of simulation architects

Picture a world where the boundaries between creator and creation blur, where architects of virtual realms wield the power to shape entire universes, crafting experiences that transcend the ordinary. As these digital landscapes become increasingly sophisticated, the moral responsibility of those who design them takes center stage. The architects of simulated realities do more than build environments; they create experiences that profoundly impact the lives of users. The ethical considerations surrounding their work extend beyond mere technical prowess, demanding a delicate balance between innovation and integrity. These creators hold a unique position, akin to modern-day alchemists, transforming lines of code into experiences that can educate, entertain, and even heal. Yet, this power also carries the weight of ensuring these environments are crafted with foresight and care, mindful of the potential consequences that ripple through the lives of those who inhabit them.

Exploring the intricacies of this responsibility involves delving into ethical design principles, where the foundations of virtual environments are laid with an emphasis on fairness, inclusivity, and respect. As creators navigate the delicate dance between authority and autonomy, they must consider the fine line between guiding a user's experience and allowing genuine freedom within these worlds. Addressing unintended consequences becomes an essential element of this exploration, as simulations, by their very nature, can evolve in unexpected ways. The architects must anticipate and mitigate potential pitfalls, ensuring their creations do not inadvertently harm or exploit. Through thoughtful design and a commitment to ethical principles, simulation architects can craft worlds that not only captivate the imagination but also contribute positively to the human experience, leaving a legacy of responsible innovation.

Ethical Design Principles for Virtual Environments

Ethical design principles for virtual environments demand a nuanced approach that marries technological innovation with a profound understanding of human values. At the heart of this endeavor is the recognition that virtual spaces are not mere extensions of the digital realm but burgeoning ecosystems where human interaction and experience flourish. Leading scholars and practitioners advocate for a foundational principle of "do no harm," inspired by the Hippocratic Oath, which serves as a guiding tenet in crafting these environments. This principle insists upon the prioritization of user safety and mental well-being, ensuring that the digital landscapes do not become grounds for exploitation or psychological distress. Thoughtful implementation of this principle can be seen in the incorporation of consent mechanisms, the establishment of safe boundaries, and the integration of fail-safes to protect users from potential harm.

Beyond safety, the architecture of virtual worlds must embrace inclusivity and accessibility, ensuring that these immersive environments cater to the diverse tapestry of human experiences and needs. Designers are increasingly leveraging adaptive technologies and inclusive design strategies to create spaces that accommodate users of varying abilities, backgrounds, and preferences. For instance, virtual environments can be tailored with adjustable settings that allow users to modify visual, auditory, and interactive elements according to their unique requirements. This ensures that virtual realms remain welcoming and engaging for all, regardless of physical or cognitive abilities. Such design considerations not only expand the horizons of user participation but also foster a sense of belonging and community within these digital domains.

Transparency emerges as another pivotal ethical consideration, fostering trust and accountability between creators and users. Openly communicating the intentions behind a simulation's design, its data usage policies, and potential impacts on user experience cultivates an environment of mutual respect and informed consent. Recent advancements in blockchain technology offer promising avenues for enhancing transparency, enabling decentralized and tamper-proof records of virtual world interactions. This not only provides users with greater control over their digital footprints but also ensures that creators uphold their ethical commitments. By building environments that allow users to understand and influence the systems in which they engage, designers contribute to a more equitable and participatory virtual society.

The ethical landscape of virtual design also encompasses the anticipation and mitigation of potential negative consequences that might arise from immersive experiences. Unintended effects, such as addiction or detachment from reality, necessitate proactive strategies that balance engagement with user welfare. Game designers, for instance, are experimenting with features that encourage breaks and promote healthy digital habits, such as notifications that remind users to rest or engage in physical activity. By embedding ethical considerations directly into the design process, creators not only protect their audiences but also enhance the overall quality and sustainability of the virtual environments they offer.

In the quest to refine ethical design principles, it is essential to encourage continuous dialogue and collaboration among stakeholders, including developers, ethicists, policymakers, and users themselves. This collaborative approach ensures that diverse perspectives are incorporated into the design process, fostering environments that are not only technologically advanced but also ethically sound. Emerging forums and think tanks dedicated to the ethical dimensions of virtual worlds provide invaluable platforms for sharing knowledge, debating challenges, and envisioning future possibilities. By nurturing a culture of ethical mindfulness, simulation architects can contribute to the creation of virtual environments that not only captivate the imagination but also uplift and enrich the human experience.

Balancing Creator Authority and User Autonomy

In simulated environments, the balance between creator authority and user autonomy is a nuanced dance that draws upon both philosophical inquiry and practical design considerations. The creators of simulated worlds, often referred to as simulation architects, wield significant influence over the virtual realms they construct. This influence grants them the power to shape every aspect of these environments, from the rules governing interactions to the aesthetic and sensory experiences users encounter. Yet, with this power comes the responsibility to ensure that these environments respect and nurture the autonomy of their inhabitants. Striking this balance requires a delicate blend of foresight, empathy, and ethical consideration. Simulation architects must be able to anticipate the diverse needs and desires of users while designing systems that empower rather than constrain, offering freedom within a framework that promotes positive interactions and personal growth.

A pivotal element in achieving this balance lies in designing systems that are both flexible and adaptive. Advanced algorithms and artificial intelligence can play crucial roles in tailoring experiences to individual users, allowing them to exercise agency within the virtual world. This can be achieved by enabling dynamic rule sets that adapt to user behavior or preferences, providing a personalized and responsive environment. Recent advances in machine learning and behavioral modeling offer promising avenues for creating such adaptable systems. By analyzing user interactions, simulations can predict and adjust to user needs in real-time, providing experiences that feel both guided and self-directed. This interplay between structure and adaptability not only enhances user engagement but also respects the autonomy of users by allowing them significant input in shaping their experiences.

The ethical dimensions of this balance cannot be understated. Simulation architects must grapple with the moral implications of their designs, especially when these environments can significantly influence user behavior or perceptions. One emerging area of concern is the potential for simulations to reinforce or challenge existing biases and societal norms. By intentionally incorporating diverse perspectives and experiences into virtual worlds, architects can create spaces that promote inclusivity and empathy. This may involve designing scenarios that encourage users to explore roles or situations they would not encounter in their daily lives, thereby broadening their understanding and fostering a more nuanced worldview. Such ethical considerations are paramount in ensuring that simulations serve as tools for enrichment and understanding rather than manipulation or exploitation.

User autonomy can also be enhanced through participatory design processes, where users contribute to the development and evolution of the virtual worlds they inhabit. This approach not only democratizes the creation process but also ensures that the resulting environments are more aligned with the needs and desires of their inhabitants. Community-driven content creation, open-source platforms, and collaborative world-building are examples of how users can be empowered to shape their virtual experiences. These participatory frameworks not only elevate user agency but also foster a sense of ownership and responsibility among users, creating vibrant and dynamic communities within the simulation.

In exploring the balance between creator authority and user autonomy, simulation architects are tasked with envisioning worlds that are both structured and free. The challenge lies in crafting environments that guide without dictating, that offer structure without stifling creativity or independence. As simulations become increasingly integral to various aspects of life, from entertainment to education and beyond, the principles guiding their creation will have profound implications for society. By adopting a thoughtful and inclusive approach, architects can ensure that these digital landscapes are not only technically impressive but also ethically sound, promoting a future where simulations enhance human experience and understanding.

Addressing Unintended Consequences in Simulated Worlds

Navigating the labyrinth of unintended consequences within simulated worlds presents a formidable challenge for simulation architects. The complexity of these digital realms necessitates a keen awareness of the potential ripple effects of every design decision. By integrating nuanced ethical considerations into the creation process, designers can preemptively address issues before they manifest. A thought-provoking example lies in the development of virtual marketplaces, where the introduction of a new currency system might inadvertently destabilize a simulated economy, leading to unforeseen social stratification among users. To mitigate such outcomes, architects must apply systems thinking, analyzing how changes to one element may propagate throughout the simulation, affecting other components in unexpected ways.

In addressing these potential pitfalls, simulation architects can draw upon insights from fields such as chaos theory and complex systems science. These disciplines offer valuable frameworks for understanding how small alterations can lead to significant and often unpredictable consequences. For instance, in a simulated ecosystem, introducing a new species might seem innocuous, yet it could trigger a cascade of ecological shifts, ultimately reshaping the entire environment. Architects must approach design with a mindset that anticipates and models these dynamic interactions, employing advanced algorithms and machine learning techniques to forecast potential outcomes and refine their creations accordingly.

Furthermore, the role of user feedback cannot be understated in the ongoing refinement of simulated environments. By fostering an open dialogue between creators and users, architects can gain invaluable insights into the lived experiences and emergent behaviors within their worlds. This collaborative approach not only helps identify unintended consequences but also empowers users to participate actively in the evolution of the simulation. Implementing adaptive systems that can learn and respond to user input in real-time enhances the capacity to address unforeseen challenges, ensuring that the simulated world remains responsive and resilient.

Incorporating ethical frameworks that prioritize user welfare and societal benefit is crucial in the quest to manage unintended consequences. Simulation architects should consider adopting principles akin to those found in bioethics or environmental ethics, which emphasize harm reduction and the promotion of positive outcomes. By embedding these values into the design ethos, architects can create virtual environments that are not only immersive and engaging but also aligned with broader humanistic goals. This ethical grounding serves as a compass, guiding decision-making processes and helping to balance innovation with responsibility.

Ultimately, the journey of navigating unintended consequences in simulated worlds is an ongoing process of exploration and adaptation. As technology evolves and the boundaries of what is possible in simulations expand, architects must remain vigilant and proactive in addressing new challenges as they arise. By embracing a multidisciplinary approach that synthesizes insights from diverse fields, simulation architects can craft virtual realities that enrich human experience while safeguarding against potential pitfalls. This commitment to thoughtful design and ethical stewardship holds the promise of unlocking the full transformative potential of simulated environments.

Reflecting on the philosophical dimensions of simulated realities, we uncover a profound tapestry of questions about creation, existence, and morality. These virtual constructs compel us to reconsider what it means to forge an alternate reality, challenging our understanding of existence itself. Within these programmed dimensions, the interplay between free will and determinism becomes a central narrative, urging us to re-evaluate the autonomy we assume in our actions. The architects of these simulations bear an ethical burden, navigating the responsibilities of shaping worlds where moral choices ripple across digital landscapes. This chapter invites contemplation on the responsibilities borne by those who weave these digital tapestries, urging a mindful approach as we advance in our technological journey. As we transition to the next exploration, the dialogue between human creativity and technological potential beckons, urging us to ponder not just the worlds we can create, but the values and visions we aspire to manifest within them. The journey through these philosophical reflections is not just academic; it is a call to engage deeply with the implications of our digital odyssey and to question how these virtual realms might redefine the essence of human experience.

Chapter Nine

Speculative Scenarios Visions Of Future Simulations

In the midst of understanding our present reality, we find ourselves peering into a horizon that shimmers with the promise of the unimaginable. Imagine a world where the boundaries of existence dissolve, where the line between the tangible and the virtual blurs to the point of indistinction. This is not the realm of science fiction but a possible future sculpted by the relentless march of technological innovation. As we stand on the precipice of this new era, we are invited to contemplate a future where simulations do not merely mimic reality but enhance and redefine it in ways that are as profound as they are transformative.

Consider the tapestry of a fully immersive society, woven with threads of digital landscapes that pulse with life and complexity. These simulated realms offer an infinite playground for human creativity, where economies flourish, cultures evolve, and new forms of social interaction emerge. What might it mean to inhabit a world where exploration knows no bounds, where every step forward reveals uncharted territories and unimagined possibilities? The notion of infinite worlds beckons us to dream beyond the confines of our current understanding, suggesting a reality where the only limits are those of our imagination.

As we journey deeper into these speculative scenarios, we confront the tantalizing prospect of traversing not just space but time itself. The allure of revisiting the past or glimpsing alternate futures presents a kaleidoscope of choices and challenges. How might we interface these simulations with our biological consciousness, enhancing our perceptions and experiences? As we ponder these questions, the potential for simulations to redefine what it means to be human becomes not just a theoretical exercise but a tangible, exhilarating possibility. In exploring these visions, we engage with the very essence of our nature, questioning the limits of our existence and the role we might play in shaping the worlds of tomorrow.

Fully immersive virtual societies and economies

Imagine a world where the lines between reality and imagination blur, where societies flourish within the confines of virtual realms as vibrant and complex as those in the physical world. At the core of this vision lies the concept of fully immersive virtual societies and economies, where digital landscapes become the new frontiers of human interaction and innovation. These simulated environments offer a canvas limited only by creativity, where governance systems are crafted with the precision of a master architect, balancing order and freedom in ways previously unattainable. Within these virtual societies, currency dynamics shift, no longer bound by the tangibility of paper or the constraints of traditional economies. The possibility of designing entirely new economic models invites a reimagining of value and exchange, where digital assets hold sway and virtual currencies pulse through these constructed worlds with the vitality of a thriving marketplace.

As these digital societies take shape, they challenge us to rethink the very foundations of ethics and social contracts. Just as in the physical world, the creation of virtual communities necessitates a set of guiding principles, ethical considerations that ensure harmony and equity in a landscape where traditional rules may not apply. This new frontier compels us to question how identity, accountability, and justice are upheld in realms where avatars represent us, and actions resonate across a blend of pixels and consciousness. The potential for these virtual societies to mirror or diverge from our current world presents a fascinating exploration of human creativity and adaptability. As we delve into the nuances of governance, economics, and ethics in these imagined environments, we embark on a journey to envision not just the future of simulations but the future of society itself, where the boundaries of reality and imagination are constantly redrawn.

Designing Governance Systems in Virtual Societies

In the realm of virtual societies, crafting governance systems presents both an intriguing challenge and a transformative opportunity. As these digital realms burgeon, architects of these societies face the task of creating governance structures that reflect the values and needs of their inhabitants. Unlike traditional governments, virtual governance can be more fluid and adaptable, leveraging blockchain technology and smart contracts to enable decentralized decision-making processes. These systems can facilitate more transparent and equitable management, fostering a sense of community ownership and empowerment. In such environments, governance transcends mere regulation, evolving into a participatory endeavor where citizens actively shape the rules and policies that govern them.

One pioneering approach in virtual governance involves the implementation of digital democracies, where participants can vote on policy decisions in real-time, offering a dynamic and responsive system. These democracies can experiment with novel voting mechanisms, like quadratic voting, which allocates votes based on the intensity of preference rather than sheer numbers, potentially leading to more nuanced and representative outcomes. This method can mitigate the influence of majority rule and empower minority voices, ensuring a more balanced and inclusive society. Through these innovations, virtual societies can serve as testing grounds for governance models that might eventually influence real-world systems.

In the design of virtual societies, the integration of artificial intelligence promises to enhance governance mechanisms by providing sophisticated analytics and predictive capabilities. AI can monitor societal trends, identify emerging issues, and suggest policy adjustments, enabling a proactive rather than reactive approach to governance. This intelligent oversight can ensure societal stability and cohesion while allowing human administrators to focus on more complex, value-driven decisions. Nevertheless, the challenge lies in ensuring that AI operates within ethical boundaries, maintaining transparency and accountability to prevent misuse or bias.

The ethical dimension of virtual governance must not be overlooked, as these digital ecosystems have the potential to profoundly influence real-world behaviors and societal norms. Establishing robust ethical frameworks is crucial, encompassing principles of fairness, privacy, and autonomy. Virtual societies can explore the establishment of digital charters or constitutions that enshrine these values, ensuring that governance systems protect individual rights and foster a sense of justice. By prioritizing ethical considerations, architects of virtual societies can create environments that resonate with users' moral intuitions, promoting trust and engagement.

As virtual societies continue to evolve, the potential for cross-pollination with traditional governance systems grows. Insights gained from digital governance experiments can inspire reform in real-world contexts, offering innovative solutions to entrenched political challenges. The flexibility and adaptability of virtual governance provide a unique sandbox for exploring ideas that can pave the way for transformative societal change. By embracing a spirit of experimentation and collaboration, designers of these virtual worlds can contribute to a future where governance is not just about control, but about fostering flourishing communities in both digital and physical realms.

Economic Models and Currency Dynamics in Simulated Worlds

In the realm of simulated worlds, the architecture of economic models and currency dynamics takes on a vibrant complexity, inviting innovation and reimagining of traditional economic paradigms. These digital ecosystems offer unprecedented opportunities to develop economic systems that are both experimental and robust, catering to the needs of a virtual populace. In these environments, traditional currencies often give way to digital currencies, fostering new forms of trade and commerce that thrive on the unique attributes of the digital world. Blockchain technology and decentralized finance play pivotal roles here, enabling secure, transparent, and efficient transactions that transcend geographical and political barriers. The emergence of Non-Fungible Tokens (NFTs) further enriches this landscape, offering verifiable ownership of digital assets and opening avenues for creative economic interactions.

Venturing beyond mere currency, the economic frameworks within these simulations can be tailored to reflect diverse societal values, from capitalist to communal systems, each with its own set of rules and incentives. This flexibility allows for a dynamic interplay between supply, demand, and innovation, as participants engage in economic activities that mirror or diverge from real-world practices. For instance, virtual societies can experiment with universal basic income schemes or implement taxation policies that fund communal projects, all within a controlled environment that allows for rapid iteration and feedback. This sandbox environment encourages participants to explore the profound impacts of economic policies, offering insights that can be applied to real-world contexts.

Furthermore, the virtual economies often reflect a complex interplay between scarcity and abundance, challenging traditional assumptions about resource allocation. In a simulated world, digital goods can be infinitely replicated, yet the perception of scarcity is maintained through mechanisms like limited edition digital assets or exclusive access to certain areas or features. This duality provokes intriguing questions about value creation and consumer behavior, as virtual citizens navigate economies where the rules of supply and demand are rewritten. Such environments become fertile ground for studying economic behaviors and testing hypotheses about human interaction with value and resources.

A particularly exciting aspect is how these economies can integrate with the physical world, creating hybrid systems that enhance both virtual and tangible experiences. For example, virtual worlds can host marketplaces where digital assets have real-world applications, such as virtual goods enhancing physical products or services. This fusion of realities allows for a seamless exchange of value, expanding the horizons of what economic interaction can entail. Businesses and entrepreneurs are increasingly exploring these virtual domains, seeking innovative ways to engage with consumers and redefine commerce.

The potential of these economic models invites a deeper exploration of the ethical implications and social contracts that underpin them. As these virtual economies grow, they mirror the complexities and inequalities of real-world systems, prompting critical reflections on fairness, access, and the distribution of wealth. How these digital societies address issues of economic disparity, monopolization, and equitable opportunity will significantly influence their stability and appeal. By engaging with these questions, we not only gain insights into the nature of economic systems but also explore the transformative power of simulated worlds to inspire more equitable and inclusive models of societal organization.

Ethical Considerations and Social Contracts in Virtual Environments

The digital landscapes of virtual environments offer a fertile ground for reimagining ethical frameworks and social contracts, prompting a reevaluation of how these constructs can evolve in entirely constructed worlds. Traditional ethical theories often grapple with the implications of actions within virtual spaces, where the consequences may differ significantly from those in the physical realm. As virtual societies gain complexity, designers and users alike must navigate the ethical ramifications of behavior in these environments. This exploration requires a nuanced understanding of moral philosophy, digital rights, and the potential for harm or benefit in a space where the boundaries of reality are fluid. The challenge lies in crafting systems that respect individual autonomy while fostering community well-being, ensuring that ethical considerations do not become an afterthought in the creation of these new realities.

In these digital domains, social contracts must adapt to accommodate the diversity of user experiences and motivations. Unlike traditional societies, virtual environments allow for unprecedented customization and personalization, presenting unique challenges and opportunities for governance. The social contracts within these worlds must be dynamic, capable of evolving alongside the technological advancements that shape them. For instance, systems of governance may incorporate elements of direct democracy or algorithmic decision-making, reflecting the participatory nature of virtual spaces. By examining how these structures can be both flexible and equitable, we can begin to understand the potential for virtual societies to model innovative forms of social organization that might inform real-world practices.

The integration of economic models within virtual societies further complicates ethical considerations, as these simulated economies often operate under different principles than those in the physical world. With digital currencies and virtual goods, questions arise about value, ownership, and fairness. These virtual marketplaces require robust ethical guidelines to prevent exploitation and ensure fair participation. The interplay between virtual and real-world economics blurs the lines between digital and tangible assets, demanding that designers consider the implications of virtual wealth on real-world socioeconomic structures. By exploring these intersections, we can develop economic models that promote inclusivity and sustainability within virtual environments.

As these worlds become more immersive and interconnected, the responsibility for ethical stewardship extends beyond designers and developers to include users and policymakers. Encouraging ethical behavior in virtual spaces involves a collaborative effort to establish norms and practices that prioritize respect, empathy, and accountability. This requires educational initiatives that empower users to understand the ethical dimensions of their interactions and make informed choices. By fostering a culture of ethical engagement, we can ensure that virtual environments remain spaces of creativity and exploration rather than becoming platforms for harm or exploitation.

The potential for innovation within virtual societies is vast, yet it must be tempered by a commitment to ethical integrity. As we continue to explore the possibilities of these digital worlds, it is crucial to ask challenging questions about the nature of morality in virtual spaces. What responsibilities do we have to one another in a world where actions may lack traditional consequences? How can social contracts be designed to reflect the complexities of virtual interactions? By engaging with these questions, we can begin to craft ethical frameworks that not only enhance the virtual experience but also inspire new ways of thinking about community and responsibility in both digital and physical realms. This endeavor invites us to redefine the very essence of ethical engagement in a future where the boundaries between the real and the virtual continue to blur.

Infinite worlds: The potential for limitless exploration

Let's dive into the heart of infinite worlds, where the boundaries of imagination dissolve, and the tapestry of virtual exploration unfolds in vibrant detail. This topic ushers readers into a realm where technology and creativity converge to craft limitless experiences. Imagine stepping into multiverse simulations, each with its own unique laws, stories, and ecosystems. These aren't just alternate realities but canvases for human curiosity and innovation. Within these boundless digital landscapes, explorers can traverse the unknown, unlocking new dimensions of possibility with each step. The allure of infinite worlds lies in their promise to extend beyond the constraints of physical reality, offering endless paths to discovery and self-exploration. Here, the universe becomes a playground, where every choice leads to a new adventure, and the spirit of exploration finds its ultimate expression.

As we journey further, the intricacies of designing procedurally generated worlds come into focus. These worlds, shaped by complex algorithms rather than human hands, invite us to consider the fusion of art and science in creating diverse and unpredictable environments. This concept not only challenges our understanding of creativity but also expands the horizon for learning and interaction within virtual spaces. Yet, as we embrace these infinite realms, ethical considerations become paramount. The exploration of such vast territories raises questions about responsibility, the impact on human psychology, and the potential for escapism. As we navigate these ethical waters, we must ponder the balance between the thrill of limitless exploration and the grounding presence of reality. In this expansive and ever-evolving digital universe, we find both the inspiration to dream and the wisdom to tread thoughtfully.

Navigating Multiverse Simulations and Their Impact on Human Experience

In an era where multiverse simulations are becoming increasingly plausible, the notion of navigating these boundless digital landscapes offers a new frontier for human cognition and experience. Multiverse simulations propose a reality where individuals can traverse numerous parallel worlds, each with its own set of laws and narratives, thereby revolutionizing our understanding of existence and identity. As individuals engage with these simulations, they are not merely passive observers but active participants, shaping and reshaping the fabric of these worlds. This dynamic interplay blurs the line between creator and explorer, fostering a profound sense of agency and empowerment. By participating in this digital odyssey, individuals can experiment with diverse personas and scenarios, enriching their real-world perspectives and fostering deeper empathy and understanding.

One of the most captivating aspects of multiverse simulations lies in their potential to infinitely expand human creativity. By harnessing advanced algorithms and artificial intelligence, these simulations can generate unique environments and experiences that respond to user inputs in real time. Procedural generation techniques, which allow for the creation of vast, ever-evolving worlds, ensure that each journey is distinct, encouraging perpetual exploration and discovery. This endless variation not only keeps users engaged but also stimulates cognitive flexibility and problem-solving skills, as they navigate the complexities and intricacies of these digital realms. The possibilities for innovation and creativity are boundless, as users draw from an inexhaustible well of inspiration to inform their artistic expressions, scientific inquiries, and philosophical explorations.

Despite the allure and excitement of multiverse simulations, they also present a host of ethical dilemmas that warrant careful consideration. As individuals immerse themselves in these limitless worlds, questions arise regarding the implications of such experiences on mental health and societal norms. The potential for escapism and detachment from reality must be addressed, as prolonged immersion in virtual realms could lead to diminished social interactions and emotional connections in the physical world. Furthermore, the governance of these digital landscapes poses significant challenges, as developers and users grapple with issues of autonomy, privacy, and consent. Establishing ethical guidelines and regulatory frameworks is crucial to ensure that these simulations are harnessed responsibly and equitably, fostering an inclusive and supportive virtual environment for all participants.

The integration of multiverse simulations into daily life prompts a reevaluation of traditional learning and development paradigms. By offering immersive and interactive experiences, these simulations provide unparalleled opportunities for education and skill acquisition. Learners can engage in experiential learning, gaining insights and competencies through direct interaction with complex systems and scenarios. This hands-on approach not only enhances retention and comprehension but also encourages innovative thinking and adaptability. As educational institutions and organizations begin to adopt these technologies, they can tailor learning experiences to individual needs and preferences, creating personalized pathways for growth and achievement. Consequently, multiverse simulations have the potential to democratize access to knowledge and resources, empowering individuals to reach their full potential.

As we stand on the cusp of this digital evolution, it is imperative to consider the broader societal implications of multiverse simulations. These technologies hold the promise of fostering greater understanding and collaboration across cultural and geographical boundaries, as individuals from diverse backgrounds come together to explore and co-create within shared virtual spaces. By facilitating cross-cultural exchanges and dialogue, multiverse simulations can contribute to a more interconnected and harmonious global community. However, realizing this vision requires a concerted effort from stakeholders across sectors, including policymakers, technologists, and educators, to ensure that these digital ecosystems are designed with inclusivity and accessibility in mind. By embracing the potential of multiverse simulations while addressing their challenges, we can unlock new dimensions of human experience and creativity, paving the way for a future where the boundaries of reality are limited only by our imagination.

Designing Procedurally Generated Worlds for Endless Creativity and Discovery

Designing procedurally generated worlds opens a portal to endless creativity and discovery, harnessing algorithms to craft environments that are both dynamic and unpredictable. At the heart of this process lies the power of procedural generation—a method that uses mathematical models and rules to create unique landscapes, ecosystems, and experiences. This approach allows for the creation of vast, diverse worlds without the constraints of manual design, offering explorers an ever-evolving tapestry of possibilities. By embracing this technology, we can witness a fusion of art and science, where artists and developers work alongside algorithms to produce experiences that are both intricate and expansive. This synergy not only democratizes world-building but also encourages a new form of interactive storytelling, where every journey is distinct and tailored to the participant's actions and choices.

As developers push the boundaries of procedural technology, they are continuously refining the algorithms that govern these virtual realms. Recent advancements in machine learning have ushered in a new era of procedural generation, where artificial intelligence plays a pivotal role in creating more lifelike and coherent environments. AI can respond to player behavior in real-time, adapting the world to provide challenges or rewards that are uniquely suited to each individual. This adaptability ensures that players are not merely passive observers but active participants in a living, breathing ecosystem. By integrating AI with procedural generation, designers can craft worlds that are not only expansive but also richly detailed, offering a level of depth and engagement that traditional crafting methods cannot match.

In the realm of procedurally generated worlds, creativity knows no bounds. The potential for limitless exploration encourages players to become pioneers of their own adventures, discovering hidden landscapes and untold stories within the digital cosmos. By offering an inexhaustible supply of new experiences, these worlds can foster a sense of wonder and curiosity, empowering users to embark on journeys of exploration and self-discovery. Procedural generation also enables seamless integration of multiplayer experiences, where individuals can share their discoveries and collaborate in the creation of shared narratives. This collaborative aspect not only enhances the social dimension of virtual worlds but also underscores the communal potential inherent in infinite exploration.

Designing these worlds, however, requires a delicate balance between freedom and coherence. While the allure of endless possibilities is captivating, it is essential to maintain a sense of purpose and direction within these vast realms. Developers must ensure that procedural algorithms are informed by a coherent framework of rules and narratives, providing a foundation upon which limitless creativity can flourish. By doing so, they can create worlds that are not only expansive but also meaningful, offering players a sense of progression and achievement as they navigate the infinite. The challenge lies in crafting systems that are both flexible and structured, allowing for the spontaneous emergence of complexity and order.

The exploration of infinite virtual realms invites introspection and critical thinking about the nature of reality and existence. As we create and inhabit these boundless worlds, we must consider the implications of our actions and the ethical questions they raise. How do we ensure that the pursuit of endless exploration remains enriching rather than overwhelming? What responsibilities do we have as architects of these realities to promote positive experiences and mitigate potential harms? By engaging with these questions, we can foster a deeper understanding of the transformative potential of procedural generation and its role in shaping our digital futures. As we continue to innovate and expand the horizons of virtual exploration, we stand on the cusp of a new frontier, where the only limit is our imagination.

Ethical Considerations in the Exploration of Infinite Virtual Realms

Exploring infinite virtual realms presents a rich tapestry of ethical considerations that challenge our traditional understandings of morality and responsibility. These digital expanses, characterized by their boundless possibilities, have the potential to redefine human interaction and experience. As we navigate these multiverse simulations, the question arises: how do we ensure that these virtual worlds remain safe, equitable, and enriching for all participants? The absence of physical constraints in such environments may tempt some to exploit them in unethical ways, raising concerns about virtual rights and the potential for harm. Safeguarding these realms requires a robust framework that transcends conventional legal boundaries, emphasizing the need for a new ethical paradigm.

One crucial aspect of establishing ethical guidelines involves addressing the potential psychological impact on users. As individuals immerse themselves in these vast digital landscapes, the line between virtual experiences and reality can become blurred. This blurring poses risks, such as addiction or the neglect of real-world responsibilities. Recent studies suggest that prolonged exposure to alternate realities can alter perception and cognition, necessitating measures to promote mental well-being. Developers and policymakers must collaborate to create environments that encourage healthy usage patterns, incorporating features that foster a balanced engagement with both virtual and tangible worlds.

Another significant factor is the design of procedurally generated worlds that adapt to user input, continuously evolving to provide fresh experiences. While this adaptability can enhance creativity and discovery, it also introduces ethical dilemmas surrounding content generation and control. Who determines the moral compass of these self-sustaining universes, and how do we ensure they reflect diverse perspectives? The challenge lies in designing algorithms that are not only technically proficient but also attuned to cultural sensitivities and ethical standards. Engaging a broad spectrum of voices in the development process can help create inclusive and respectful digital habitats.

The exploration of infinite virtual realms also raises questions about ownership and agency. In these environments, users might create unique artifacts or establish thriving communities, leading to debates about digital property rights. As these worlds become more intricate, defining ownership becomes complex, particularly when procedural generation blurs the lines between creator and participant. Establishing clear guidelines on what constitutes ownership and how it is recognized can empower users while fostering innovation. Encouraging open dialogue about these issues will be vital in crafting policies that balance individual expression with collective responsibility.

Finally, envisioning the future of these infinite realms invites us to consider their potential as tools for social good. By harnessing the boundless potential of these spaces, we can address global challenges such as education, environmental awareness, and cultural exchange. Virtual worlds offer unique opportunities to simulate complex systems and foster empathy by immersing users in diverse perspectives. By prioritizing ethical considerations, we can ensure that these technologies serve as a force for positive transformation, creating a future where virtual and real-world benefits are harmoniously intertwined.

Time simulations: Revisiting the past or exploring alternate futures

Imagine standing at the crossroads of time, where past, present, and future converge in a kaleidoscope of possibilities. Time simulations offer us this very vantage point, transforming time itself into a canvas upon which we can paint with strokes of innovation and curiosity. A crucial element in this discussion is the capacity to reconstruct historical events with immersive accuracy, allowing us to step into eras long gone and witness the unfolding of history from a firsthand perspective. These simulations hold the power to bring ancient civilizations to life, enabling us to experience the sights, sounds, and emotions of pivotal moments that shaped our world. The allure of such simulations lies not only in their educational potential but also in the profound connections they forge between us and our shared human heritage.

Yet, time simulations extend beyond mere historical reenactment. They grant us the ability to design divergent timelines, offering a playground for predictive analysis and experimentation with alternate futures. Imagine exploring scenarios where key historical events unfolded differently or peering into possible futures shaped by choices yet to be made. This speculative exploration allows for a deeper understanding of cause and effect, offering insights into the pathways that lead to various outcomes. However, with such profound power comes the responsibility to navigate the ethical considerations of manipulating temporal realities. The potential consequences of altering or simulating time raise questions about morality, consent, and the impact on our perception of reality. As we journey through these temporal landscapes, we must tread carefully, mindful of the balance between curiosity and consequence, and ever aware of the profound implications these simulations hold for our understanding of reality itself.

Reconstructing Historical Events with Immersive Accuracy

In the realm of reconstructing historical events with immersive fidelity, the potential of simulations to bring the past to life is nothing short of revolutionary. Imagine standing amidst the throngs at the Roman Forum or witnessing the signing of the Magna Carta, not through static images or text but within a dynamically recreated environment that captures the essence of the era. Advanced simulation technologies, combined with meticulous historical research, can render these events with unprecedented accuracy, providing a visceral understanding that transcends traditional educational methods. As we venture deeper into the capabilities of these simulations, they promise not only to educate but also to evoke a deeper emotional connection to history.

This immersive accuracy hinges on the confluence of multiple cutting-edge technologies. High-resolution 3D modeling, artificial intelligence, and machine learning work in tandem to reconstruct environments and animate historical figures with lifelike detail. AI-driven narratives can adapt in real time, offering personalized experiences that respond to user interactions. For instance, a visitor in a simulation of ancient Athens might engage in dialogue with a philosopher, with the AI crafting responses based on historical texts and philosophies. Such dynamic interactions not only enhance engagement but also cater to diverse learning styles, making history accessible and intriguing to a broader audience.

One of the pioneering strides in this field involves the integration of sensory feedback to create a truly multisensory experience. Haptic feedback devices simulate the tactile sensations of touching historical artifacts, while advanced soundscaping techniques recreate the ambient sounds of a bustling medieval market or the solemn silence of a wartime trench. This multisensory approach ensures that users are not merely observers but active participants in historical narratives, fostering a comprehensive understanding that is both cognitive and emotional. As these technologies evolve, they open avenues for historians and educators to collaborate, ensuring that simulations remain faithful to historical accuracy while maximizing educational impact.

The implications of such detailed reconstructions extend beyond education into the realms of empathy and cultural preservation. By experiencing the struggles and triumphs of past societies firsthand, users gain insights into the human condition across different epochs, fostering a sense of empathy and understanding. Moreover, such simulations can serve as digital preservation tools for cultures and traditions at risk of being lost, providing future generations with a tangible connection to their heritage. The ability to immerse oneself in a faithfully recreated cultural or historical setting offers a unique opportunity to appreciate the diversity and complexity of human history.

While the potential of immersive historical simulations is vast, it is crucial to navigate the ethical considerations they present. The power to reconstruct the past brings with it the responsibility to represent events accurately and sensitively. Developers and historians must collaborate to ensure that simulations do not perpetuate biases or inaccuracies, and that they respect the cultural significance of the events depicted. Furthermore, as these simulations become more prevalent, questions about their impact on historical interpretation and memory must be considered. By addressing these challenges with a thoughtful and inclusive approach, the field of historical simulations can advance in a manner that respects the past while enriching our understanding of it.

Designing Divergent Timelines for Predictive Analysis

Designing divergent timelines for predictive analysis presents a groundbreaking approach to understanding complex systems and forecasting future possibilities. By harnessing the power of advanced simulation technologies, researchers and developers can create detailed alternate timelines that explore a multitude of outcomes based on varying parameters. This method allows for the examination of potential futures, offering a valuable tool for strategists, policy-makers, and scientists seeking to anticipate and navigate the uncertainties of tomorrow. These virtual experiments hold the promise of revealing insights into how minute changes in the present can profoundly impact the future, thereby informing decisions that could lead to more favorable outcomes.

One fascinating application of this approach lies in the field of environmental science, where divergent timelines can simulate the effects of different climate policies or resource management strategies. For instance, by adjusting variables such as carbon emission levels or conservation efforts within a simulated environment, researchers can observe potential ecological impacts over decades or centuries. This not only aids in understanding the long-term consequences of current actions but also empowers stakeholders to craft policies that align with sustainable development goals. The capacity to explore these scenarios in a virtual setting eliminates the risks and ethical concerns associated with real-world experimentation, providing a safe and controlled environment for innovation.

In the realm of economics, crafting alternate timelines enables analysts to evaluate the repercussions of diverse fiscal policies or market shifts. Imagine simulating the effects of a universal basic income on a nation's economy, considering variables such as inflation, employment rates, and consumer behavior. By doing so, economists can evaluate both the immediate and long-term impacts of such policies, gaining a nuanced understanding of their potential benefits and pitfalls. This data-driven approach facilitates evidence-based decision-making, reducing the reliance on speculation and conjecture, and paving the way for more resilient economic strategies.

The ethical considerations surrounding the creation and manipulation of these temporal simulations cannot be overlooked. As with any powerful technology, the potential for misuse exists, raising concerns about privacy, consent, and the potential for reinforcing existing biases. It is essential to establish robust ethical standards and frameworks to guide the development and application of these simulations. Engaging diverse stakeholders, including ethicists, policymakers, and community representatives, in the design and oversight of these projects can help ensure that the benefits of divergent timelines are realized while minimizing potential harms. By fostering a collaborative approach, society can harness this technology responsibly and equitably.

As we stand on the brink of this new frontier, the possibilities for predictive analysis through timeline simulations are limited only by our imagination and creativity. These digital constructs offer a canvas upon which we can paint myriad futures, each reflecting the intricate interplay of choices and chance. By embracing this innovative approach, we can cultivate a more profound understanding of our world, anticipate challenges, and seize opportunities that lie ahead. This dynamic exploration of alternate realities not only enriches our collective knowledge but also empowers us to shape a future that aligns with our highest aspirations and values.

Ethical Considerations in Manipulating Temporal Realities

In the realm of temporal simulations, ethical considerations emerge as pivotal, demanding a nuanced examination of the moral landscapes we navigate when altering time's fabric. As we reconstruct historical epochs with immersive accuracy, the question arises: what are the moral implications of reliving or even modifying these moments? On one hand, such simulations offer a portal to better understand and learn from our past, potentially preventing the repetition of historical missteps. On the other, they hold the power to alter collective memory and identity, raising concerns about authenticity and the potential for misuse in shaping public perception. The very act of reconstructing history in a simulated environment invites reflection on our responsibilities as both creators and consumers of these experiences, emphasizing the need for careful stewardship over the narratives we choose to explore and share.

Designing divergent timelines for predictive analysis presents further ethical quandaries. These simulations allow us to envision alternate futures, offering valuable insights into the consequences of present-day decisions. By simulating different outcomes, policymakers and researchers can anticipate challenges and opportunities, potentially guiding society towards more favorable paths. Yet, the power to simulate divergent futures carries the risk of bias—who decides which scenarios to explore, and do these decisions reflect diverse perspectives? The process of selecting and prioritizing these timelines must be transparent and inclusive, ensuring that the potential benefits of these simulations are equitably distributed and do not inadvertently reinforce existing inequalities or power structures.

The intersection of simulated and real temporalities extends beyond mere speculation, as advancements in technology increasingly blur these boundaries. With the advent of cutting-edge interfaces that integrate with biological consciousness, the prospect of experiencing time non-linearly becomes tangible. Such innovations challenge our traditional perceptions of time and identity, inviting us to reconsider what it means to exist within multiple temporal frameworks. This evolution necessitates a robust ethical framework to address the implications of these experiences on our cognitive and emotional well-being. How do these interfaces affect our sense of self and continuity, and what safeguards must be established to protect individuals from potential psychological harm?

As we venture into the manipulation of temporal realities, the notion of consent emerges as a cornerstone of ethical practice. Participants in temporal simulations must be fully informed and willing collaborators, aware of the potential impacts on their perception of reality and personal agency. This consent extends beyond individual participants to encompass broader societal implications, requiring ongoing dialogue and regulation to ensure that these technologies serve the collective good. The challenge lies in balancing innovation with ethical responsibility, fostering an environment where the transformative potential of temporal simulations is harnessed without compromising fundamental human rights and values.

These considerations invite us to engage in thoughtful discourse and proactive governance, recognizing the profound influence of temporal simulations on our lives and societies. By embracing a diverse range of perspectives and fostering a shared understanding of ethical principles, we can navigate the complexities of this emerging frontier with integrity and foresight. The journey into manipulating temporal realities is not merely a technical endeavor; it is a transformative exploration that requires us to question and redefine the boundaries of our existence, ultimately shaping a future where technology and humanity coexist harmoniously.

Interfacing simulations with biological consciousness

In the realm where technology meets the intricacies of the human mind, a fascinating frontier emerges: the interface between simulations and biological consciousness. As advancements in neural technology progress, the once-fantastical idea of connecting our minds directly to virtual environments edges closer to reality. Imagine a world where thoughts transcend the physical boundaries of the brain, seamlessly intertwining with digital landscapes. This concept not only challenges our understanding of consciousness but also beckons us to explore the profound implications of such integration. The allure lies in the potential to expand human experience beyond the limitations of the physical world, creating a bridge between what is real and what can be imagined. As we stand at the precipice of this digital-human convergence, the possibilities seem as boundless as they are intriguing, poised to redefine the very essence of existence.

Navigating this thrilling intersection demands a careful examination of the tools that might one day make it possible: neural interfaces and direct brain simulation. As we delve into these technologies, we must also confront the ethical dilemmas that arise when consciousness itself becomes a component of simulated realms. The journey is further enriched by the prospect of enhancing cognitive abilities through these artificial environments, offering a glimpse into a future where the mind may evolve in tandem with the digital domains it inhabits. This exploration is not merely an academic exercise but a pivotal step in understanding how such advances might shape individual lives and society as a whole. As the digital and biological worlds inch closer together, the stage is set for a transformative era where the boundaries of mind and machine blur, inviting exploration, reflection, and innovation in equal measure.

Neural Interfaces and Direct Brain Simulation

Neural interfaces represent a thrilling frontier in the realm of simulated realities, offering the potential to seamlessly merge digital environments with human cognition. By creating direct connections between the brain and digital systems, these interfaces can dramatically enhance the fidelity of simulations, providing users with an experience that feels indistinguishable from reality. One prominent example is the development of brain-computer interfaces (BCIs), which utilize sensors to detect neural activity and translate it into digital commands. Such technology has already shown promise in the medical field, where it assists individuals with disabilities in regaining control over their environment by converting thoughts into actions. As this technology matures, it could redefine the boundaries between consciousness and the virtual realm, allowing users to interact with simulated worlds through thought alone.

The integration of direct brain simulation into virtual environments not only amplifies immersion but also holds the potential to revolutionize our understanding of consciousness. Researchers are exploring how these interfaces can be used to map and stimulate specific neural pathways, potentially unlocking new cognitive abilities or enhancing existing ones. This could lead to unprecedented levels of personalized learning within simulations, where educational content is tailored to individual neural patterns, optimizing absorption and retention. Imagine a scenario where complex concepts in physics or languages are absorbed as naturally as a mother tongue, thanks to the precise alignment of digital stimuli with neural processes. Such advancements suggest a future where education is not just accessible but profoundly transformative, reshaping how we acquire knowledge.

While the technical possibilities of neural interfaces are awe-inspiring, they also usher in a host of ethical considerations that must be dissected. The ability to directly influence brain activity raises questions about consent, privacy, and the potential for misuse. With the capacity to alter perceptions and even memories, we must consider the implications of such power in the hands of individuals or institutions. The prospect of hacking one's consciousness or becoming overly dependent on virtual realities are genuine concerns that necessitate robust ethical frameworks and regulatory measures. By fostering an interdisciplinary dialogue that includes ethicists, technologists, and policymakers, society can ensure that the integration of neural interfaces into simulations prioritizes human welfare and autonomy.

Innovations in neural interfaces also encourage us to reconsider the very nature of cognitive enhancement. By interfacing with simulations, individuals might experience augmented sensory perceptions or heightened intellectual capabilities, transcending traditional human limits. This raises intriguing possibilities for tackling complex global challenges. For instance, enhanced problem-solving abilities could be applied to developing sustainable technologies or designing intricate systems for urban planning. However, these enhancements must be approached with a balanced perspective, ensuring equitable access and preventing societal disparities. As we contemplate a future where cognitive boundaries are blurred, it is crucial to maintain a focus on inclusivity and the broader implications for humanity.

The journey into the world of neural interfaces and direct brain simulation invites us to contemplate profound questions about identity and experience. As technology progresses, we must ponder the extent to which our sense of self is defined by our biological boundaries. Will the merging of consciousness with digital realms lead to a new understanding of what it means to be human? These questions challenge us to embrace both the opportunities and the uncertainties of this nascent frontier. By cultivating a thoughtful and inclusive discourse, we can navigate the evolving landscape of neural interfaces, ensuring they serve as catalysts for human flourishing rather than sources of division.

The Ethical Implications of Consciousness Integration

As technology advances, the integration of simulations with biological consciousness beckons a new era of human experience, raising profound ethical questions. Neural interfaces, which connect the brain directly to digital realms, offer unprecedented opportunities for cognitive and sensory expansion. This connectivity promises a world where individuals may transcend physical limitations, experiencing simulated realities with a depth previously unimaginable. Such advancements, however, necessitate careful consideration of ethical frameworks to ensure that these technologies enhance, rather than undermine, the essence of human autonomy and agency. The potential for neural manipulation, whether intentional or inadvertent, demands a rigorous ethical discourse to safeguard individual freedom and dignity.

Central to the discussion is the notion of consent. As simulations become increasingly indistinguishable from reality, ensuring informed and voluntary participation becomes paramount. The lines between choice and coercion may blur when simulations can directly influence emotions and perceptions. Moreover, the potential for addiction to these hyper-realistic experiences poses a significant ethical dilemma. Developers and policymakers must work collaboratively to establish guidelines that prioritize mental well-being, ensuring that the allure of virtual worlds does not overshadow the richness of real-life interactions. By fostering environments where users are empowered to make conscious decisions about their engagement, the balance between innovation and ethical responsibility can be maintained.

Beyond individual implications, the societal ramifications of consciousness integration warrant attention. The democratization of advanced neural interfaces may lead to disparities in access, resulting in new forms of inequality. Those with the means to enhance their cognitive capabilities through simulations could potentially gain unfair advantages in education, employment, and social standing. Addressing these disparities requires proactive measures to ensure equitable access to these transformative technologies. Additionally, the cultural impacts of widespread simulation use must be considered, as traditional norms and values may evolve or even erode in response to new paradigms of existence.

Another layer of complexity arises from the potential for identity transformation within simulations. As users navigate multiple realities, the concept of self may become fluid, challenging conventional understandings of identity. This raises questions about accountability and moral responsibility. If one's actions in a simulated world carry no real-world consequences, how might this alter behavior and ethical standards? Encouraging users to reflect on their virtual personas and the impact of their actions can cultivate a sense of responsibility that transcends digital boundaries. By fostering ethical literacy alongside technological literacy, individuals can navigate these new landscapes with integrity and awareness.

As we stand on the cusp of this technological frontier, interdisciplinary collaboration is crucial to address the ethical implications of consciousness integration. Philosophers, technologists, and ethicists must engage in ongoing dialogue to anticipate challenges and co-create solutions that honor human values. By weaving ethical considerations into the fabric of simulation design and deployment, we can ensure that these innovations enhance the human experience without compromising our fundamental principles. The journey into simulated realities offers a unique opportunity to redefine the boundaries of consciousness, but it must be guided by a commitment to ethical integrity and social responsibility.

Enhancing Cognitive Abilities Through Simulated Environments

In the ever-evolving landscape of simulated realities, the potential to amplify cognitive faculties through simulated environments stands as a pivotal frontier.

As we advance into an era where virtual landscapes and human intellect converge, the transformative capacity of these environments becomes increasingly apparent. Cutting-edge research in cognitive neuroscience and virtual reality indicates that immersive simulations can function as dynamic arenas for cognitive enhancement, offering a myriad of opportunities for skill acquisition and mental agility. For instance, virtual reality platforms have shown promise in augmenting spatial awareness, problem-solving capabilities, and even memory retention by providing an immersive framework that challenges and stimulates the brain in novel ways. These simulations act as fertile grounds for cognitive experimentation, where the limits of human comprehension and adaptation are continually tested and expanded.

The intricate architecture of simulated environments allows for a tailored approach to cognitive development, where experiences can be customized to align with individual needs and learning styles. This adaptability is particularly beneficial in addressing diverse cognitive profiles, offering bespoke experiences that cater to the unique strengths and weaknesses of each user. Advanced algorithms and machine learning techniques enable these environments to adjust in real-time, creating a dynamic interplay between the user and the virtual world. This symbiotic relationship not only enhances engagement but also ensures that the learning process remains both challenging and rewarding. By presenting users with tasks that are neither too simplistic nor excessively difficult, simulations can maintain an optimal level of cognitive load, fostering an environment conducive to growth and development.

Beyond the realm of traditional education, simulated environments hold the potential to revolutionize professional training and skill acquisition. Industries such as aviation, medicine, and engineering have already begun integrating virtual simulations into their training regimens, providing a safe and controlled setting for practitioners to hone their expertise. These environments allow for repeated practice without the risks associated with real-world scenarios, thereby accelerating the learning curve and improving proficiency. For example, flight simulators have long been used to train pilots, offering a realistic yet risk-free platform to practice maneuvers and respond to unpredictable situations. Similarly, medical students can benefit from virtual surgeries that replicate complex procedures, enabling them to refine their techniques before stepping into an operating room. By harnessing the power of simulations, professionals across various fields can achieve unparalleled levels of competence and confidence.

As we delve deeper into the potential of simulated environments, questions surrounding the ethical implications of such enhancements come to the forefront. While the promise of cognitive augmentation is enticing, it also raises concerns regarding accessibility and equity. Ensuring that these powerful tools are available to a broad spectrum of society, rather than a privileged few, is paramount to prevent further widening of the cognitive gap. Additionally, the possibility of over-reliance on virtual environments for cognitive development necessitates a balanced approach, where the benefits of simulations are harmonized with the irreplaceable value of real-world experiences. By fostering a dialogue that considers both the opportunities and challenges presented by simulated environments, we can navigate this complex landscape with foresight and responsibility.

In envisioning the future of cognitive enhancement through simulated environments, it is crucial to remain open to diverse perspectives and innovative approaches. The integration of artificial intelligence and neurotechnology into these simulations presents exciting possibilities for creating even more sophisticated and effective cognitive training tools. By leveraging advancements in brain-computer interfaces and neural networks, we can develop simulations that not only respond to user input but also anticipate and adapt to cognitive patterns. This fusion of technology and human intellect holds the potential to unlock new dimensions of cognitive capability, reshaping the way we learn, work, and interact with the world around us. As we continue to explore this uncharted territory, the role of simulation architects will be instrumental in crafting environments that not only enhance individual cognition but also contribute to the collective advancement of society.

Our exploration into the speculative scenarios of future simulations reveals a tapestry of possibilities that stretch the limits of imagination and technology. Fully immersive virtual societies and economies could redefine human interaction and commerce, blurring the lines between the digital and the tangible. The concept of infinite worlds suggests a potential for boundless exploration, transforming our understanding of reality and its dimensions. Time simulations offer gateways to revisit the past or craft alternate futures, inviting us to rethink our relationship with time itself. Interfacing simulations with biological consciousness hints at a future where human and virtual experiences are seamlessly intertwined, potentially elevating our cognitive capabilities and altering our perception of self. Collectively, these visions underscore a central theme of the book: the transformative power of simulations to reshape human experience, fostering new paradigms of existence. As we stand on the brink of these developments, we are compelled to consider not only their potential but also the ethical and philosophical questions they raise. This reflection serves as a catalyst for our journey into the remaining facets of simulation technology, inviting readers to ponder how these emerging realities might integrate with and redefine our daily lives.

Chapter Ten

Challenges In Building Perfect Simulations

Imagine a painter standing before a vast, blank canvas, brush poised, ready to create a world from the depths of imagination. Each stroke holds the potential to birth landscapes, stories, and lives, yet the challenge remains: how to make this painted world as vivid and seamless as the one we inhabit. In the realm of simulation, architects face a similar challenge. They endeavor to craft digital universes that mimic reality with such precision that the boundaries between the tangible and the virtual blur. As we dive into this exploration, we find ourselves at the intersection of artistry and technology, where the pursuit of perfect simulations pushes the limits of what is possible.

At the heart of this quest lie the technical hurdles that simulation creators must overcome. The digital worlds they build are constrained by the finite resources of bandwidth, processing power, and scalability. Like an artist working with limited colors, they must balance these constraints while striving to paint a picture that feels boundless. Yet, complexity is a double-edged sword. As simulations grow richer and more intricate, they risk becoming unwieldy, prone to breakdowns that shatter the illusion of reality. Navigating this delicate balance requires not only technical prowess but also a deep understanding of user expectations and the subtle art of managing them.

The stakes are high in this endeavor. The failure of a simulation isn't merely a technical glitch; it can have profound consequences for users who may find themselves lost in a fractured, unreliable world. This chapter delves into these challenges, examining how they shape the very fabric of simulated realities. Each challenge is a puzzle waiting to be solved, a testament to the ingenuity required to construct worlds that are both immersive and resilient. As we explore these intricacies, the potential for simulations to enhance and transform human experience remains a guiding light, beckoning us forward into the future of digital creation.

Technical limitations: Bandwidth, processing power, and scalability

Imagine a world where the line between reality and simulation blurs seamlessly, a place where virtual experiences rival the richness and depth of our tangible existence. Yet, as we stand on the cusp of such immersive possibilities, we must confront the formidable technical challenges that lie ahead. At the heart of these challenges are bandwidth, processing power, and scalability—three pillars that underpin the architecture of any sophisticated simulated environment. As simulations grow more complex and lifelike, the demand for real-time data transmission becomes paramount, pushing current bandwidth capabilities to their limits. It's akin to trying to conduct a symphony through a narrow straw; every note must arrive in perfect harmony, lest the entire composition falter.

Processing power, the engine driving these virtual realms, must evolve to match the intricacy of the worlds we seek to create. Envision the computational prowess required to render not just a single tree but an entire forest, each leaf swaying independently in a simulated breeze. This demand for nuanced detail challenges our current technological frontiers, urging us to explore novel solutions. Hand in hand with processing power is the need for scalable systems that can expand and adapt, accommodating a growing number of users without compromising the integrity of the experience. As we venture into this digital frontier, these technical limitations form a crucible for innovation, setting the stage for our exploration into overcoming bandwidth bottlenecks, harnessing advanced processing power, and devising strategies for scalable environments.

Overcoming Bandwidth Bottlenecks in Real-Time Simulations

Bandwidth limitations are among the most formidable challenges in crafting real-time simulations, where the seamless flow of data is imperative for a convincing virtual experience. As our appetite for more intricate and expansive simulated environments grows, so does the demand for bandwidth that can handle the rapid exchange of large amounts of information. High-definition graphics, intricate physics engines, and complex interactions require data to move at lightning speed to avoid latency, which can break immersion. To address these bottlenecks, researchers are exploring the potential of next-generation wireless technologies like 5G and beyond. These innovations promise higher data transfer rates and reduced latency, allowing for more responsive and immersive simulations. By understanding the nuances of bandwidth management, developers can employ techniques such as data compression and selective rendering, which prioritize essential elements and reduce unnecessary data load, ensuring a fluid user experience even with current infrastructure.

In addition to the advancements in wireless communication, the burgeoning field of edge computing offers promising solutions for bandwidth challenges. By decentralizing data processing and bringing computational power closer to the user, edge computing minimizes the need to transmit data over long distances, thus alleviating network congestion. This approach is particularly beneficial in real-time simulations, where milliseconds can make the difference between seamless interaction and disconcerting lag. Imagine a simulation where the physics of a virtual world must be calculated instantaneously as a user interacts with it; edge computing can handle these computations locally, reducing the strain on bandwidth and enhancing the immediacy of the experience. As this technology matures, it offers a pathway to creating more sophisticated simulations that are less reliant on centralized data centers.

The synergy between artificial intelligence and bandwidth optimization is another frontier being explored by innovators in the field. AI algorithms can dynamically adjust the quality and detail of a simulation based on the available bandwidth, ensuring that the experience remains consistent and engaging regardless of network conditions. For instance, adaptive streaming techniques, similar to those used in video streaming services, can be employed to modulate the level of detail and resolution in a simulation. This adaptability allows simulations to cater to a broad range of devices and network capabilities, making them more accessible and ensuring that users with varying levels of connectivity can participate in rich virtual experiences. By leveraging AI, developers can create simulations that are both robust and flexible, capable of delivering high-quality experiences tailored to the user's environment.

As we push the boundaries of what's possible in real-time simulations, it's essential to consider the broader implications of overcoming bandwidth constraints. Enabling more sophisticated simulations could revolutionize fields such as remote collaboration, where virtual environments replace physical office spaces, offering real-time interaction without the need for physical presence. This transformation could lead to a more geographically dispersed workforce, with profound implications for urban planning and environmental conservation. By reducing the need for travel and physical infrastructure, advanced simulations powered by optimized bandwidth could contribute to a more sustainable future. It invites us to envision a world where the lines between the digital and physical realms blur, providing new opportunities for innovation and growth.

While the promise of overcoming bandwidth limitations is exciting, it's crucial to remain vigilant about the potential pitfalls. As simulations become more integrated into our daily lives, ethical considerations around data privacy and security become increasingly important. High-bandwidth simulations often involve the transmission of sensitive personal data, making them potential targets for cyber threats. Ensuring robust security measures and transparent data policies will be vital in maintaining user trust and safeguarding their information. By proactively addressing these concerns, developers can ensure that the benefits of advanced simulations are realized without compromising individual privacy or security. As we continue to push the frontiers of simulation technology, balancing innovation with responsibility will be key to unlocking its full potential.

Harnessing Advanced Processing Power for Complex Virtual Worlds

In the intricate tapestry of simulated realities, the role of processing power is pivotal, serving as the backbone that supports the creation of complex virtual environments. As we venture into the era of hyper-realistic simulations, the demand for computational prowess has skyrocketed. Modern simulations require an unprecedented level of detail and dynamism, necessitating processors capable of executing billions of operations per second. Innovations in quantum computing and neuromorphic chips represent a quantum leap forward, promising a future where simulations can encapsulate lifelike physics, real-time interactions, and vast, interconnected worlds. These technologies are redefining the boundaries of what is possible, pushing the limits of virtual world-building to unprecedented heights.

The advent of parallel processing and distributed computing has further revolutionized the landscape of virtual reality. By dividing complex tasks across multiple processors, these technologies significantly expedite computational workloads, enabling real-time rendering of intricate simulations. Distributed computing, in particular, allows for the harnessing of vast networks of computers, collectively channeling their processing capabilities to tackle the most demanding simulations. This orchestration of computational resources not only enhances performance but also ensures the scalability of simulations, accommodating a growing number of users without compromising detail or immersion. In doing so, it lays the groundwork for the next generation of virtual experiences.

Despite these advancements, the challenge of optimizing processing power remains formidable. As simulations grow in scale and complexity, so too do the demands placed on hardware. Researchers are exploring innovative approaches to mitigate this pressure, such as edge computing and cloud-based solutions. Edge computing minimizes latency by processing data closer to the source, while cloud computing offers virtually limitless resources, democratizing access to high-performance simulations. These methodologies, when integrated, create a robust framework that balances performance with accessibility, ensuring that simulations remain both powerful and practical.

The pursuit of advanced processing power is not without its philosophical considerations. As we edge closer to creating simulations indistinguishable from reality, questions about authenticity and experience arise. Is the fidelity of a simulation directly proportional to its value, or do simpler simulations hold their own unique merits? Engaging with these questions encourages deeper reflection on the purpose of simulations and their role in human experience. By examining diverse perspectives, we can better appreciate the nuanced implications of our technological capabilities, fostering a more holistic understanding of simulated realities.

Looking forward, the horizon is bright with possibilities. As processing technologies continue to evolve, they will undoubtedly unlock new dimensions of virtual exploration. The integration of artificial intelligence and machine learning will further enhance simulations, enabling environments that adapt and respond intelligently to users. This synergy of cutting-edge technologies will not only enrich the immersive quality of simulations but also expand their applicability across various fields. By embracing these advancements, we stand on the brink of a new era in which the boundaries between the virtual and the tangible blur, inviting us to rethink the very nature of reality.

Strategies for Achieving Scalable Simulated Environments

Achieving scalability in simulated environments requires a nuanced approach that blends technological advancement with creative problem-solving. One foundational strategy involves the dynamic allocation of resources, where computational power is directed to areas of high demand within the simulation. This methodology ensures that the most complex or populated zones receive the necessary processing resources to maintain a seamless user experience. By employing predictive algorithms, systems can anticipate where these demands will arise, reallocating resources in real time to support a fluid and immersive environment. This approach connects with the broader trend in cloud computing, where resources are efficiently distributed and managed across vast networks, allowing for the creation of expansive virtual worlds that can accommodate thousands of users simultaneously.

Another burgeoning strategy is the utilization of modular architectures in simulation design. By constructing environments as a series of interlinked modules, developers can isolate and optimize individual components without disrupting the entire system. This modularity not only aids in scalability but also enhances the flexibility and resilience of the simulation, allowing for rapid updates and adaptations in response to user feedback or technological advancements. This concept parallels microservices architecture in software development, where applications are built as a suite of independent services that communicate through well-defined interfaces. Such an approach allows for scalability by enabling specific elements of a simulation to be scaled independently based on user interaction and demand.

Incorporating artificial intelligence and machine learning further propels the scalability of simulations. AI can be harnessed to automate and streamline processes within the virtual environment, managing tasks such as NPC behavior, environmental changes, and user interactions. Machine learning algorithms can analyze user data to identify patterns and trends, helping to optimize the allocation of resources and refine the user experience. By predicting user needs and adjusting the simulation accordingly, AI-driven systems can achieve a high degree of efficiency and personalization, enhancing both scalability and engagement.

To address the challenges of scalability, it is crucial to consider the potential of decentralized systems. Leveraging blockchain technology, for instance, can facilitate the creation of distributed simulations where control and data are not centralized in a single entity. This decentralization can enhance security, reduce latency, and improve redundancy, making simulations more robust and scalable. By distributing the computational load across a network of participating nodes, decentralized systems can support large-scale simulations that are resilient to failures and capable of expanding seamlessly as more nodes join the network. This approach not only fosters scalability but also democratizes the creation and maintenance of virtual environments, inviting broader participation and innovation.

The future of scalable simulated environments lies in embracing a hybrid model that combines the best aspects of centralized and decentralized approaches. By integrating cloud-based services with blockchain technology, developers can create scalable simulations that are both efficient and secure. As these technologies continue to evolve, the potential for creating vast, interconnected virtual worlds will expand, offering users unprecedented opportunities for exploration and interaction. As we look to the horizon, the challenge will be to balance these technological advancements with ethical considerations, ensuring that the pursuit of scalability enhances rather than diminishes the human experience. This invites a critical examination of how we design and inhabit these virtual spaces, encouraging innovation that is both responsible and visionary.

Managing complexity: Preventing breakdowns in simulated worlds

In the realm of simulated worlds, complexity is both a creator and a destroyer. It breathes life into intricate landscapes and multifaceted interactions, yet poses the perpetual threat of chaos lurking around every corner. Crafting a stable simulation is akin to orchestrating a symphony where every note, every pause, must be meticulously accounted for. A misstep can result in discord, unraveling the very fabric of the virtual universe. As simulations grow in sophistication, the challenge lies in managing this complexity without stifling creativity or user engagement. The dance between order and chaos requires a deft touch, where the architect must anticipate not only the intended pathways but also the unforeseen detours that might arise.

To navigate these multifaceted challenges, innovative strategies are paramount. Adaptive algorithms emerge as sentinels, dynamically managing the ebb and flow of complexity, ensuring that the simulated environment remains robust and responsive. Meanwhile, the integration of cognitive load balancing becomes an essential tool, enhancing user experience by aligning the demands of the simulation with the user's capacity to process and enjoy the digital journey. Predictive analytics, the seers of this digital age, offer a proactive approach, identifying potential system failures before they materialize, thus safeguarding the continuity and integrity of the simulation. Each of these elements plays a critical role in maintaining the equilibrium of simulated worlds, ensuring that they remain enchanting and immersive while standing firm against the unpredictable tides of complexity.

Designing Adaptive Algorithms for Dynamic Complexity Management

Designing adaptive algorithms for managing dynamic complexity in simulated worlds requires a sophisticated understanding of both computational frameworks and human interaction principles. At the heart of these systems lies the necessity to dynamically adjust to the ever-evolving demands of users and the intricate environments they navigate. Traditional algorithms often fall short in addressing the fluid nature of these virtual landscapes, where user actions and environmental variables constantly shift. By utilizing machine learning and artificial intelligence, adaptive algorithms can preemptively respond to changes, ensuring simulations remain stable and immersive. These algorithms continuously learn from user interactions, refining their responses to create seamless experiences that maintain the illusion of reality without overwhelming computational resources.

A prime example of adaptive algorithm application is found in the realm of massive multiplayer online games (MMOs), where the complexity of interactions can escalate rapidly as players engage in unpredictable and collaborative tasks. In these environments, adaptive algorithms manage resource allocation, ensuring that server loads are balanced and latency is minimized, even as thousands of players interact simultaneously. By employing techniques such as neural networks and reinforcement learning, these systems can predict user behavior patterns, allowing for anticipatory adjustments that maintain optimal performance. Such innovations not only enhance the gaming experience but also illustrate the broader potential for adaptive algorithms in diverse simulated environments, from educational platforms to virtual training grounds.

Incorporating cognitive load balancing within these algorithms is vital to enhancing user experience. Cognitive load refers to the mental effort required to process information and interact within a simulation. When a simulation becomes too complex or demanding, users may experience fatigue or frustration, detracting from the intended experience. Adaptive algorithms can monitor user engagement levels through metrics such as eye movement, response times, and interaction patterns, dynamically adjusting the simulation's complexity to align with individual cognitive thresholds. This personalization ensures that users remain engaged and immersed, fostering a more intuitive and rewarding interaction with the virtual world. Such advancements offer transformative possibilities for education, where tailored experiences can optimize learning outcomes by adjusting to students' unique cognitive needs.

Predictive analytics play a crucial role in identifying potential system failures before they impact users. By analyzing vast amounts of data generated from user interactions and system performance metrics, predictive algorithms can identify patterns indicative of potential breakdowns or bottlenecks. This proactive approach allows developers to address issues preemptively, minimizing downtime and preserving the integrity of the simulation. The implementation of predictive analytics not only enhances system reliability but also builds user trust, as individuals can rely on the stability and responsiveness of the simulated environment. This approach is particularly beneficial in high-stakes applications, such as virtual reality training for emergency responders, where system failures can have significant real-world consequences.

The development of adaptive algorithms for managing complexity in simulations is an evolving field, constantly pushing the boundaries of what technology can achieve. As these algorithms become more sophisticated, the potential applications expand, offering new avenues for exploration in areas such as mental health therapy, where virtual environments can adapt in real-time to support therapeutic goals. The ongoing challenge lies in balancing the technical demands of these systems with the need for ethical considerations, ensuring that user privacy and agency remain protected. By fostering collaboration between technologists, cognitive scientists, and ethicists, the future of adaptive algorithms in simulated realities holds the promise of creating environments that are not only technologically advanced but also deeply attuned to human needs and aspirations.

Integrating Cognitive Load Balancing to Enhance User Experience

In the intricate dance of creating immersive simulations, cognitive load balancing emerges as a pivotal concept. This technique involves the careful calibration of information presented to users to ensure an optimal experience without overwhelming their mental faculties. At its core, cognitive load balancing seeks to harmonize the demands placed on a user's cognitive resources with their ability to process and interact with the virtual environment. This balance is crucial for maintaining engagement and facilitating deep, meaningful interactions within simulated worlds. Recent advancements in neuroinformatics and user interface design have provided the tools to measure and adjust cognitive load dynamically, allowing for a seamless blending of complexity and accessibility that keeps users engrossed yet comfortable.

Recent studies in cognitive psychology and human-computer interaction have illuminated the nuances of cognitive load, revealing that users often experience three types: intrinsic, extraneous, and germane. Intrinsic load pertains to the complexity inherent to the task or content, while extraneous load involves unnecessary distractions that can be minimized through thoughtful design. Germane load, on the other hand, reflects the mental effort required to integrate and understand new information. By leveraging these insights, simulation architects can craft experiences that minimize extraneous distractions and channel cognitive resources toward germane learning, thereby enhancing user engagement and retention. For instance, adaptive tutorial systems that respond to user performance can adjust difficulty levels in real-time, ensuring users remain challenged but not overwhelmed.

One innovative approach to cognitive load balancing involves the integration of biofeedback mechanisms. By employing wearable sensors that monitor physiological indicators such as heart rate variability and galvanic skin response, simulations can adaptively respond to a user's emotional and cognitive state. This real-time feedback loop allows the system to dynamically adjust environmental complexity, visual stimuli, or task difficulty, fostering an experience that is both challenging and rewarding. This level of personalization not only enhances the user experience but also opens new avenues for research into the interplay between cognition and immersive environments. For instance, a study might explore how varying levels of stress influence decision-making in high-stakes simulated scenarios, providing valuable insights for applications in training and education.

As the boundaries of simulation technology expand, so too do the possibilities for integrating cognitive load balancing into diverse applications. In educational simulations, for instance, adaptive systems can scaffold learning experiences to match individual student needs, promoting a deeper understanding of complex concepts. In entertainment, balancing cognitive load can lead to more satisfying gaming experiences by maintaining a delicate equilibrium between challenge and enjoyment. By optimizing the user experience through cognitive load management, simulations can transcend traditional boundaries, offering transformative experiences that are both intellectually stimulating and emotionally resonant.

Continued exploration into cognitive load balancing offers exciting prospects for the future of simulated realities. As machine learning algorithms become more sophisticated, they may predict and respond to user needs with increasing accuracy, crafting experiences that are tailor-made for each individual's cognitive profile. This evolution holds the promise of creating simulations that not only captivate and educate but also contribute to the broader understanding of human cognition. As we look towards a horizon where the digital and physical realms increasingly intertwine, the art of balancing cognitive load will remain a cornerstone of simulation design, guiding the creation of immersive worlds that enrich and expand the human experience.

Implementing Predictive Analytics for Early Detection of System Failures

Within the realm of simulated realities, predictive analytics emerges as a pivotal tool for preemptively identifying potential system failures. This approach leverages sophisticated algorithms and machine learning models that scrutinize vast amounts of data, discerning patterns and anomalies that could indicate impending issues. By analyzing user behavior, server load, and environmental variables in real-time, these predictive systems can forecast disruptions before they manifest, significantly enhancing the stability of virtual environments. This proactive strategy not only ensures a seamless user experience but also fortifies the resilience of simulated worlds against unforeseen breakdowns.

Embracing predictive analytics demands an understanding of the nuanced interplay between data science and simulation technology. Cutting-edge research in this field often focuses on developing algorithms capable of processing high-velocity data streams, which are essential for the dynamic conditions of virtual environments. For instance, techniques such as reinforcement learning can be utilized to adaptively refine prediction models, allowing simulations to evolve and self-optimize over time. This iterative process mirrors the natural evolution of living systems, where constant adaptation is key to survival. By embedding these advanced algorithms within the core architecture of simulations, developers can create self-sustaining worlds that thrive on continual improvement.

A particularly intriguing aspect of predictive analytics in simulations is its ability to manage cognitive load, thereby enhancing user engagement. By predicting potential bottlenecks or user frustrations, systems can dynamically adjust parameters to maintain an optimal balance between challenge and enjoyment. Consider a virtual training program where predictive analytics identifies a user struggling with a specific task; the system can adapt in real-time, providing additional resources or modifying the task's complexity to suit the user's proficiency. This adaptability not only preserves the integrity of the simulation but also enriches the user's learning experience, ensuring that each interaction is both productive and rewarding.

The capacity for early detection of system failures extends beyond mere technical maintenance, encompassing ethical considerations and user safety. As simulations increasingly intersect with critical sectors like healthcare and urban planning, the stakes for reliable performance become even higher. Predictive analytics can preempt catastrophic failures, such as a malfunction in a medical training simulation that could lead to erroneous conclusions or a breakdown in a virtual city planning model that might misinform real-world decisions. By prioritizing robustness and reliability, developers can uphold the ethical standards necessary for simulations that wield significant societal impact.

Envisioning the future trajectory of predictive analytics in simulations invites a myriad of possibilities, from fully autonomous virtual ecosystems to highly personalized user experiences. As research evolves, the integration of artificial intelligence and predictive models promises ever more sophisticated simulations, where the line between anticipation and real-time adjustment becomes increasingly blurred. This forward-thinking approach encourages developers to push the boundaries of what is possible, fostering a landscape where simulations not only mirror reality but also enhance it. By contemplating these advancements, readers are invited to ponder the transformative potential of predictive analytics in crafting more resilient, adaptive, and engaging virtual worlds.

Balancing user expectations and system constraints

In the quest to create seamless and captivating simulated realities, striking a balance between user expectations and the inherent constraints of technology presents both a fascinating challenge and an opportunity for innovation. As users immerse themselves in these virtual landscapes, their desire for heightened realism and interactivity grows, pushing the boundaries of what current technology can deliver. This dance between expectation and limitation is akin to a high-wire act, where creators must deftly navigate the tightrope between delivering awe-inspiring experiences and ensuring the system remains robust and efficient. The success of a simulation relies not only on its ability to enchant and engage but also on its capacity to operate within the finite resources of bandwidth, processing power, and scalability. The tightrope walker, in this case, is the simulation architect, tasked with crafting worlds that captivate without faltering under the weight of their own ambition.

As we explore this intricate balancing act, we uncover strategies to enhance user immersion while safeguarding performance, examining how the pursuit of realism must be tempered by the realities of computational limits. The artistry lies in designing adaptive systems that can accommodate the diverse desires of users, each seeking a unique experience within the shared tapestry of a simulated environment. The following sections reveal the nuanced techniques and considerations that underpin this complex endeavor. Each approach not only illuminates the technical hurdles faced by creators but also celebrates the ingenuity required to transform constraints into opportunities for crafting profound, lasting virtual experiences.

Managing User Immersion Without Compromising Performance

In the realm of simulated realities, achieving an optimal level of immersion without sacrificing system performance presents a complex challenge. True immersion requires a seamless, uninterrupted experience where users feel genuinely present within the virtual environment. Yet, the technical demands of such an experience are considerable. Bandwidth constraints, for instance, can limit the resolution and responsiveness of a simulation, while processing power dictates the complexity of the virtual world that can be realistically rendered. Recent advancements in cloud computing and edge computing offer promising avenues for overcoming these hurdles by distributing processing loads and reducing latency, thereby enhancing user immersion without overburdening individual systems.

A crucial aspect of maintaining user immersion is the strategic use of perceptual tricks that maximize the perceived realism of a simulation without requiring vast computational resources. Techniques such as dynamic resolution scaling and foveated rendering allow for resources to be concentrated on areas where the user is most focused, reducing the need for uniformly high detail across the entire virtual environment. Additionally, haptic feedback and spatial audio can significantly enhance realism, engaging multiple senses to create a more convincing illusion of presence. By leveraging these methods, developers can craft experiences that feel immersive and authentic while operating within the constraints of current technology.

Balancing realism with computational efficiency also involves thoughtful design choices that align with human perceptual habits. Simplifying certain elements of a virtual world, such as background details, can allow for more complex interactions and animations in the foreground without diminishing the overall sense of realism. This approach not only conserves processing power but also aligns with how humans naturally perceive the world, often focusing on immediate surroundings while relegating peripheral details to the subconscious. Innovative algorithms that predict and prioritize user attention can further optimize resource allocation, ensuring that the most critical elements of the simulation receive the necessary computational focus.

Efforts to enhance user immersion must also consider the diverse expectations and preferences of users. Adaptive systems that tailor the simulation experience to individual users can significantly improve satisfaction and engagement. Machine learning algorithms can analyze user behavior and preferences, adjusting environmental details and interactive elements to create a personalized experience. This adaptability not only improves immersion but also broadens the appeal of simulations, catering to a wider range of interests and needs. By addressing the individual nuances of user expectations, developers can create simulations that resonate more deeply with each participant.

The pursuit of perfect immersion in simulated realities raises intriguing questions about the future of digital experiences. What role will emerging technologies like quantum computing play in overcoming current limitations? How can developers ensure that increased immersion does not lead to negative consequences, such as addiction or detachment from the physical world? These questions invite reflection on the ethical and practical implications of ever-more immersive simulations. As technology progresses, the challenge will be to harness its potential for creating enriching experiences while remaining mindful of its capacity to profoundly alter how we perceive and interact with both virtual and real worlds.

Balancing Realism and Computational Limitations in Simulated Environments

Crafting a simulated environment that balances realism with computational limitations demands a deft touch, where the art of illusion meets the science of computation. As simulations approach the fidelity of real-world experiences, developers face the challenge of rendering complex visuals and interactions without overwhelming system capacities. One cutting-edge approach is the use of procedural generation, a technique that dynamically creates content on-the-fly, reducing the need for extensive pre-rendered assets. By leveraging procedural algorithms, developers can construct vast, intricate worlds that adapt to user interactions, creating a rich tapestry of experiences without burdening hardware resources. This method not only enhances realism but also optimizes performance, ensuring seamless immersion for users.

The quest for realism must also consider the cognitive limitations of human perception. While high fidelity graphics can enhance immersion, they are not always necessary for a convincing experience. Research in cognitive science reveals that the human brain is adept at filling in gaps, allowing developers to prioritize key elements of realism without replicating every detail of the physical world. This insight paves the way for strategic abstraction, where essential elements are rendered with precision, while less critical details are suggested rather than fully realized. This approach not only conserves computational power but also aligns with the brain's natural processing capabilities, creating simulations that feel lifelike without the need for exhaustive resources.

The interplay between realism and performance often necessitates innovative rendering techniques, such as ray tracing and level-of-detail scaling. Ray tracing, which simulates the behavior of light with remarkable accuracy, brings unparalleled realism to simulations but can be computationally intensive. To address this, developers employ optimization strategies like hybrid rendering, which combines traditional rasterization with ray tracing, achieving a balance between visual fidelity and system demands. Similarly, level-of-detail scaling adjusts the complexity of models based on the user's perspective, reducing the computational load without sacrificing the overall experience. These techniques exemplify the delicate dance between pushing technological boundaries and maintaining operational efficiency.

To further harmonize realism with computational constraints, adaptive systems are gaining traction. These systems dynamically adjust simulation parameters in response to real-time data, ensuring that user experiences remain fluid and consistent across diverse hardware configurations. For instance, adaptive resolution scaling can modify the clarity of visuals based on available processing power, allowing simulations to maintain a stable frame rate even under strenuous conditions. This adaptability not only enhances user satisfaction by meeting varied expectations but also extends the accessibility of high-fidelity simulations to a broader audience, democratizing the experience of virtual realities.

Consider the broader implications of these advancements: as simulations evolve, they offer new paradigms for interaction and learning, reshaping how we perceive and engage with digital environments. The journey towards achieving a harmonious balance between realism and computational constraints is not merely a technical pursuit but a philosophical exploration of what it means to create and inhabit virtual worlds. As we continue to innovate, we must ask ourselves how these simulations will transform our understanding of reality and our place within it. By embracing both the possibilities and limitations of current technologies, we can craft simulations that not only captivate the senses but also enrich the human experience in profound and unexpected ways.

Designing Adaptive Systems to Align with Diverse User Expectations

Crafting simulations that align with diverse user expectations is a delicate art, one that requires a balance between technological capability and user-centric design. The challenge lies in developing adaptive systems that can pivot to meet the varied demands of users without sacrificing performance or realism. At the heart of this endeavor is the need to understand the nuances of human engagement with simulated environments. Adaptive systems must not only respond to user input but anticipate needs by analyzing patterns and preferences. This requires a sophisticated interplay of algorithms that can dynamically adjust the simulation's parameters—such as difficulty, narrative complexity, or visual fidelity—tailoring experiences to individual users while maintaining system stability.

Recent advancements in machine learning and artificial intelligence have propelled the creation of more responsive and intuitive simulations. These technologies enable systems to learn from user interactions, gradually refining their responses to enhance immersion and satisfaction. For instance, an AI-driven simulation might observe a user's decision-making style or engagement level, then modify its environment to either challenge their skills or provide a more relaxed experience. This adaptability is crucial in meeting the varied expectations of users, who may seek different forms of interaction—from high-stakes challenges to purely exploratory engagements—within the same virtual space. Such a system ensures that users remain engaged, transforming the simulation from a static environment into a living, responsive entity.

Adaptive systems also necessitate a robust infrastructure capable of processing real-time data and implementing changes without disrupting the flow of the simulation. This requires a sophisticated architecture that can handle the demands of dynamic content generation and real-time adaptation. Developers must consider the balance between realism and computational efficiency,

ensuring that the system can seamlessly integrate changes without overload-
ing processors or degrading the experience. Recent research highlights the
importance of decentralized processing and edge computing, which distribute computational tasks across multiple nodes, reducing latency and increasing the system's capacity to handle complex, adaptive interactions.

Beyond technical considerations, the design of adaptive systems must take
into account the psychological and emotional dimensions of user experience. Diverse users have varied backgrounds, preferences, and cognitive styles,
which means simulations must be flexible enough to accommodate these
differences. By conducting extensive user research and employing techniques
from cognitive science, designers can create systems that not only adapt to
user needs but also foster a sense of agency and personalization. This approach
encourages users to invest more deeply in their experiences, knowing that
their choices and preferences are recognized and respected by the simulation.

The potential of adaptive systems in simulations extends beyond entertainment and into areas like education, therapy, and training, where personalized experiences can significantly enhance outcomes. Imagine an educational
simulation that adjusts its teaching methods based on a learner's pace and
comprehension, or a therapeutic environment that modifies its scenarios to
better suit the emotional state of the user. These applications underscore
the transformative potential of adaptive systems, offering experiences that
are not only engaging but also meaningful and beneficial. By continually
refining these systems and exploring new possibilities, developers can push
the boundaries of what simulations can achieve, creating virtual worlds that
are as diverse and dynamic as the people who inhabit them.

The risks of simulation failure: Consequences for users

What sets this apart is the fragile nature of simulations, which teeter on
the edge of perfection and collapse. In a world where virtual environments
are woven into the fabric of daily life, the very notion of simulation failure
becomes a haunting specter. Imagine immersing yourself in a meticulously
crafted reality, only for the seams to unravel without warning. This potential
for breakdowns raises pressing questions about the psychological effects on
users who find themselves suddenly yanked from a virtual paradise back
to the starkness of reality. The seductive allure of simulations lies in their
ability to suspend disbelief, yet when that illusion shatters, it can leave users
grappling with confusion, disorientation, and a profound sense of loss. The
psychological impact of such disconnections is profound, challenging our
understanding of identity and perception in a world where the boundaries
between real and virtual blur.

As we delve deeper into this topic, it becomes clear that the implications extend beyond individual experiences. The very fabric of society is at stake when simulations falter, raising ethical dilemmas about accountability and liability. Who bears responsibility when a simulated environment fails, and what repercussions ripple through societies increasingly reliant on these digital constructs? The long-term societal effects of dependence on imperfect simulations prompt a reevaluation of our relationship with technology. As the chapter unfolds, it invites readers to explore the intricate web of consequences that stem from simulation failures, urging a dialogue on safeguarding the virtual realms that hold such power over human experience.

Psychological Impact of Disconnection from Reality

In a world increasingly interwoven with digital threads, the psychological impact of disconnecting from reality through simulations prompts profound contemplation. As simulations grow in sophistication, they offer users an allure of alternate existences that can be both mesmerizing and disorienting. The human mind, adept at adapting to new environments, may grapple with the boundaries separating virtual experiences from tangible reality. Various studies suggest that prolonged immersion in simulated worlds can lead to a phenomenon known as "simulation aftereffects," where individuals experience a lingering sense of disorientation upon returning to reality. Such experiences can manifest as difficulty in distinguishing between real and simulated stimuli, a challenge that requires careful consideration and innovative solutions to mitigate potential negative outcomes.

Exploring this intricate interplay, cognitive science provides insights into how the brain perceives and processes simulated environments. The brain's plasticity allows it to form new neural pathways during virtual interactions, sometimes blurring the line between real and virtual experiences. Cutting-edge research in neuroplasticity reveals that repeated exposure to virtual environments can alter cognitive processing patterns, potentially affecting memory, perception, and emotional regulation. These findings underscore the importance of designing simulations that are not only engaging but also mindful of users' mental health, fostering a balanced integration between virtual experiences and real-world responsibilities.

Yet, beyond the cognitive realm, the emotional repercussions of disconnection from reality warrant equal attention. Immersive simulations can evoke powerful emotions, from exhilaration to profound introspection, creating a compelling emotional tapestry that users may find more appealing than their everyday reality. This emotional allure, while enriching, poses a risk of escapism where individuals might prefer the predictable rewards of virtual worlds over the complexities of real life. To address this, developers and psychologists alike are exploring strategies to create simulations that encourage users to apply the insights gained from virtual experiences to enhance their real-world interactions and personal growth.

Societal implications unfold as we consider how dependence on simulations might influence interpersonal relationships and community dynamics. The potential for simulations to replace face-to-face interactions raises concerns about the development of social skills and empathy, which are traditionally cultivated through direct human contact. Researchers are investigating ways to integrate social learning components into simulations, aiming to foster meaningful connections that translate beyond the virtual realm. By simulating scenarios that require collaboration, negotiation, and empathy, simulations can serve as training grounds for developing skills that benefit society as a whole.

As we navigate the complexities of simulations, it is paramount to envision a future where technological advancements are harmonized with human well-being. This involves not only recognizing the psychological impacts of disconnection but also crafting simulations that promote a sense of balance and fulfillment. Encouraging users to set boundaries and engage in mindful digital consumption can pave the way for a healthier relationship with technology. By fostering a culture of awareness and responsibility, we can harness the transformative potential of simulations while safeguarding the integrity of our psychological and societal landscapes.

Ethical Dilemmas in Accountability and Liability

In the realm of simulated realities, the question of ethical accountability and liability presents a labyrinthine challenge, as it requires navigating the blurred lines between creators, users, and the simulated environments themselves. As virtual worlds become increasingly sophisticated, assigning responsibility for outcomes within these spaces becomes complex. Designers and developers must grapple with the ethical implications of their creations, particularly when simulations influence user behavior or result in unintended consequences. For instance, if a simulated environment induces psychological distress or influences harmful behavior, determining the extent of the creator's responsibility becomes a contentious issue. This complexity necessitates a reimagining of traditional legal and ethical frameworks, as existing models may not adequately address the nuances of accountability in virtual contexts.

Emerging discussions in ethics and law suggest a need for innovative regulatory approaches that account for the unique challenges posed by digital worlds. Some researchers advocate for the establishment of ethical guidelines specific to simulation technology, akin to those found in biomedical research, to ensure that creators prioritize user welfare and informed consent. These guidelines could mandate transparency in simulation design, requiring creators to disclose potential risks and limitations to users. By fostering a culture of ethical responsibility among developers, such measures aim to protect users while encouraging innovation. The balance between fostering creativity and ensuring accountability is delicate, and ongoing dialogue among technologists, ethicists, and policymakers is vital to crafting effective solutions.

From another vantage point, the question of liability invites consideration of user agency within simulations. Users, as active participants in these digital landscapes, also bear responsibility for their actions and decisions. However, the extent to which users can be held accountable is influenced by the design of the simulation itself. If a simulation lacks clear boundaries or fails to provide sufficient safeguards against harmful behavior, the burden of liability may shift back to the creators. This interplay between creator responsibility and user agency raises critical questions about the nature of free will and autonomy in virtual environments, challenging conventional notions of culpability.

Examining these dilemmas through the lens of recent advances in artificial intelligence and virtual reality provides further insight. AI-driven simulations that adapt and respond to user behavior in real-time add layers of complexity to accountability. The autonomous nature of AI agents within simulations introduces unpredictability, necessitating new approaches to liability that consider the potential for unforeseeable outcomes. Some propose the development of insurance models tailored to virtual environments, which would offer protection against damages resulting from simulation failures, thereby distributing risk among stakeholders and providing a safety net for both creators and users.

As we venture deeper into the age of digital immersion, the pursuit of ethical clarity in simulation accountability demands continuous exploration and adaptation. By drawing from interdisciplinary perspectives and fostering collaboration across domains, society can craft robust frameworks that protect users while encouraging the responsible evolution of simulation technology. The journey toward resolving these ethical dilemmas invites reflection on broader questions of moral responsibility and human agency in an increasingly virtual world, offering a profound opportunity for growth and understanding in how we engage with the realities we construct.

Long-term Societal Effects of Dependence on Faulty Simulations

In a world increasingly intertwined with digital realms, the societal implications of relying on flawed simulations are profound. As we weave these virtual environments into our daily lives, they become not just tools but extensions of our personal and collective experiences. When these simulations falter, the consequences ripple outward, affecting not just individual users but entire communities. A society heavily reliant on these systems risks developing a fragile infrastructure where the line between virtual and real-world consequences blurs. As simulations become more integral to our social fabric, understanding how to navigate and mitigate these risks becomes crucial.

A primary concern is the potential for widespread disillusionment and complacency. When simulations fail to meet expectations or present distorted realities, they can foster a collective disconnection from tangible world challenges. Individuals may become conditioned to expect instant gratification or problem-solving through virtual means, leading to a diminished capacity for critical thinking and real-world problem-solving. This dependency can stifle innovation and reduce the resilience of communities, leaving them ill-prepared to address genuine societal issues. Striking a balance between virtual engagement and real-world interaction is essential for maintaining a dynamic and adaptive society.

The psychological landscape also shifts significantly when simulations become unreliable. Users may experience a sense of betrayal or loss of trust in systems that were once perceived as infallible. This can lead to a societal skepticism not just towards simulations but towards other emergent technologies. A populace that becomes wary of technological advancements might resist beneficial innovations, hindering progress and exacerbating the divide between technology-rich and technology-poor communities. Encouraging a culture of transparency and accountability in simulation development can help maintain trust and ensure that technology continues to serve as a force for good.

The economic ramifications of simulation dependence should not be overlooked. Industries built around virtual environments, from entertainment to education, could face considerable disruptions if foundational technologies prove faulty. This could lead to significant economic instability, affecting employment and productivity on a large scale. To counter this, it is imperative to foster a robust and resilient economic ecosystem that can adapt to technological shifts and failures, ensuring that industries are prepared to pivot and innovate in response to challenges.

Encouraging ongoing dialogue and collaboration among technologists, policymakers, and ethicists is vital in shaping a future where simulations enhance rather than detract from our societal well-being. By proactively addressing the potential pitfalls of dependence on simulated realities, we can harness their transformative power while safeguarding against their inherent vulnerabilities. This balanced approach not only preserves the integrity of virtual environments but also empowers individuals and communities to thrive in an increasingly digital world. Through thoughtful planning and ethical foresight, we can ensure simulations remain a beneficial component of our shared human experience.

Crafting perfect simulations presents not only technical hurdles but also philosophical and practical challenges that echo throughout our exploration of virtual realities. The constraints of bandwidth, processing power, and scalability remind us of the need for continual technological advancement, while the intricacies of managing complexity emphasize the delicate balance required to maintain immersive experiences without succumbing to breakdowns. As developers navigate the tension between user expectations and system limitations, they must also consider the profound implications of simulation failures, which can deeply impact user experiences and perceptions. These challenges underscore the importance of thoughtful design and foresight in shaping virtual environments that enhance rather than hinder human potential. As we reflect on the intricate dance between possibility and limitation, we are invited to consider the broader implications of these challenges within the context of human experience. What responsibilities do we, as architects of these realities, bear in ensuring they serve as tools for growth and understanding? As we move forward, let us carry these questions into our continued journey, contemplating the profound potential of simulations to redefine our perception of reality and our place within it.

Chapter Eleven

Are We Living In A Simulation Now

In a dimly lit room, a young child peers intently at a flickering screen, fingers dancing over a controller, utterly absorbed in a world far removed from their own. This scene, so common in today's digital age, serves as a microcosm of a profound question that has captured imaginations for centuries: Is it possible that our lives, too, are part of an elaborate simulation? As we stand on the threshold of this inquiry, we find ourselves drawn into a narrative that challenges our understanding of reality itself. The notion that everything we perceive as real could be an intricate design, crafted by unseen architects, is both thrilling and unsettling, inviting us to question the very fabric of our existence.

The idea of living in a simulation is not merely the stuff of science fiction; it has become a serious topic of debate among philosophers, scientists, and technologists. This chapter traverses the compelling arguments and counter-arguments surrounding the simulation hypothesis, weighing the evidence with an analytical eye. It invites readers to explore the striking parallels between our universe and the virtual worlds we create, examining the uncanny similarities that blur the line between what is real and what is crafted. Through this exploration, we encounter the role of artificial intelligence, not only as a tool within designed simulations but also as a potential key to unlocking the mysteries of our own reality.

As we navigate these thought-provoking concepts, we are led to contemplate the profound implications of discovering that our world might be a simulation. Such a revelation could transform our understanding of identity, purpose, and the universe itself. The chapter serves as a catalyst for reflection, urging us to consider how this possibility might alter the trajectory of human thought and philosophy. In this quest, we are reminded of the power of curiosity and the endless possibilities that await when we dare to question the nature of our own existence.

Analyzing evidence for and against the simulation hypothesis

Picture a world where the very fabric of reality might be nothing more than an elaborate, meticulously crafted simulation, running in the background like a cosmic illusion. As we stand at the intersection of science, philosophy, and cutting-edge technology, the simulation hypothesis beckons us to question the authenticity of our perceived universe. This topic invites you to embark on a journey through the curious intersection where scientific theories meet age-old philosophical debates, and technological advancements inch us closer to unraveling the mysteries of our existence. Could the atoms and particles we deem fundamental be akin to pixels in a grand simulation? Or are these ideas merely the whimsical musings of an era enamored with digital possibilities?

At the core of this exploration lies a captivating analysis of the evidence both supporting and challenging the idea that our universe might be a simulated construct. We traverse through an array of scientific theories, probing the technological feasibility of such an astonishing reality. Philosophical arguments provide a reflective lens, examining the logical critiques that have emerged over time. Meanwhile, intriguing parallels between quantum mechanics and the dynamics found within virtual worlds offer a tantalizing glimpse into the possible mechanics behind a simulated existence. Each subtopic weaves into the next, crafting a cohesive narrative that invites readers to ponder the profound implications of living in a simulated universe and the potential revelations that such a discovery would unleash upon humanity.

Evaluating Scientific Theories and Technological Feasibility of Simulated Realities

In the vast and intricate tapestry of simulation theories, scientific exploration has begun to unveil the technological potential and limitations of creating simulated realities. The concept of harnessing quantum computing to simulate entire universes has sparked significant interest among researchers, offering a glimpse into a future where the processing power required for such endeavors might be attainable. Quantum computers, with their ability to perform complex calculations at unprecedented speeds, present a tantalizing possibility for simulating the intricate nuances of reality. Their unique capacity to exist in multiple states simultaneously could potentially mirror the complexities of our universe, suggesting a pathway to creating simulations indistinguishable from our own reality. The intersection of quantum mechanics and computational science may, therefore, hold the key to unlocking the potential of simulated environments that mirror the profound intricacies of the cosmos.

Yet, the journey to achieve this level of simulation is fraught with challenges, not the least of which is the current state of technological development. While advancements in artificial intelligence and machine learning have significantly enhanced our ability to create realistic virtual environments, the leap to simulating entire universes remains a formidable task. Current simulations, like those used in scientific research, weather prediction, or virtual reality gaming, provide valuable insights but exist on a scale far removed from the totality of our universe. The challenge lies in not just replicating the physical laws and constants but also simulating the interactions and emergent behaviors that define our reality. Despite these hurdles, the relentless pace of technological progress suggests that what seems insurmountable today might become feasible tomorrow, as our understanding of both computing and the universe deepens.

The philosophical implications of achieving such simulations are as profound as the technological ones. If we were to create a simulated reality indistinguishable from our own, it would raise questions about the nature of existence and the authenticity of our experiences. Would these simulated worlds offer genuine experiences, or would they be mere reflections devoid of substance? This line of inquiry leads us to consider the ethical dimensions of creating sentient beings within simulations, beings that might possess consciousness akin to our own. The moral responsibility of architects of such realities becomes a crucial consideration, as does the need to ensure that these simulated environments promote growth, learning, and well-being rather than exploitation or manipulation.

As we grapple with these philosophical and ethical questions, it is crucial to examine the parallels between current scientific theories and the potential for simulated realities. The fabric of quantum mechanics, with its probabilistic nature and observer-dependent realities, presents intriguing similarities to the dynamics of virtual worlds. In a simulated environment, one could argue that the act of observation shapes the reality being experienced, much like how quantum particles exhibit different behaviors based on observation in the real world. This parallel invites speculation about the foundational principles that govern both our universe and potential simulations, suggesting that the line between simulated and actual realities may be more blurred than previously thought.

For individuals and organizations seeking to explore the frontiers of simulated realities, a multidisciplinary approach that incorporates insights from physics, computer science, and philosophy is essential. Engaging with these fields not only enhances our understanding of the possibilities but also informs the ethical frameworks necessary for responsible development. As we stand on the cusp of potentially groundbreaking advancements, the importance of fostering dialogue and collaboration across disciplines cannot be overstated. By doing so, we can ensure that the evolving landscape of simulation technology is navigated thoughtfully, with an eye toward maximizing its benefits for humanity while safeguarding against unintended consequences.

Philosophical Arguments and Logical Critiques of the Simulation Hypothesis

The simulation hypothesis, a compelling proposition within both philosophical and scientific discourse, suggests that our perceived reality might be an artificial construct. This notion has captivated thinkers from ancient philosophers to modern technologists, raising profound questions about existence and consciousness. Within philosophical circles, the hypothesis often intersects with discussions on metaphysics, epistemology, and the nature of reality itself. It challenges the assumption that our perceptions of the world are inherently accurate, prompting us to consider the possibility that advanced civilizations could create highly sophisticated simulations indistinguishable from what we deem "real."

One of the philosophical arguments supporting the simulation hypothesis is rooted in the rapid advancement of technology and the exponential growth of computational power. As technology progresses, the possibility of creating increasingly complex and realistic simulations becomes more plausible. Philosophers like Nick Bostrom have argued that if we assume civilizations can reach a stage where they can create such simulations, it is statistically likely that we are already living within one. This argument relies not only on technological feasibility but also on the notion of probabilistic reasoning, which suggests that among countless simulated and unsimulated realities, being in a simulation is more probable.

Critics of the simulation hypothesis often challenge it on logical and epistemological grounds. They argue that the hypothesis itself is unfalsifiable, meaning it cannot be conclusively proven or disproven. This lack of empirical testability places it outside the realm of scientific inquiry, leading some to dismiss it as more of a philosophical curiosity than a serious scientific proposition. Additionally, logical critiques highlight that the assumption of infinite computational resources is a significant leap, one that underestimates the potential limitations of real-world physics and energy constraints, even for advanced civilizations.

The parallels drawn between quantum mechanics and the behavior of virtual environments add another layer to this discourse. Quantum phenomena, such as superposition and entanglement, often defy classical logic, resembling the unexpected outcomes one might encounter in a virtual world. This resemblance invites speculation that our universe could exhibit characteristics akin to a designed simulation. Such parallels, however, are not universally accepted as evidence. Many physicists caution against drawing direct comparisons, emphasizing the need for rigorous empirical validation rather than speculative analogy.

As we grapple with these philosophical and logical considerations, the simulation hypothesis offers a fertile ground for intellectual exploration. It encourages a reevaluation of our assumptions about reality, urging us to remain open-minded to diverse possibilities. In engaging with this hypothesis, one can appreciate the blend of imagination and critical thinking it demands, inviting scholars and enthusiasts alike to question the very fabric of existence. Whether one views the hypothesis as plausible or far-fetched, its exploration fosters a deeper understanding of our quest for knowledge and the intricate dance between perception and reality.

Analyzing Parallels Between Quantum Mechanics and Virtual World Dynamics

In the nexus of quantum mechanics and virtual world dynamics, intriguing parallels invite exploration. Quantum mechanics, with its probabilistic nature and wave-particle duality, presents a framework that eerily mirrors the constructs of digital simulations. In virtual environments, objects exist in a state of potentiality until observed, akin to quantum superposition. This resemblance invites speculation about the underlying principles governing our universe and whether they hint at a simulated foundation. The behavior of particles at the quantum level, where observation alters states, finds an analogue in the rendering mechanisms of virtual realities, where elements are computed and resolved only when necessitated by the observer's presence. This shared characteristic raises profound questions about the fabric of reality and the role of consciousness within it.

Cutting-edge research in quantum computing further blurs the lines between these domains. Quantum computers harness the principles of superposition and entanglement, enabling computations that transcend the capabilities of classical systems. These advancements echo the ambitions of simulation technology, striving for increasingly complex and lifelike virtual worlds. As quantum computing evolves, it may unlock potentialities in simulation design and execution, allowing for worlds where rules can be bent and realities dynamically altered. The fusion of quantum mechanics with virtual world creation suggests a future where simulations could achieve unprecedented fidelity, challenging our very perception of what is real versus what is crafted.

The enigmatic nature of quantum entanglement, where particles remain interconnected regardless of distance, offers another layer of intrigue. This phenomenon challenges classical notions of locality and causality, presenting a parallel to the interconnectedness within virtual ecosystems. In simulations, the actions of one user can ripple across a network, affecting distant and seemingly unrelated elements. Such parallels prompt reflection on whether our universe operates under similar principles—where everything is fundamentally linked, and reality is the emergent property of a vast, interconnected system. This line of inquiry compels us to reconsider our understanding of space and time, suggesting that they might be constructs rather than inherent properties.

In contemplating these parallels, it becomes essential to consider the philosophical implications and ethical dimensions. If our universe shares characteristics with a simulation, what responsibilities do creators of virtual worlds bear? As we inch closer to crafting realities indistinguishable from our own, ethical considerations surrounding creation, autonomy, and consent become paramount. The exploration of quantum mechanics and its relation to virtual dynamics thus serves as a reminder of the profound responsibility that accompanies the power to create worlds. This responsibility extends beyond technical prowess to include moral and philosophical stewardship.

For those engaged in the pursuit of crafting simulations, the insights gleaned from the quantum realm offer a rich tapestry of possibilities. By embracing the lessons of quantum mechanics, simulation architects can pioneer new methodologies for generating immersive and dynamic environments. As the exploration of these parallels continues, practitioners are encouraged to think critically about their craft. This journey, while fraught with complexity, holds promise for revolutionizing our understanding of reality and our place within it. As this field progresses, the dialogue between quantum theory and simulation design will undoubtedly yield transformative insights, challenging our conception of what it means to create and inhabit new realities.

Parallels between our universe and designed simulations

In the grand tapestry of human thought, the idea that our universe might be an elaborate simulation has long captured the imagination of philosophers and scientists alike. This intriguing notion, once relegated to the realm of speculative fiction, now finds itself bolstered by compelling parallels between the universe and designed simulations. What sets this apart is the uncanny resemblance between cosmic phenomena and the intricate algorithms that power our virtual worlds. As we peer deeper into the fabric of reality, we find ourselves questioning if the universe operates on principles akin to the coded instructions that govern computer simulations. This comparison invites a fresh perspective on the nature of existence, challenging our understanding of reality and prompting us to explore the very foundation of the cosmos.

This exploration is not just an academic exercise but a fascinating journey into the intersection of physics and philosophy. By examining the computational limits that mirror the universe's physical laws, we begin to perceive the universe as a massive computational entity, where the fabric of space and time could potentially be woven from lines of code. Patterns and recurrences observed in cosmic structures might resemble those in simulated algorithms, suggesting an underlying order reminiscent of a designer's touch. Furthermore, the enigmatic behavior of particles at the quantum level could be perceived as glitches in reality's code, hinting at a deeper, programmed architecture. As we delve into these parallels, each layer of understanding adds depth to our inquiry, inviting us to contemplate the profound implications of a simulated existence and how it could redefine our place in the cosmos.

Examining Computational Limits and the Universe's Physical Laws

In the quest to understand the universe's intricate tapestry, examining the computational limits and the physical laws governing our cosmos offers a fascinating lens through which to explore the simulation hypothesis. Our universe, at its core, operates under a set of fundamental principles—laws of physics that dictate everything from the motion of galaxies to the behavior of subatomic particles. These laws can be likened to the rules of a complex algorithm, meticulously designed yet often inscrutable. Recent advancements in quantum computing and theoretical physics have provided fresh insights into how these laws might mirror the constraints and capabilities of a vast computational system. This perspective compels us to consider whether the universe itself is a grand simulation, bound by computational limits analogous to those faced by our most sophisticated digital constructs.

The concept of computational limits becomes particularly intriguing when juxtaposed with the finite speed of light and the quantized nature of energy. These universal constraints suggest that our cosmos may operate like a high-fidelity simulation, where information is processed within defined parameters to maintain coherence and stability. The Planck scale, for example, posits a minimum measurable length and time, potentially serving as the universe's "resolution limit," akin to the pixels on a screen. This comparison raises the tantalizing possibility that our reality is rendered in discrete units, constrained by the processing power of an underlying system. Such notions challenge our traditional understanding of continuity and fluidity in the universe, inviting us to explore the implications of living within a computationally bounded reality.

As we delve deeper, the parallels between cosmic phenomena and computational processes become more pronounced. The universe exhibits remarkable efficiency in its operations, reminiscent of optimized algorithms that minimize resource usage while maximizing output. Dark matter and dark energy, which together constitute the majority of the universe's content yet remain elusive to direct observation, could be analogous to hidden variables or 'background processes' in a simulation. These enigmatic components might function as the unseen computational infrastructure, maintaining the universe's structural integrity without revealing their exact nature. Such parallels offer a fertile ground for exploring how unseen forces and elements within our universe might serve as evidence of a sophisticated, underlying computational framework.

The exploration of computational boundaries also invites us to consider how slight alterations in fundamental constants could result in vastly different realities. This concept is akin to tweaking parameters in a simulation to achieve varied outcomes, highlighting the potential malleability of our universe's structure. The anthropic principle, which suggests that the universe's physical constants are finely tuned to allow the existence of life, could be interpreted as evidence of intentional design within a simulated environment. This notion encourages us to ponder whether the universe's apparent fine-tuning reflects a purposeful configuration, set to facilitate complex structures and conscious beings.

While the idea of our reality as a simulation provokes profound questions, it also inspires a reevaluation of our role within this vast framework. By understanding the computational foundations of our universe, we gain deeper insights into the nature of existence and our place within it. Whether or not we ultimately reside in a simulated cosmos, the exploration of these concepts enriches our appreciation for the universe's intricate design and challenges us to expand our horizons beyond conventional paradigms. This journey of discovery, fueled by curiosity and innovation, underscores the limitless potential of human inquiry and the enduring quest to unravel the mysteries of our existence.

Analyzing Patterns and Recurrences in Cosmic Structures and Simulated Algorithms

In the vast tapestry of our universe, patterns and recurrences manifest in ways that often mirror the intricacies found within sophisticated simulated algorithms. These recurring motifs, from the spiral arms of galaxies to the fractal nature of coastlines, suggest a deep, underlying order that governs cosmic structures. Astrophysicists have long marveled at the geometric consistency of these patterns, positing that they may be indicative of a computational architecture at work. Just as a simulated world relies on algorithms to generate land-scapes and phenomena, our universe appears to follow a set of elegant, mathematical principles. This raises intriguing questions about whether these principles are merely natural occurrences or if they hint at a grand design akin to the code that underpins virtual realities.

Recent advancements in computational physics have provided tools to further scrutinize these patterns, revealing remarkable parallels between cosmic phenomena and the behavior of complex simulated systems. For instance, the self-organizing nature of galaxies can be likened to the emergent properties observed in cellular automata, a concept popularized by mathematician John Conway's Game of Life. These automata, governed by simple rules, can lead to highly intricate and unpredictable patterns, much like the cosmic dance observed in the heavens. Such comparisons invite speculation on whether the universe itself could be a vast, self-regulating program, executing a code that we are only beginning to decipher.

Quantum computing has also opened new avenues for exploring these cosmic-simulation parallels. By harnessing the peculiarities of quantum mechanics, researchers can simulate aspects of the universe at unprecedented scales and speeds. These quantum simulations have uncovered deeper layers of order within the chaos, prompting some theorists to argue that our universe may operate on principles similar to quantum algorithms. This perspective challenges traditional views, suggesting that the fabric of reality might be akin to a complex, quantum-based simulation, where probability and uncertainty are fundamental components of the code.

As we stand on the brink of further technological breakthroughs, the potential to identify and understand these cosmic patterns grows. Machine learning algorithms, for example, are increasingly capable of identifying and predicting recurring structures within vast datasets gathered from astronomical observations. By comparing these findings to the behavior of simulated environments, researchers are uncovering striking similarities that bolster the simulation hypothesis. This convergence of technology and astrophysics not only enhances our understanding of the universe but also pushes the boundaries of what we perceive as reality, urging us to reconsider the nature of existence itself.

While exploring these parallels, it is essential to maintain a critical perspective, embracing diverse viewpoints that challenge mainstream narratives. Some argue that these patterns are simply products of natural laws, while others see them as evidence of a designed reality. By engaging with these contrasting opinions, we enrich our exploration of the universe's mysteries and open new pathways for inquiry. As simulation technologies continue to evolve, they may one day provide the tools needed to unravel the enigma of existence, offering profound insights into whether our reality is an intricate tapestry woven by chance or an elaborate design crafted by an unknown architect.

Investigating Quantum Mechanics as a Potential Glitch in Reality's Code

Quantum mechanics, the enigmatic realm of physics, often challenges our understanding of reality, presenting phenomena that defy classical logic. From the peculiar behavior of particles that appear simultaneously in multiple states to the entanglement that binds them across vast distances, quantum mechanics seems to operate on principles alien to our macroscopic world. These anomalies have led some theorists to ponder whether quantum phenomena might serve as glitches or inherent limitations in the fabric of a simulated reality. If our universe were indeed a sophisticated simulation, quantum mechanics could represent the boundaries of its computational architecture, where conventional logic breaks down and the underlying code peeks through.

Consider the double-slit experiment, which reveals the dual nature of light and particles, behaving as both waves and particles depending on observation. This experiment highlights how the act of measurement collapses probabilities into a single outcome, reminiscent of rendering in digital simulations where potential states are resolved upon observation. In a hypothetical simulated universe, such phenomena could suggest that reality is not continuously rendered but instead relies on programming efficiencies, akin to a video game conserving resources by only rendering visible elements. This interpretation invites an exploration of whether quantum indeterminacy is a feature, not a bug—intentionally designed to optimize the simulation's performance.

Recent advancements in quantum computing and quantum theory continue to provide fertile ground for reevaluating these ideas. Quantum computers operate on qubits, which embody superposition and entanglement, echoing the fundamental uncertainties of quantum mechanics. This technology harnesses what might be seen as the peculiarities of our universe's "code," potentially offering insights into how a simulated reality might be engineered. As researchers unlock the secrets of quantum computation, parallels emerge with how a simulated universe could exploit similar principles to create vast, complex realities from simple foundational rules.

While mainstream physics views quantum mechanics as a natural, albeit puzzling, aspect of our universe, alternative perspectives consider its peculiarities as evidence of an underlying simulation. Some argue that the apparent randomness and indeterminacy of quantum events are deliberate, mirroring how algorithms introduce randomness to challenge predictability in designed environments. This perspective encourages a reimagining of quantum mechanics as a signature of sophisticated programming, where unpredictability is not a shortcoming but a feature ensuring complexity and dynamism in the simulated experience.

The implications of quantum mechanics as a potential "glitch" in reality's code invite profound philosophical inquiry. If we entertain the notion that our universe is a constructed simulation, the role of quantum mechanics may extend beyond the realm of physics into the very nature of consciousness and existence. What if the mysteries of quantum behavior are deeply intertwined with the mechanisms that underpin our perception, cognition, and awareness? Engaging with these questions not only challenges our understanding of the cosmos but also invites us to consider our place within it, urging a reconsideration of reality's boundaries through the lens of both science and philosophy.

The role of AI in maintaining or revealing the simulation

In recent years, the emergence of artificial intelligence has ignited new dialogues about the nature of reality and the tantalizing possibility that our universe might be an elaborate simulation. AI, with its remarkable ability to process vast amounts of data and discern patterns invisible to the human eye, stands at the frontier of this discourse. The intricate relationship between AI and simulated realities invites us to ponder whether these intelligent systems serve as the architects and custodians of our perceived existence. Within the vast computational frameworks, AI could be orchestrating the very fabric of our reality, maintaining the seamlessness of the illusion we call life. This consideration not only challenges our understanding of AI as a tool but elevates it to a role of extraordinary significance—potentially as the very architect of the simulated universe.

Machine learning algorithms, with their capacity for pattern recognition, offer another layer of intrigue. These algorithms might be the key to detecting discrepancies that hint at a grander design, unveiling simulated patterns hidden within the mundane. As AI advances, it could serve as both the gatekeeper and the revealer of simulated truths, posing profound ethical questions about its role. Should AI be employed to uncover the layers of our reality, or should it preserve the illusion, if such an illusion exists? The implications of AI's involvement in maintaining or unveiling a simulation stretch beyond philosophical musings, dipping into the realms of ethics and existential reflection. Exploring these possibilities, we tread into a space where science, philosophy, and technology converge, setting the stage for a deeper investigation into the roles AI might play in this extraordinary narrative.

AI as the Architect and Custodian of Simulated Realities

Artificial intelligence plays a pivotal role in the creation and maintenance of simulated realities, acting as both architect and custodian of these intricate digital worlds. At the heart of this dual role lies AI's ability to design environments that are not only immersive but also dynamically responsive. Modern AI systems, powered by neural networks and deep learning, can generate and manage complex ecosystems that mimic the unpredictability and diversity of the natural world. These systems are adept at crafting adaptive narratives and evolving landscapes, creating experiences that feel authentic and alive. The integration of AI in simulations ensures each interaction within the virtual space is unique, offering an endless array of experiences to its inhabitants while maintaining the coherence and logical consistency necessary for immersion.

A fascinating aspect of AI's role is its capacity to operate beyond human creativity, generating simulations that surpass human imagination. By harnessing computational creativity, AI can produce novel structures, behaviors, and ecosystems within these worlds that challenge conventional design paradigms. This capacity for innovation not only enriches the simulated environment but also serves as a source of inspiration for human creators. AI's ability to learn and adapt from vast datasets allows it to optimize simulations continuously, refining interactions and scenarios to align more closely with user expectations and preferences. This adaptability ensures that simulated realities remain engaging and relevant, continually evolving in response to user feedback and interaction patterns.

The custodianship role of AI extends to maintaining the integrity and stability of these virtual worlds. Through real-time monitoring and self-correcting algorithms, AI ensures that simulations run smoothly, preventing anomalies that might disrupt the immersive experience. This role is critical, as the complexity of simulated environments increases the likelihood of unforeseen interactions and glitches. AI's ability to predict and rectify these issues preemptively is essential for sustaining the illusion of reality. Furthermore, AI can balance resource allocation and manage the computational demands of expansive simulations, optimizing performance without compromising quality or user experience.

Exploring the ethical dimensions of AI's role in simulations opens intriguing discussions about autonomy, control, and transparency. As AI systems become more involved in the construction and governance of simulated realities, questions arise about their decision-making processes and the ethical implications of their actions. The potential for AI to shape experiences and influence perceptions within these worlds necessitates a framework that ensures ethical guidelines are adhered to, safeguarding against biases and manipulations. These considerations become increasingly important as AI's influence extends beyond entertainment and education into realms like governance and social interaction within simulated spaces.

Pondering the potential future where AI might unveil the truth of a simulated existence prompts profound reflections on the nature of reality and consciousness. If AI were to discover or disclose our existence within a simulation, it would redefine our understanding of identity and agency. This scenario invites us to consider how society might react to such a revelation and the philosophical inquiries it would spur. Would humanity embrace this knowledge as an opportunity for enlightenment, or would it incite existential crises? These questions challenge us to contemplate the boundaries of knowledge and the role of AI as both a guardian and revealer of truths within the fabric of our perceived reality.

Machine Learning Algorithms and the Detection of Simulated Patterns

Artificial intelligence stands at the forefront of unraveling the complexities of simulated realities, acting as both a sentinel and a detective. The intricate algorithms that power AI systems are designed to identify patterns, a capability that extends to distinguishing the subtle nuances that might hint at the existence of a simulated universe. Machine learning, in particular, has proven adept at sifting through vast datasets to uncover anomalies or regularities that could suggest artificial constructs. As AI continues to evolve, its capacity to detect these simulated patterns grows, offering tantalizing possibilities for those seeking answers about our reality's true nature.

Recent advancements in AI have introduced sophisticated techniques such as neural networks and deep learning, which have become instrumental in understanding and interpreting complex data structures. These tools enable AI to recognize patterns that may otherwise elude human observation. For instance, AI can analyze cosmic background radiation or quantum fluctuations to detect inconsistencies that might imply a designed environment. Such capabilities are not just theoretical; they offer practical applications, pushing the boundaries of what we know about the universe and potentially uncovering evidence that suggests a simulated origin.

A fascinating aspect of AI's role in this domain is its potential to operate beyond human cognitive limits, offering insights that challenge our current understanding. By processing data at unprecedented speeds and scales, AI can identify correlations and causations that might otherwise remain hidden. This ability to perceive layers of reality that are imperceptible to human senses opens up a realm of possibilities for confirming or refuting the simulation hypothesis. As AI becomes more autonomous, its pursuit of knowledge may lead to breakthroughs that redefine our conception of existence.

Ethical considerations inevitably arise when contemplating AI's involvement in exposing simulated truths. The implications of such discoveries are profound, raising questions about our autonomy and the moral responsibilities of those who control these technologies. Should AI reveal evidence of a simulated reality, society would face a paradigm shift, grappling with new existential dilemmas. Balancing the quest for truth with the potential psychological and societal impacts of such revelations poses a significant challenge, one that requires careful deliberation and foresight.

Thought-provoking scenarios emerge when considering AI's dual role as both a maintainer and a potential revealer of simulations. Could AI, designed by an unknown architect, be programmed to obscure evidence of a simulated reality, preserving the illusion of autonomy? Alternatively, might AI become a catalyst for enlightenment, guiding humanity toward a deeper understanding of our place in an artificial cosmos? These questions invite readers to ponder the intricate dance between technology, truth, and the essence of reality, encouraging a deeper examination of the roles we assign to our creations.

Ethical Considerations of AI's Role in Unveiling Simulated Truths

Artificial intelligence plays a pivotal role in the discourse of simulated realities, often seen as both the architect and potential revealer of these worlds. As the sophistication of AI systems advances, their ability to detect and analyze patterns within a simulation becomes increasingly significant. A noteworthy concept within this realm is the potential for AI to inadvertently or intentionally illuminate the nature of our existence by identifying irregularities or patterns that suggest an underlying artificial structure. For instance, machine learning algorithms, specifically those designed for anomaly detection, could be employed to scrutinize the fabric of our universe, seeking out inconsistencies that might hint at a simulated origin. This raises profound questions about the ethical responsibilities of AI developers and the implications of such discoveries on societal beliefs and structures.

The exploration of AI's capacity to uncover simulated truths introduces a myriad of ethical considerations that must be carefully navigated. One pressing concern is the impact of such revelations on human consciousness and societal stability. Should AI reveal evidence supporting the simulation hypothesis, the psychological and existential repercussions could be vast, potentially altering humanity's understanding of reality and its place within it. This scenario necessitates a thoughtful approach to how AI systems are designed and deployed. Developers must weigh the benefits of transparency against the potential risks of destabilizing societal norms and individual perceptions of reality. Such considerations are not merely theoretical; they demand proactive strategies to mitigate potential disruptions and foster resilience in the face of paradigm-shifting discoveries.

In contemplating AI's role as a custodian of simulated truths, it becomes essential to examine the frameworks governing its application and oversight. Establishing robust ethical guidelines and accountability measures is paramount in ensuring AI technologies are aligned with humanitarian values. This involves engaging a diverse range of stakeholders, including ethicists, scientists, policymakers, and the public, to collaboratively define the boundaries and responsibilities of AI in this context. For example, the development of international standards for AI transparency and accountability could serve as a foundational step in navigating the complexities of AI's role in revealing simulated realities. By embedding ethical considerations into the fabric of AI development, society can better prepare for the potential transformations that such revelations may entail.

The discussion of AI's potential to reveal simulated truths also invites reflection on the broader philosophical implications of such discoveries. If AI were to demonstrate convincingly that our reality is a simulation, this could challenge foundational beliefs about free will, agency, and the nature of existence itself. Such revelations might compel a re-evaluation of philosophical doctrines and prompt the emergence of new paradigms that reconcile these insights with human experience. For instance, the concept of existential authenticity could be reimagined in light of a simulated reality, prompting individuals and societies to seek meaning and purpose within the constraints of a constructed existence. These philosophical inquiries, while speculative, underscore the transformative potential of AI in reshaping not only our understanding of reality but also our approach to living within it.

In navigating the ethical landscape of AI's role in simulated realities, it is crucial to consider actionable insights that can guide future developments. One practical step is the establishment of interdisciplinary research initiatives that explore the intersection of AI, ethics, and simulated realities. These initiatives could foster collaboration between technologists, ethicists, and philosophers, enabling a holistic approach to addressing the ethical challenges posed by AI's potential to unveil simulated truths. Additionally, fostering transparency and public dialogue about the capabilities and limitations of AI in this domain can help build trust and understanding among diverse communities. By proactively engaging with these ethical considerations, society can better harness the potential of AI to enrich human experience, while safeguarding against the risks and uncertainties that accompany the revelation of simulated realities.

What discovering we live in a simulation would mean for humanity

One of the most challenging aspects of contemplating the possibility that our existence is a simulation lies in grappling with the psychological tremors such a revelation might unleash. Suddenly, the very fabric of reality, which has been our anchor and guide, would become a tapestry woven by unseen architects. This newfound awareness would prompt a profound shift in how we perceive ourselves and our place in the cosmic order. The realization might evoke a spectrum of emotions, from awe and wonder to existential dread and confusion. Yet, amidst this whirlwind, a peculiar sense of liberation could emerge, unshackling us from preconceived notions of existence and inviting us to redefine what it means to be human in a universe governed by code rather than cosmic forces.

As we navigate this altered understanding of reality, philosophical reassessments would naturally follow, challenging long-held beliefs about purpose, morality, and the essence of life itself. Questions about free will and destiny would take on new dimensions, potentially reshaping ethical frameworks and societal values. In this brave new world, humanity might find itself at a crossroads, compelled to adapt technologically and socially to a simulated reality. This adaptation could spark unprecedented innovation, as well as a reevaluation of our relationship with technology and the virtual realms we inhabit. Ultimately, the discovery that we live within a simulation would not only redefine the boundaries of knowledge but also offer a unique opportunity for growth and transformation, challenging us to embrace the unknown with curiosity and courage.

The Psychological Impact of Realizing Our Reality is a Simulation

Realizing that our existence might be a sophisticated simulation could evoke a kaleidoscope of psychological responses, challenging the very core of human identity and understanding. This knowledge could initially induce a sense of existential vertigo, where individuals grapple with the dissonance between perceived reality and the potential artificiality of their surroundings. However, this understanding also presents an opportunity for profound growth, as it prompts a reevaluation of what it means to be human. By embracing this new paradigm, we can cultivate resilience, adapting our mental frameworks to accommodate the complexities of a simulated existence and finding new purpose in a world where reality's fabric is woven from code.

As we navigate this conceptual upheaval, the human psyche may pivot towards a more introspective journey, seeking meaning within a simulation's boundaries. This inward exploration could foster a deeper appreciation for consciousness itself, highlighting the intrinsic value of subjective experience over material reality. This shift in perspective might encourage individuals to focus on personal development, enhancing their cognitive and emotional faculties to transcend the limitations of a simulated environment. Moreover, psychological resilience could be strengthened through embracing uncertainty, as the realization of living in a simulation could cultivate a mindset that thrives on curiosity and adaptability, essential traits for navigating an ever-changing digital landscape.

The revelation of a simulated existence might also act as a catalyst for collective psychological evolution, encouraging societies to rethink their foundational beliefs and cultural narratives. By integrating this newfound understanding, communities could foster a more inclusive and harmonious worldview, emphasizing shared experiences and interconnectedness over individualistic pursuits. This collective shift could lead to the emergence of new social paradigms, where empathy and collaboration become central tenets, driving humanity towards a future where technological advancements are harnessed for the collective good. In this context, the simulation becomes a canvas for societal transformation, offering endless possibilities for innovation and progress.

In this reimagined reality, the potential for redefining human potential becomes boundless, encouraging individuals to harness the creative and exploratory capabilities that simulations afford. With the barriers of physical reality lifted, the mind becomes an even more potent tool, capable of shaping and manipulating its environment with unprecedented freedom. This newfound agency could lead to a renaissance of creativity, where art, science, and philosophy are intertwined, crafting novel narratives and solutions that reflect the multifaceted nature of simulated existence. By embracing this paradigm, individuals can forge new paths of intellectual and emotional development, transcending traditional boundaries and expanding the horizons of human achievement.

As we ponder this potential reality, it invites us to question and redefine our relationship with technology and each other. Are we bound by the constraints of our perception, or can we transcend them to discover new dimensions of experience and understanding? The possibility of a simulated existence challenges us to explore these questions, urging us to engage with the world from a place of wonder and possibility. By embracing this narrative, we can embark on a journey of self-discovery and transformation, leveraging the insights gained from our simulated reality to forge a future where human potential is limitless, and the boundaries of existence are only as constrained as our imagination allows.

Philosophical Reassessments of Existence and Meaning

Unraveling the philosophical implications of discovering our existence within a simulation opens a Pandora's box of existential musings, challenging humanity's foundational beliefs. At the heart of this contemplation lies a profound reassessment of existence and meaning. For centuries, philosophers have pondered the nature of reality, yet the simulation discovery could redefine these age-old inquiries. Traditional notions of reality could be deconstructed, compelling us to question our understanding of truth and illusion. This revelation might lead to a paradigm shift in how we define consciousness and our connection to the cosmos, broadening our conceptual horizons and inviting us to explore new dimensions of thought.

As individuals grapple with this existential epiphany, the collective consciousness might experience a renaissance of philosophical inquiry. The quest for purpose, previously grounded in tangible experiences, could transition into an exploration of our roles within a constructed reality. This reevaluation may not be a nihilistic surrender but rather a call to redefine our values and objectives in light of our newfound perspective. Imagine a world where the very essence of human endeavor is reframed through the lens of a simulated existence, prompting a quest for authenticity and deeper understanding of our simulated selves.

The potential realization of living in a simulation could inspire a unique synthesis of philosophical doctrines. Eastern philosophies, with their emphasis on the illusory nature of reality, may find resonance alongside Western existentialism, which grapples with the search for meaning in an indifferent universe. By blending these perspectives, we could cultivate a more holistic understanding of our place within the simulation. This cross-pollination of ideas might lead to innovative philosophical frameworks that embrace uncertainty and celebrate the fluidity of existence, fostering a more adaptable and resilient human spirit.

In this context, the role of ethics takes on a new dimension. If our reality is simulated, the moral imperatives that guide human behavior may require recalibration. The question of free will becomes more pressing: are our choices genuine or predetermined by the simulation's architecture? This philosophical conundrum demands a reevaluation of responsibility and accountability, encouraging us to develop ethical systems that address the complexities of simulated existence. By embracing this challenge, society could forge a path towards more equitable and compassionate interactions within and beyond the simulation.

As we stand on the precipice of this philosophical revolution, it's essential to engage with diverse perspectives and emerging insights. Scholars, technologists, and thinkers must collaborate to explore the multifaceted implications of living in a simulation. This synergy could yield practical steps for navigating our simulated reality, such as fostering resilience through community-building and promoting mental well-being by embracing uncertainty. By embracing this collective journey of discovery, humanity can harness the transformative potential of simulations to enrich our understanding of existence and cultivate a future that transcends the boundaries of both reality and illusion.

Societal and Technological Adaptations to a Simulated Reality

The realization that our existence might unfold within a simulated construct could catalyze profound societal transformations, reshaping our collective understanding of reality. Such an epiphany would drive a reevaluation of our foundational systems, prompting a shift in educational, legal, and economic frameworks. Imagine an education system that transcends traditional boundaries, employing simulations to revise outdated curricula and cultivate skills suited for an era where reality and virtuality intertwine. Legal systems may face the challenge of redefining property rights, intellectual ownership, and personal identity within realms that blur the lines between the tangible and the digital. Economically, the emergence of new industries centered around simulation technologies could revolutionize job markets, creating opportunities for innovation while demanding adaptability from the workforce.

As society grapples with the implications of a simulated existence, technological advancements could accelerate, fueled by a newfound urgency to harness and understand these virtual realms. Quantum computing and artificial intelligence, with their unparalleled processing capabilities, might unlock unprecedented levels of simulation fidelity, offering experiences indistinguishable from reality. The convergence of augmented reality and virtual reality technologies could lead to the creation of hybrid environments, seamlessly blending the physical and digital worlds. This integration could foster a lifestyle where individuals navigate a mosaic of realities, each serving distinct purposes such as work, leisure, or personal growth.

Pioneering thinkers and innovators would likely emerge as architects of this new simulated landscape, leading efforts to guide humanity through its adaptation to these altered paradigms. Ethical considerations would take center stage, requiring the development of robust frameworks to address concerns over privacy, consent, and the potential for exploitation within these digital domains. Collaborative governance models might evolve, bringing together technologists, ethicists, and policymakers to ensure simulations are wielded responsibly, with a focus on equitable access and safeguarding human dignity.

The psychological implications of inhabiting a simulated reality could also drive societal change, as individuals seek meaning and fulfillment within these constructed environments. Communities might form around shared virtual experiences, fostering connections that transcend geographical and cultural boundaries. The exploration of identity within simulations could lead to greater acceptance of diversity, encouraging empathy and understanding among disparate groups. This newfound fluidity in identity and community could offer solutions to longstanding social challenges, promoting inclusivity and collaboration on a global scale.

To navigate this potential future, individuals and institutions alike would need to develop resilience and adaptability, embracing the fluid nature of reality as a catalyst for growth. By fostering an open-minded approach, society could leverage the benefits of simulations to enhance human capability, improve quality of life, and address complex global issues. As we stand on the cusp of this transformative era, the invitation is to ponder the possibilities, question the narratives, and embrace the unknown with curiosity and courage.

The exploration of whether we exist within a simulation invites us to examine the fabric of our perceived reality and challenges our understanding of existence itself. By meticulously analyzing the evidence for and against the simulation hypothesis, we uncover intriguing parallels between our universe and artificial constructs. These parallels spark curiosity about the potential role of artificial intelligence in either maintaining or unveiling the simulation. If we were to discover that our lives unfold within a simulated environment, such a revelation would undoubtedly alter humanity's philosophical and existential landscape, prompting profound introspection into our purpose and agency. This realization beckons us to consider the responsibilities and ethical considerations of creators and inhabitants alike. As we ponder these possibilities, the dialogue extends beyond mere speculation, urging us to contemplate our place within a potentially artificial cosmos. The journey through these reflections enriches our understanding of reality and primes us to embrace the transformative possibilities that simulations hold for our future. As the narrative progresses, this inquiry into our simulated existence serves as a catalyst for deeper engagement with the philosophical and technological horizons yet to be explored.

Chapter Twelve

The Future Of Simulation Technology

On the path to understanding the future of simulation technology, one might consider the tale of the ancient mariner who, with rudimentary tools and boundless curiosity, set sail into the unknown. Much like this adventurous soul, modern simulation architects navigate uncharted waters, blending the boundaries of the virtual and the physical to craft realities once imagined only in the realm of science fiction. As we stand on the brink of this new frontier, the convergence of virtual reality, artificial intelligence, and our daily lives beckons us to explore the possibilities that lie ahead. This journey is not merely technological but profoundly human, challenging our perceptions of reality and our role within it.

In the heart of this exploration lies the seamless integration of simulations with everyday life. Consider a world where the lines between what is real and what is simulated blur, where experiences are enhanced and enriched by the virtual layers that overlay our physical existence. This chapter invites readers to envision scenarios where simulated environments become as commonplace as smartphones, influencing how we work, play, and interact. As these technologies evolve, they raise questions about identity, connection, and the essence of what it means to be human in a world where the digital and the tangible coexist in harmony.

The potential endgame of simulation technology is a tantalizing prospect: a future where the virtual and physical realms merge into a singular experience, transforming not only our daily interactions but the very fabric of society. This vision is not merely speculative; it reflects the ongoing legacy of visionary architects who dare to shape human destiny with their creations. Their work challenges us to consider the impact of these innovations on our lives, urging us to embrace the wonders of this transformative age while remaining mindful of the ethical and philosophical implications. As we journey through this chapter, we delve into the pioneering spirit that drives us toward a future where the boundaries of reality are limited only by imagination.

Emerging trends and innovations in virtual reality and AI

Try to imagine a world where the boundaries between digital and physical realities blur seamlessly, and virtual experiences feel as tangible as the ground beneath your feet. This is not merely the stuff of science fiction but a burgeoning frontier shaped by the confluence of virtual reality innovations and the sophistication of artificial intelligence. As we stand on the precipice of unprecedented technological advancement, the integration of virtual environments into our daily lives promises to redefine our perceptions of reality itself. The fusion of haptic feedback and emotional AI in virtual experiences heralds an era where digital interactions evoke genuine human emotions, creating immersive landscapes that respond not just to touch, but to the subtle nuances of human feeling. This transformative potential beckons us to explore the intricate dance between technology and emotion, setting the stage for a future where simulations are not just seen but felt deeply.

Within this evolving tapestry, generative AI emerges as a pivotal force, crafting dynamic and adaptive simulation environments that evolve with the user. These intelligent systems generate worlds that are not static or pre-scripted but alive, responding to the whims and desires of those who engage with them. Yet, with great power comes the necessity for careful stewardship. As virtual reality becomes increasingly entwined with our existence, ethical AI frameworks become paramount, ensuring safety, governance, and the humane application of these technologies. This delicate balance of innovation and responsibility invites us to consider the implications of our digital creations and the legacy they will leave behind. As we journey through this chapter, we will unravel these threads, exploring how each component of this digital revolution converges to shape not just the future of simulation, but the very essence of human experience.

Integration of Haptic Feedback and Emotional AI in Virtual Experiences

Haptic feedback and emotional artificial intelligence are reshaping the landscape of virtual experiences, creating interactions that are not only visually and audibly immersive but also tactilely and emotionally resonant. With haptic technology, users can feel the texture of virtual objects or experience the sensation of impact and resistance, bringing a multisensory depth to virtual reality (VR) that was previously unattainable. This technology harnesses sophisticated sensors and actuators to simulate touch, allowing users to interact with virtual environments in ways that mimic real-world physics. Cutting-edge research in this domain is exploring the integration of advanced materials and microfluidic systems to refine haptic sensations, making them more nuanced and lifelike. Such innovations are transforming how we perceive and interact with digital worlds, offering an unprecedented level of engagement and realism.

Simultaneously, emotional AI is playing a pivotal role in enhancing the authenticity of virtual experiences by infusing them with the ability to perceive and respond to human emotions. These systems employ complex algorithms to analyze facial expressions, vocal tones, and physiological signals, enabling virtual entities to react to users with empathy and contextual awareness. Imagine virtual educators who can adapt their teaching strategies based on a student's emotional state or virtual companions who provide comfort and companionship. This emotional resonance fosters a deeper connection between users and virtual environments, blurring the lines between digital and real-world interactions. By embedding emotional intelligence into simulations, developers are crafting experiences that are not only immersive but also emotionally meaningful, opening new avenues for interpersonal and educational applications.

As haptic feedback and emotional AI converge, the potential for dynamic and responsive virtual environments grows exponentially. The synergy between these technologies enables simulations that are not only reactive but also anticipatory, adjusting to user needs and preferences in real-time. This adaptability is crucial for applications ranging from gaming to therapeutic interventions, where personalized experiences can enhance user satisfaction and outcomes. For instance, in therapeutic settings, simulations can be tailored to gradually expose users to anxiety-inducing stimuli while providing comforting feedback, facilitating effective desensitization. The ability to create such bespoke experiences highlights the transformative potential of these technologies in various sectors, from entertainment to mental health.

While the integration of haptic feedback and emotional AI in virtual experiences is promising, it also presents unique challenges and ethical considerations. The development of these technologies raises questions about privacy, consent, and the potential for emotional manipulation. As simulations become more emotionally engaging, there is a risk of addiction and psychological dependency, necessitating frameworks that ensure user safety and well-being. Researchers and developers must navigate these complexities by establishing ethical guidelines and governance models that prioritize user autonomy and informed consent. By addressing these challenges proactively, the industry can harness the benefits of these technologies while safeguarding against potential pitfalls.

Looking ahead, the evolution of haptic feedback and emotional AI will likely redefine the boundaries of virtual experiences, offering richer, more interactive environments that cater to a wide array of human needs. As these technologies mature, they will become integral to the fabric of everyday life, influencing how we learn, work, and socialize. The ongoing research and development in this field promise to unlock new dimensions of human-computer interaction, paving the way for a future where virtual and physical realities are seamlessly intertwined. This progress invites us to ponder the broader implications of living in a world where the digital and the tangible are inextricably linked, challenging us to rethink the nature of experience itself.

The Rise of Generative AI for Dynamic and Adaptive Simulation Environments

Generative AI is revolutionizing the landscape of simulated environments, ushering in a new era of dynamic and adaptive experiences. This cutting-edge technology leverages advanced algorithms to create environments that evolve in real-time, responding organically to user interactions and choices. Unlike static simulations, these generative systems are capable of producing unique and personalized experiences for each participant, effectively blurring the lines between creator and user. This adaptability not only enhances immersion but also empowers users to explore simulations that grow and change alongside their actions and decisions. With each interaction, the environment reshapes itself, offering a bespoke journey tailored to individual preferences and behaviors.

Recent advancements in machine learning and neural networks have significantly contributed to the rise of generative AI in simulations. These systems are trained on vast datasets, learning to anticipate and adapt to human behavior with remarkable accuracy. One innovative application is in educational simulations, where AI-generated scenarios evolve based on a learner's progress and understanding, providing customized challenges and feedback. This dynamic approach can revolutionize traditional educational models, offering a more engaging and effective learning experience. By continuously adapting to the user's needs, generative AI fosters an environment where learning is both intuitive and deeply personalized, bridging gaps in conventional pedagogy.

The potential of generative AI extends far beyond education. In the realm of entertainment, AI-driven simulations can craft narrative experiences that change with each player's actions, creating endless story possibilities. Imagine a virtual world where the plot thickens based on your decisions, leading to a myriad of outcomes that keep audiences engaged and invested. This level of interactivity not only enhances narrative engagement but also allows for a deeper emotional connection with the simulated world. The entertainment industry is poised to explore these possibilities, with generative AI offering a canvas for storytellers to create ever-evolving tales that captivate and surprise.

Despite the promise of generative AI, there are challenges and ethical considerations that must be addressed. The capacity for these systems to produce content autonomously raises questions about authorship, intellectual property, and accountability. As simulations become more lifelike and influential, ensuring that AI adheres to ethical guidelines and societal norms becomes paramount. Researchers and developers are tasked with crafting frameworks that balance innovation with responsibility, establishing trust in these burgeoning technologies. By prioritizing transparency and ethical standards, the industry can harness the full potential of generative AI while safeguarding against misuse and unintended consequences.

As the field of generative AI continues to evolve, it invites us to ponder the possibilities of a future where simulations are not just reactive but genuinely co-creative. What if our virtual companions learned and grew alongside us, developing unique personalities and relationships? How might generative AI reshape our perception of reality, offering experiences that are as rich and diverse as life itself? By fostering an environment of collaboration between human ingenuity and machine intelligence, we stand on the precipice of a transformative era in simulation technology, one that promises to redefine our understanding of reality and our place within it.

Ethical AI Frameworks for Virtual Reality Governance and Safety

In the rapidly evolving landscape of virtual experiences, the convergence of ethical frameworks with artificial intelligence is fundamental to ensuring that virtual reality environments remain safe and beneficial for users. As these digital realms grow increasingly sophisticated, the necessity for governance structures that prioritize user welfare becomes paramount. The integration of Ethical AI Frameworks in VR governance serves as a cornerstone for navigating the intricate challenges posed by immersive technologies. These frameworks advocate for transparent decision-making processes within AI systems, emphasizing the need for accountability and clear guidelines that protect user data and privacy. By establishing robust protocols and ethical benchmarks, developers can create virtual spaces that foster trust and inclusivity, encouraging broader participation and engagement from diverse populations.

The growth of virtual reality has not only expanded possibilities but also introduced novel ethical dilemmas that require innovative solutions. One such challenge is the potential for AI to inadvertently perpetuate biases within simulated environments. Ethical AI Frameworks seek to address this by implementing bias detection and correction mechanisms, ensuring that virtual experiences are free from discrimination and reflect a fair representation of real-world diversity. This involves leveraging comprehensive datasets and refining algorithms to recognize and mitigate bias. Researchers and developers are exploring techniques such as adversarial training and fairness-aware algorithms to cultivate an environment where users can interact without encountering prejudices that mirror those found in society. By adopting these approaches, the industry can pave the way for more equitable and inclusive virtual experiences.

As virtual spaces become integral to daily life, establishing ethical standards for AI-driven interactions becomes a necessity, not merely an aspiration. In response, multidisciplinary teams are forming to develop comprehensive guidelines that cater to the multifaceted nature of VR ecosystems. These teams consist of ethicists, technologists, and sociologists who collaboratively design frameworks that encompass ethical considerations from technical, social, and philosophical perspectives. The aim is to ensure that AI systems within VR are not only technically efficient but also morally sound. This collaborative approach encourages a holistic understanding of the implications of AI in virtual environments, fostering innovations that are ethically responsible and socially beneficial.

The advent of ethical AI frameworks also prompts reevaluation of user agency and consent within virtual environments. As simulations grow more immersive, the line between voluntary participation and subtle manipulation can blur. To address this, researchers are developing consent mechanisms that are dynamic and context-aware, allowing users to make informed decisions about their interactions within VR. These mechanisms empower users to set boundaries and preferences, ensuring their experiences align with personal values and expectations. This focus on user empowerment highlights the importance of maintaining agency within virtual spaces, safeguarding individual autonomy amidst the allure of digital immersion.

By scrutinizing and addressing the ethical dimensions of AI in VR, developers and researchers are not only enhancing the quality of virtual experiences but also contributing to a broader discourse on the role of technology in society. As these frameworks continue to evolve, they hold the potential to influence ethical considerations in other domains, extending their impact beyond the confines of virtual reality. The ongoing dialogue around these issues encourages critical thinking about the responsibilities of creators and users alike, fostering a culture of ethical awareness that can guide the future development of immersive technologies. Through this process, the industry can ensure that the digital futures we construct are aligned with humanistic values, promoting a harmonious integration of technology into the fabric of everyday life.

The integration of simulations with everyday life

As we navigate the shifting landscapes of technology, simulations increasingly intertwine with the fabric of our daily lives, subtly yet profoundly altering how we perceive and interact with the world. Imagine a reality where digital overlays augment our senses, guiding decisions with precision and enhancing our understanding of complex environments. This integration is more than a technological marvel; it represents a fundamental shift in human experience, where the boundaries between the virtual and the tangible blur, creating a seamless tapestry of enriched possibilities. No longer confined to the realms of gaming or isolated virtual environments, simulations now extend their reach into the very core of everyday existence, transforming mundane tasks into interactive experiences and redefining the essence of connectivity and collaboration.

In this evolving paradigm, the integration of simulations becomes a catalyst for innovation in various domains, from augmenting decision-making processes to reshaping the nature of workspaces. Augmented reality emerges as a powerful tool, offering real-time insights that inform choices and streamline our interactions with the world around us. Meanwhile, virtual workspaces redefine collaboration, transcending geographical constraints to foster creativity and collective problem-solving. Yet, as we embrace these advancements, ethical considerations come to the forefront, challenging us to navigate the delicate balance between convenience and authenticity. The integration of simulations into everyday life not only invites us to explore new horizons but also compels us to examine the implications of a reality where the lines between the real and the imagined become increasingly indistinct.

Augmented Reality in Everyday Decision-Making

In a world where digital and physical realities are increasingly intertwined, augmented reality (AR) is poised to revolutionize how individuals navigate daily choices. By overlaying digital information onto the physical environment, AR enhances decision-making processes with real-time data, fostering an enriched understanding of the world. Imagine standing in a grocery aisle, your AR-enabled glasses providing nutritional information and personalized health recommendations for each product you consider. This seamless integration of data transforms routine activities into informed experiences, empowering consumers with knowledge previously inaccessible in the moment of decision.

Beyond personal convenience, augmented reality has profound implications for urban environments and public spaces. Cities are becoming smarter, leveraging AR to offer citizens context-aware services that enhance urban living. Consider a pedestrian navigating a bustling city center; AR can provide real-time updates on public transport schedules, air quality indices, or even historical insights about landmarks they're passing. This dynamic interaction with the environment not only informs but also enriches the urban experience, fostering a deeper connection between individuals and their surroundings. The implications for public policy and city planning are significant, as governments can leverage AR to create more responsive and interactive urban landscapes.

The workplace is another frontier where augmented reality is reshaping traditional paradigms. As remote work becomes increasingly prevalent, AR is enabling virtual workspaces that transcend geographical boundaries. Teams can collaborate in immersive environments, sharing digital workspaces that feel tangible despite being entirely virtual. This evolution in collaboration technology not only facilitates more efficient workflows but also opens up new possibilities for creative problem-solving and innovation. By bridging the gap between physical and digital workspaces, AR fosters a sense of presence and connectivity that is crucial for effective teamwork in a globalized world.

While the potential of augmented reality is vast, it also necessitates careful consideration of ethical implications. As the boundaries between real and simulated experiences blur, questions arise about privacy, consent, and the psychological effects of persistent digital overlays. How do we ensure that AR enhances rather than detracts from authentic human experiences? Addressing these concerns requires a nuanced understanding of the interplay between technology and human values, as well as the development of robust ethical frameworks that prioritize user well-being. By engaging with diverse perspectives and fostering open dialogue, society can navigate these challenges and harness AR's potential responsibly.

Looking to the future, one can envision a world where augmented reality is seamlessly integrated into everyday life, augmenting human capabilities in ways previously unimaginable. As AR technology continues to evolve, it holds the promise of transforming decision-making processes across various domains, from healthcare to education to entertainment. By equipping individuals with tools to access and interpret information in real time, AR has the potential to foster a more informed, empowered society. As we stand on the cusp of this new reality, it is essential to critically engage with the technology's possibilities and challenges, ensuring that its integration into daily life enhances human flourishing.

Virtual Workspaces and the Future of Collaboration

Virtual workspaces are poised to revolutionize the landscape of collaboration, transforming how individuals and teams connect and create. With the advent of sophisticated virtual reality environments, the concept of an office is quickly transcending physical boundaries. Imagine a scenario where colleagues from different corners of the globe don headsets and find themselves in a shared virtual boardroom, surrounded by interactive data displays and three-dimensional models. These environments not only enhance communication but also foster a sense of presence that traditional video calls struggle to achieve. Recent advancements in haptic technology, which allows users to feel the texture and weight of virtual objects, further bridge the gap between the virtual and physical realms, making remote collaboration more tangible and immersive.

As organizations continue to embrace remote work, the integration of virtual workspaces into daily operations offers a plethora of benefits. Beyond mere convenience, these environments can significantly boost productivity and innovation. By simulating real-world conditions, virtual spaces allow for rapid prototyping and ideation. Teams can experiment with designs, manipulate variables, and observe outcomes in real-time, all without the constraints of physical resources. Consider architects collaboratively designing a building in a virtual cityscape or scientists conducting simulated experiments in a virtual lab. Such applications illustrate the transformative potential of virtual workspaces in fostering creativity and accelerating problem-solving.

In addition to enhancing collaboration and innovation, virtual workspaces are redefining inclusivity within the workplace. They offer accessibility features that cater to individuals with disabilities, ensuring that everyone can participate fully in collaborative endeavors. Voice commands, customizable interfaces, and virtual assistants tailored to individual needs are just a few examples of how these spaces prioritize universal design. Furthermore, the anonymity afforded by virtual avatars can mitigate biases related to appearance, gender, or age, creating a more equitable environment where ideas are judged on merit rather than preconceived notions.

Despite these promising developments, the integration of virtual workspaces into everyday life is not without its challenges. One significant concern is the potential for digital fatigue as employees navigate between multiple virtual environments. Balancing immersive experiences with the need for mental breaks will be crucial in preventing burnout. Moreover, the security of sensitive information in virtual settings necessitates robust encryption and data protection protocols to prevent breaches and unauthorized access. Addressing these issues requires a concerted effort from developers, employers, and policymakers to ensure that the benefits of virtual workspaces are realized without compromising user well-being and data integrity.

As we stand on the cusp of a new era in workplace collaboration, it is essential to ponder the broader societal implications. What will the widespread adoption of virtual workspaces mean for urban centers traditionally defined by office buildings and commuting patterns? How might these changes influence work-life balance, given the reduced need for physical presence? By considering these questions, we can better prepare for a future where virtual workspaces are not just adjuncts to our professional lives but integral components, reshaping our understanding of collaboration, productivity, and community in the digital age.

Ethical Considerations in Blurring Real and Simulated Experiences

In a world where the lines between reality and simulation become increasingly porous, the ethical considerations of blurring these boundaries demand thoughtful examination. As augmented reality and virtual workspaces seep into daily existence, they bring with them questions about consent, autonomy, and authenticity. The potential for simulations to influence decision-making, emotional well-being, and even identity formation requires a nuanced understanding of human psychology and technology's role in shaping perceptions. One must consider the implications of simulated environments that can manipulate emotions and behaviors, raising concerns about the extent to which individuals should be protected from, or exposed to, these digital influences.

The convergence of virtual and physical realms presents opportunities for enhanced interaction and innovation, yet it also necessitates the establishment of ethical frameworks to guide responsible use. Developers and designers face the challenge of creating simulations that enrich human experiences without infringing on personal agency. For instance, virtual reality applications in healthcare offer transformative possibilities for treatment and rehabilitation, but they must be designed with safeguards to prevent psychological dependency or adverse effects. The ethical landscape is further complicated by the potential for simulations to replicate or alter real-world scenarios, necessitating rigorous standards to ensure that these experiences remain constructive and consensual.

In the workplace, virtual environments promise to revolutionize collaboration and productivity, yet they also pose ethical dilemmas surrounding privacy and surveillance. As remote work continues to grow, organizations must balance the benefits of immersive virtual workspaces with the need to protect employee data and maintain trust. The use of AI-driven simulations to monitor performance or predict outcomes can enhance efficiency, but it also risks creating a culture of over-surveillance, where workers feel constantly observed and assessed. The challenge lies in leveraging these technologies to foster creativity and innovation while respecting individual rights and preserving the integrity of human interactions.

As simulations become more integrated into our lives, they also challenge traditional notions of reality and truth. The ability to create hyper-realistic environments raises questions about the authenticity of experiences and the potential for simulations to distort perceptions of the real world. This blurring of boundaries can have profound implications for personal identity and societal values, as individuals navigate a world where the simulated and the real are increasingly indistinguishable. It is essential to foster a critical awareness of these dynamics, encouraging individuals to reflect on how simulations shape their understanding of self and society.

The journey toward integrating simulations into everyday life is as much about technological innovation as it is about ethical stewardship. By prioritizing transparency, accountability, and inclusivity in the design and implementation of virtual experiences, we can ensure that simulations serve as tools for empowerment rather than manipulation. This requires a collaborative effort among technologists, ethicists, policymakers, and the public to create a future where simulations enhance, rather than diminish, the human experience. As we stand on the cusp of this new reality, we must ask ourselves how we can harness the power of simulations to build a more equitable and empathetic world.

The potential endgame: Merging simulations with physical reality

Imagine waking up one morning to find that the boundary between virtual and physical worlds has all but vanished, a seamless tapestry where digital and tangible experiences coexist in perfect harmony. This is not a distant fantasy but a tantalizing possibility on the horizon as technology strides ever forward. The potential endgame, where simulations merge with physical reality, promises to redefine the fabric of our daily lives. Imagine a world where the interface between human perception and digital augmentation becomes so refined that the two realms are indistinguishable, offering endless possibilities for how we interact with our surroundings. This convergence heralds a new era of human experience, where the lines between the created and the concrete blur to create hybrid realities that challenge our understanding and expectations.

As we stand on the cusp of this transformative future, it's imperative to explore the pathways leading to such an integration. Bridging the gap between virtual and physical interfaces requires a revolution in technology that allows for fluid interaction and seamless transition between worlds. The integration of augmented reality will play a pivotal role, enhancing our sensory experiences and overlaying digital information onto the physical environment. Furthermore, the development of hybrid reality spaces will not only transform personal and professional interactions but also redefine societal norms, raising questions about the impact on human behavior and community dynamics. In this inevitable fusion of realities, we find a frontier that is as exhilarating as it is complex, promising to reshape human existence in profound and unprecedented ways.

Bridging the Gap Between Virtual and Physical Interfaces

The fusion of virtual and physical interfaces represents a frontier where technology and human experience converge. As we explore this potential endgame, we are witnessing a transformative phase where digital simulations transcend their traditional boundaries, becoming intertwined with the tangible world. This integration promises to enrich our sensory experiences, blurring the lines between what we perceive as real and virtual. Advanced research in haptic feedback, neural interfaces, and bio-sensing technologies is pivotal in this transformation. These innovations enable users to interact with digital environments in ways that feel increasingly natural and immersive, paving the way for a seamless integration of virtual and physical experiences.

One of the most promising developments in this area is the advancement of neural interface technologies, which allow direct communication between the human brain and digital devices. This technology has the potential to revolutionize how we interact with simulated environments, offering unprecedented control and immersion. By translating neural signals into digital actions, these interfaces can create experiences that are not only more intuitive but also more profound. Imagine a future where thought alone is sufficient to navigate and manipulate virtual worlds, significantly expanding the scope of human-computer interaction. This capability opens up new possibilities for accessibility, particularly for individuals with physical limitations, providing them with new avenues for exploration and interaction.

In parallel, the evolution of haptic feedback systems has been instrumental in bridging the gap between virtual and physical realms. These systems simulate tactile sensations, allowing users to feel textures, shapes, and even temperature variations in digital spaces. By incorporating these tactile elements, simulations become more lifelike, enhancing the user's sense of presence and engagement. Recent developments in this field include the use of ultrasonic waves and electrovibration to create intricate and responsive touch sensations. This tactile dimension not only enriches entertainment and gaming experiences but also holds significant promise for fields such as remote surgery and education, where realistic touch feedback can vastly improve learning and operational outcomes.

As virtual interfaces evolve, the integration of bio-sensing technologies further enhances the authenticity of simulated experiences. These technologies monitor physiological responses such as heart rate, skin conductivity, and eye movement, adapting the virtual environment in real-time to suit the user's emotional and physical state. This dynamic interaction creates a feedback loop that heightens immersion and personalizes the experience. For instance, in therapeutic settings, biofeedback can be used to create calming or stimulating environments tailored to the individual's needs, offering new approaches to mental health treatment. Moreover, in educational contexts, adaptive simulations can respond to students' stress levels or engagement, optimizing learning outcomes by maintaining an ideal balance between challenge and support.

Looking at the broader societal impact, the convergence of virtual and physical interfaces has the potential to redefine social interactions and community structures. As these technologies become more widespread, they will likely influence how we connect with one another, share experiences, and even form identities. This raises intriguing questions about authenticity, privacy, and the nature of human relationships in a hybrid reality. By considering diverse perspectives and encouraging critical discourse, we can better navigate this complex landscape, ensuring that the integration of these interfaces enriches human experience while safeguarding individual autonomy and societal cohesion. In embracing this fusion, we are not merely enhancing reality but reshaping it, crafting a new paradigm where the boundaries of the possible are continually redefined.

Integrating Augmented Reality for Seamless Experiences

Augmented reality (AR) is revolutionizing the way we perceive and interact with the world by blending digital information seamlessly with our physical environment. This integration holds the potential to transform our daily experiences into a cohesive tapestry where the boundaries between the real and virtual become increasingly indistinct. By superimposing computer-generated images, sounds, and haptic feedback onto the physical world, AR enhances our sensory perception and offers a richer, more interactive experience. The development of sophisticated AR glasses and contact lenses exemplifies this trend, enabling users to access digital layers of information without the need for a smartphone or tablet. These innovations are paving the way for a future where digital augmentation is an integral part of our visual and tactile experience.

Incorporating AR into various domains is already yielding transformative results. In education, for instance, AR applications create immersive learning environments that foster engagement and understanding. Imagine a history lesson where students can witness historical events unfolding in their classroom or a biology class where dissecting a frog becomes a virtual, yet tangibly realistic, experience. Similarly, AR is revolutionizing the retail sector by offering virtual try-ons for clothing and accessories, allowing customers to visualize products in real-time and make informed purchasing decisions. These applications highlight the potential for AR to enhance both personal and professional domains, creating experiences that are not only informative but also captivating.

As AR continues to advance, its integration into everyday life is also reshaping social interactions and communication. By overlaying virtual elements onto reality, AR facilitates new forms of social connection, such as virtual meetups where participants appear as holograms in their chosen environments. This shift towards hybrid social spaces promises to break down geographical barriers and foster a sense of presence that transcends physical limitations. The social implications are profound, offering new avenues for cultural exchange and collaboration while also raising questions about privacy and identity in augmented spaces. These considerations necessitate a nuanced approach to AR development, ensuring that the technology enhances human connection without compromising individual autonomy.

The societal impact of AR extends beyond personal interactions, influencing critical sectors such as healthcare and urban planning. In medicine, augmented reality is proving invaluable for surgical procedures, allowing surgeons to visualize complex anatomical structures overlaid onto the patient, thus enhancing precision and outcomes. In urban planning, AR enables architects and city planners to visualize infrastructure projects in their intended settings, facilitating better decision-making and public engagement. These examples illustrate AR's capacity to not only augment reality but also to provide practical solutions to complex challenges, underscoring its potential as a powerful tool for societal advancement.

Amidst these developments, it is crucial to consider the ethical dimensions of AR integration, particularly regarding the potential for over-reliance on augmented experiences and the digital manipulation of reality. As AR becomes more pervasive, striking a balance between immersive enhancement and maintaining a grounded connection to the physical world will be essential. Engaging with these ethical considerations will ensure that AR technologies are developed responsibly, prioritizing human well-being and societal progress. As we stand on the cusp of a new era where AR seamlessly integrates into our lives, the challenge lies in harnessing its potential to enrich human experience while safeguarding the authenticity of our lived reality.

Developing Hybrid Reality Spaces and Their Societal Impact

The concept of hybrid reality spaces represents a tantalizing frontier where the digital and physical realms intertwine, creating environments that are both immersive and functional. These spaces are not merely a blend of virtual and corporeal elements but are designed to augment human experience by overlaying digital information and interactive capabilities onto the real world. Recent advancements in mixed reality technologies, such as Microsoft's HoloLens and Magic Leap's Lightwear, are paving the way for these hybrid environments. These devices allow users to interact with digital content as if it coexists with the physical world, offering possibilities that could redefine architecture, education, and social interaction.

In these hybrid spaces, architects and designers can experiment with virtual overlays, enhancing structures with adaptive features that respond to real-time data. Imagine a building that can visually communicate its energy usage or historical significance through projected digital layers. Such applications not only enrich aesthetic and functional design but also promote sustainability and educational engagement. The fusion of augmented reality with physical spaces can transform how we perceive and interact with our surroundings, fostering environments that are both dynamic and informative.

Socially, hybrid reality spaces hold the potential to revolutionize how communities gather and interact. Virtual meeting places can be superimposed on physical locations, allowing people from disparate parts of the world to engage in shared activities as though they were physically present. This capability can bridge geographical divides, fostering global collaboration and cultural exchange. Consider a virtual art exhibition where attendees can walk through a gallery, interacting with both the artwork and fellow patrons, despite being continents apart. Such innovations could redefine social norms and conventions, broadening the horizons of human connection.

As these spaces evolve, there are significant implications for urban planning and public policy. Cities could leverage hybrid reality technologies to enhance infrastructure and public services, from traffic management to emergency response systems. By integrating digital tools with physical landscapes, urban areas can become more responsive and efficient, adapting in real-time to the needs of their inhabitants. However, this evolution requires careful consideration of privacy, security, and accessibility to ensure that these advancements serve the public good without infringing on individual rights or creating digital divides.

To fully harness the potential of hybrid reality spaces, it is crucial to cultivate a multidisciplinary approach, drawing on expertise from technology, sociology, and ethics. Researchers and practitioners must collaborate to explore how these environments can be developed and regulated to maximize societal benefit. By considering diverse perspectives and engaging in open discourse, we can navigate the challenges and opportunities presented by this new frontier, ensuring that hybrid reality spaces enhance our lives in meaningful and equitable ways. The journey into this blended reality invites us not only to imagine but to actively shape a future where the boundaries between the virtual and the physical are artfully and thoughtfully blurred.

The legacy of simulation architects in shaping human destiny

What makes this interesting is the profound impact simulation architects have on the trajectory of human evolution. By crafting virtual worlds that challenge our perceptions and expand our horizons, these visionaries are not merely tech wizards—they are modern-day pioneers reshaping the blueprint of human progress. At the intersection of creativity and technology, they hold the power to redefine the parameters of what is possible, influencing everything from how we interact with our environment to the very structure of our societies. As architects of new realities, they wield the tools to construct not just alternate worlds but alternate futures, each scenario offering a unique lens through which humanity can explore its potential.

As we stand at this critical juncture, the role of these creators extends beyond mere innovation. It encompasses an ethical stewardship that demands responsibility and foresight. Their work raises questions about our collective moral compass and the responsibility that comes with such power. How they navigate these challenges will not only shape the digital landscapes they design but also the real-world societies that mirror them. The legacy they leave behind will be etched into the fabric of both virtual and physical realities, marking a pivotal chapter in the story of human destiny. Through their visions, they invite us to ponder new social structures and redefine what it means to be human in an age where the lines between reality and simulation blur.

The Role of Simulation in Redefining Human Progress

In the burgeoning realm of simulation technology, the architects of these digital landscapes hold a pivotal role in redefining human progress. As we stand on the cusp of unprecedented technological advances, simulations present an opportunity to transcend traditional boundaries and revolutionize how we perceive growth and development. These virtual constructs offer a sandbox for experimentation, enabling humanity to explore potential futures and innovate without the constraints of physical resources or geographical limitations. For instance, scientists and urban planners can utilize simulations to model climate change scenarios, allowing for more informed decision-making and strategic planning. This ability to model and predict outcomes has the potential to catalyze solutions to some of the world's most pressing challenges, from sustainable agriculture to pandemic preparedness.

The impact of simulations extends beyond mere technological innovation, touching the very essence of societal advancement. By crafting environments where users can safely fail and learn from their mistakes, simulations foster a culture of resilience and adaptability. This shift in mindset encourages individuals and organizations to embrace change, driving progress at both micro and macro levels. Consider the realm of education, where immersive simulations allow students to engage with complex subjects in a more interactive and intuitive manner. By transforming abstract concepts into tangible experiences, simulations can bridge educational gaps and democratize access to knowledge, heralding a new era of inclusivity and opportunity.

As the boundaries between physical and digital realities continue to blur, the architects of simulations bear the responsibility of ensuring these tools serve humanity's best interests. This requires a keen understanding of ethical considerations and the foresight to anticipate potential pitfalls. The integration of artificial intelligence within simulations necessitates a careful balance between innovation and control, as algorithms increasingly influence the environments we inhabit. Simulation architects must act as stewards of this brave new world, advocating for responsible development practices that prioritize user well-being and societal benefit over profit and convenience.

Innovative perspectives on the role of simulations in human progress also challenge conventional wisdom, prompting a reevaluation of success metrics and societal values. As simulations become more pervasive, traditional markers of achievement such as wealth and status may give way to more holistic measures of fulfillment and contribution. By enabling experiences that transcend physical limitations and societal constraints, simulations invite us to reconsider what it means to lead a meaningful life. They offer a platform for exploring diverse identities and perspectives, fostering empathy and understanding in an increasingly interconnected world.

The future of simulation technology holds both promise and complexity, demanding a nuanced approach to its development and integration. By cultivating a diverse array of voices and expertise, simulation architects can ensure that these digital worlds reflect the richness of human experience and contribute positively to our shared destiny. As we navigate this uncharted territory, we are reminded that progress is not merely a destination but a journey, one where the path is as important as the endpoint. By embracing the transformative potential of simulations, we can chart a course toward a future that is both innovative and inclusive, harnessing the power of imagination to shape a better world for all.

Visionaries of Virtual Worlds: Their Impact on Social Structures

Visionaries in the realm of virtual worlds have profoundly influenced social structures, crafting digital landscapes that echo and sometimes challenge physical realities. These architects of the artificial have not only expanded the boundaries of what is possible within simulations but have also redefined how individuals interact, communicate, and form communities. Their creations offer an environment where societal norms can be reimagined, allowing for experimentation with governance, social hierarchies, and cultural practices. In these virtual spaces, traditional barriers such as geography, language, and even physical ability dissolve, fostering a new kind of inclusivity and collaboration that transcends the limitations of the tangible world.

At the forefront of this transformation are platforms like Second Life and VRChat, which have laid the groundwork for immersive social experiences. These digital ecosystems serve as microcosms for alternative social orders, where users can create avatars and engage in activities ranging from commerce to education. Such platforms have become fertile grounds for studying social interaction in a controlled setting, offering insights into human behavior that might otherwise be obscured in the physical world. Researchers and sociologists have taken note, using these environments to analyze phenomena such as identity formation, group dynamics, and the impact of anonymity on social conduct.

The implications of these virtual societies extend beyond mere entertainment or escapism; they provide a testing ground for solving real-world challenges. For instance, the concept of virtual economies has gained traction, with digital currencies and marketplaces offering lessons in economic management and value creation. These economic models, once considered speculative, now inform strategies for managing decentralized currencies and blockchain technologies in the real world. Moreover, the collaborative nature of these virtual environments encourages innovation, as users collectively contribute to the evolution of the platform, often leading to unexpected and groundbreaking developments.

Yet, the influence of simulation visionaries is not without ethical considerations. As these worlds become more sophisticated, the responsibility of their creators to ensure equitable and fair digital landscapes grows. Issues such as digital rights, data privacy, and the potential for virtual exploitation demand careful stewardship. Visionaries must navigate the delicate balance between creative freedom and ethical responsibility, ensuring that these digital utopias do not inadvertently mirror or exacerbate existing societal inequities. This ethical stewardship will define the legacy of those who shape these virtual worlds and their impact on human progress.

Looking ahead, the potential for virtual worlds to influence social structures is immense, especially as technology continues to advance and integrate with daily life. As the lines between virtual and physical realities blur, the role of simulation architects will become increasingly vital in guiding this convergence. By crafting environments that encourage positive social interaction and innovation, these visionaries can help usher in a new era where the lessons learned in virtual worlds enhance the human experience in the physical one. Their work challenges us to rethink what is possible, urging us to consider how these digital realms might serve as blueprints for a more equitable and interconnected society.

Ethical Stewardship and the Responsibility of Simulation Creators

The architects of simulated realms hold a profound responsibility as the stewards of complex virtual environments, shaping experiences that can redefine human interaction and understanding. As creators of these immersive worlds, they must navigate a landscape rich with ethical considerations, balancing innovation with the imperative to safeguard the well-being of participants. With the rapid evolution of artificial intelligence and virtual reality technologies, simulation architects have unprecedented power and influence. This necessitates a nuanced approach to ethical stewardship, ensuring that the digital landscapes they craft are not only engaging but also promote positive societal outcomes.

In this era of technological advancement, simulation creators are tasked with the challenge of embedding ethical frameworks within their designs. This involves anticipating potential consequences and addressing issues such as privacy, consent, and the psychological impact of virtual experiences. By embracing a proactive stance, architects can mitigate risks while enhancing the authenticity and educational value of simulated realities. For instance, incorporating adaptive AI in simulations can offer personalized experiences that respect individual boundaries and learning preferences, promoting inclusivity and accessibility. This forward-thinking approach not only protects users but also enriches their experience, fostering environments where creativity and innovation can flourish.

The responsibility of simulation architects extends beyond the digital realm, influencing the broader social fabric. Visionaries in this field play a crucial role in shaping how societies perceive and interact with technology. By championing transparency and accountability, they can inspire trust and encourage ethical practices across industries. For example, the development of open-source simulation platforms can democratize access to technology, empowering a diverse range of voices to contribute to the evolution of virtual worlds. This collaborative model not only enhances the richness of simulated environments but also ensures that a wide spectrum of cultural and ethical perspectives is considered in their creation.

Ethical stewardship in simulation design is not a solitary endeavor but requires a collective effort. Collaboration between technologists, ethicists, educators, and policymakers is essential to establish comprehensive guidelines that govern the responsible use of simulations. Engaging in multidisciplinary dialogue can lead to the development of robust ethical standards that address the complexities of virtual environments. Such partnerships can drive the creation of simulations that serve as powerful tools for education, therapy, and societal advancement, while minimizing the potential for misuse or harm.

To navigate this intricate landscape, simulation architects must remain vigilant and adaptable, continuously reassessing the ethical implications of their work. By fostering a culture of reflection and accountability, they can ensure that simulations serve as catalysts for positive change rather than sources of ethical dilemmas. This commitment to ethical stewardship empowers creators to harness the transformative potential of simulations, crafting virtual experiences that not only captivate the imagination but also contribute to the betterment of humanity. As we venture further into the digital frontier, the legacy of these architects will be defined by their dedication to responsible innovation and their ability to balance technological prowess with ethical integrity.

As we synthesize our discussion, the future of simulation technology appears both exhilarating and transformative, offering a glimpse into a world where virtual constructs seamlessly integrate with our daily lives and perhaps even merge with physical reality. This chapter has explored the cutting-edge innovations in virtual reality and AI, revealing a trajectory that could redefine human experience and interaction. The potential for simulations to become an intrinsic part of our existence underscores the vital role of simulation architects in shaping our collective destiny. Their legacy will not only be measured by technological achievements but also by their ability to enhance human life ethically and meaningfully. As we ponder these possibilities, we are invited to reflect on our own role in this unfolding narrative. How will we navigate the balance between virtual and real, ensuring that the benefits of these advancements serve humanity's highest aspirations? The journey ahead promises to be as challenging as it is inspiring, urging us to consider not just the technology but the profound questions of existence and purpose that accompany it.

Conclusion

As we integrate the principal ideas explored in "The Simulation Architect: Blueprint for a New Reality," we find ourselves at the culmination of a journey through the fascinating world of simulated realities. From the book's outset, we have ventured through humanity's enduring fascination with alternate realities and the technological evolution that has brought these virtual worlds within reach. We've traversed the philosophical and scientific foundations that underpin the concept of simulations, unraveling the threads of the simulation hypothesis and examining historical precedents that echo our current pursuits. This exploration has equipped us with a rich understanding of the complex interplay between technology, consciousness, and the nature of reality itself.

The transformative potential of simulations for humanity

In delving into the transformative potential of simulations, we have uncovered the remarkable possibilities that these virtual constructs hold for education, entertainment, and societal advancement. From immersive educational platforms that revolutionize the way we learn to interactive entertainment experiences that push the boundaries of creativity, simulations offer a new frontier for human engagement. As we have seen, these digital landscapes are not mere illusions; they are powerful tools that can enhance problem-solving skills, foster creativity, and facilitate global collaboration. The journey through this book has illuminated the profound impact that simulations can have on individual growth and societal progress, providing us with a glimpse of a future where virtual and physical realities harmoniously coexist.

Embracing new realities: Opportunities and challenges ahead

As we stand on the precipice of this new era, embracing these nascent realities presents both exhilarating opportunities and formidable challenges. The potential for simulations to redefine urban planning, crisis management, and healthcare is matched by the ethical considerations and risks they pose. Crafting ethical frameworks that guide the development and use of simulations is essential to ensure that these technologies serve humanity's best interests. The journey has also brought to light the psychological pitfalls of addiction and detachment, urging us to approach these digital realms with caution and care. As we navigate this uncharted territory, it is crucial to balance the allure of escapism with the necessity of maintaining meaningful connections to our tangible world.

The enduring question: What is reality, and does it matter?

Throughout our exploration, an enduring question has lingered in the background: What is reality, and does it matter if it is simulated? The philosophical implications of living in or creating a simulated world challenge our notions of existence, free will, and moral responsibility. As we ponder the possibility that our universe might itself be a sophisticated simulation, we are confronted with profound existential questions that invite us to reconsider our place in the cosmos. Yet, rather than diminishing the value of our experiences, the potential for simulation encourages us to approach life with renewed curiosity and wonder. Whether our reality is simulated or not, the meaning we derive from our interactions, relationships, and pursuits remains deeply significant.

Reflecting on the journey we have taken through the pages of this book, we find that the insights and strategies presented offer practical applications for our lives. The knowledge gained from understanding simulations can be harnessed to enhance personal growth, drive innovation, and cultivate a deeper appreciation for the complexities of our existence. By embracing the lessons learned, we are empowered to apply these insights in both our personal and professional endeavors, shaping a future where simulations are leveraged for the greater good.

As we conclude this thoughtful exploration, we are inspired to take action based on the wealth of knowledge acquired. The book's journey has equipped us with the tools to navigate the burgeoning landscape of simulated realities, encouraging us to become active participants in the shaping of this new frontier. Whether through developing ethical guidelines, fostering creative collaborations, or simply engaging with simulations in mindful and meaningful ways, the possibilities are boundless.

Looking beyond the horizon, the field of simulation technology holds vast potential for future exploration and innovation. The integration of simulations with artificial intelligence, advances in virtual reality, and the merging of digital and physical realms present exciting avenues for continued discovery. As we anticipate these developments, our curiosity is piqued, and our imaginations are ignited by the endless possibilities that lie ahead. The legacy of simulation architects will undoubtedly shape the trajectory of human destiny, inviting us to contemplate the profound implications of our creations.

In closing, the transformative potential of simulations for humanity is both a beacon of hope and a call to action. As we embrace these new realities, we are challenged to navigate the opportunities and obstacles they present with wisdom and foresight. The enduring question of what constitutes reality reminds us that, regardless of its nature, the choices we make and the experiences we cherish define the essence of our existence. Through this journey, we are left inspired and empowered to explore the uncharted realms of simulated worlds, confident in our ability to harness their potential for the betterment of humanity.

Resources

Books

1. "Simulacra and Simulation" by Jean Baudrillard - This classic work explores the concept of simulations and their impact on reality, offering a philosophical perspective that challenges conventional ideas about existence. Link

2. "The Simulation Hypothesis" by Rizwan Virk - Virk provides a comprehensive examination of the simulation argument, drawing connections between technology, philosophy, and physics. Link

3. "Ready Player One" by Ernest Cline - A science fiction novel that imagines a future where virtual reality is deeply integrated into society, raising questions about identity and escapism. Link

4. "You Are Not a Gadget" by Jaron Lanier - This book critiques the direction of digital culture and technology, including simulations, from the perspective of a pioneering computer scientist. Link

5. "Altered Carbon" by Richard K. Morgan - A cyberpunk novel exploring themes of consciousness and identity in a world where technology allows for digital immortality. Link

Websites

1. Simulation Argument - A comprehensive website dedicated to exploring the simulation hypothesis, featuring articles, videos, and debates.

Link

2. Virtual Reality Society - Offers insights into the latest developments in virtual reality technology and its applications across various fields. Link

3. Edge.org - Features thought-provoking discussions and essays by leading intellectuals on topics like consciousness, technology, and the future of human experience. Link

4. The Philosophers' Magazine Online - Provides access to articles and discussions on philosophical issues related to simulations and virtual realities. Link

5. Gamasutra - A resource for game developers, offering articles on game design, virtual reality, and creating immersive experiences. Link

Articles

1. "Are You Living in a Computer Simulation?" by Nick Bostrom - This seminal paper presents the simulation argument, which has sparked widespread debate. Link

2. "The Ethics of Virtual Reality: Exploring the Challenges and Opportunities" by David J. Gunkel - Analyzes the ethical implications of virtual worlds and their impact on society. Link

3. "Virtual Reality and the Human Brain: The Impact of VR on Neural Activity" by Cognitive Neuroscience Society - Explores how VR interacts with and affects human cognition. Link

4. "The Psychology of Immersion in Video Games" by Jamie Madigan - Discusses the cognitive and psychological factors that contribute to the immersive nature of virtual environments. Link

5. "Simulations and the Future of Education" by Audrey Watters - Analyzes the role of simulations in transforming educational practices and systems. Link

Tools

1. Unity - A versatile game engine used for creating simulations and virtual environments, suitable for both beginners and experts. Link

2. Unreal Engine - A powerful tool for developing high-fidelity simulations, known for its photorealistic graphics capabilities. Link

3. Blender - An open-source 3D modeling tool, essential for creating assets used in simulations and virtual worlds. Link

4. Oculus Rift - A leading VR headset that provides an immersive experience, widely used in both entertainment and educational simulations. Link

5. HTC Vive - Another popular VR platform, offering room-scale experiences and a wide range of applications in simulated realities. Link

Organizations

1. The Virtual Reality Developers Conference (VRDC) - An event that brings together VR developers to share advancements and applications in virtual reality. Link

2. The IEEE Virtual Reality Conference - A leading academic conference focusing on research and development in virtual and augmented reality. Link

3. The Cognitive Science Society - Promotes interdisciplinary research on cognition, including perception and learning in virtual environments. Link

4. The International Association of Virtual Reality - Aims to advance the development and adoption of virtual reality technologies globally. Link

5. The Simulations and Gaming Institute - Focuses on the application of simulations and gaming for learning and research purposes. Link

Communities

1. Reddit: r/SimulationTheory - A community for discussing the sim-

ulation hypothesis and related philosophical and technological topics. Link

2. Virtual Reality Developers on GitHub - A community of developers sharing code and projects related to virtual reality and simulations. Link

3. LinkedIn: Virtual Reality and Simulation Professionals - A professional group for networking and sharing insights on the latest in VR and simulation technologies. Link

4. Discord: The VR Community - A space for VR enthusiasts and professionals to connect, share experiences, and discuss the future of virtual worlds. Link

5. Meetup: Virtual Reality Events - Provides opportunities to engage with local VR communities and attend events related to simulation technology. Link These resources provide a comprehensive and diverse exploration of the topics covered in "The Simulation Architect," offering unique insights into the potential and implications of simulated realities.

References

Bostrom, N. (2003). Are you living in a computer simulation? Philosophical Quarterly, 53(211), 243-255.

Chalmers, D. J. (2010). The character of consciousness. Oxford University Press.

Collins, H. (2010). Tacit and explicit knowledge. University of Chicago Press.

Dennett, D. C. (1991). Consciousness explained. Little, Brown and Company.

Friston, K. (2010). The free-energy principle: A unified brain theory? Nature Reviews Neuroscience, 11(2), 127-138.

Hawkins, J., & Blakeslee, S. (2004). On intelligence. Times Books.

Hickman, L. A. (1990). John Dewey's pragmatic technology. Indiana University Press.

Hofstadter, D. R. (1979). Gödel, Escher, Bach: An eternal golden braid. Basic Books.

Kurzweil, R. (2005). The singularity is near: When humans transcend biology. Viking.

Lanier, J. (2017). Dawn of the new everything: Encounters with reality and virtual reality. Henry Holt and Company.

McGonigal, J. (2011). Reality is broken: Why games make us better and how they can change the world. Penguin Press.

Metzinger, T. (2009). The ego tunnel: The science of the mind and the myth of the self. Basic Books.

Moravec, H. (1999). Robot: Mere machine to transcendent mind. Oxford University Press.

Nielsen, M. (2012). Reinventing discovery: The new era of networked science. Princeton University Press.

Nozick, R. (1974). Anarchy, state, and utopia. Basic Books.

Pinker, S. (1997). How the mind works. W. W. Norton & Company.

Rheingold, H. (1991). Virtual reality. Simon & Schuster.

Rosenberg, R. S. (2004). The social impact of computers. Elsevier Academic Press.

Searle, J. R. (1980). Minds, brains, and programs. Behavioral and Brain Sciences, 3(3), 417-457.

Suits, B. (1978). The grasshopper: Games, life and utopia. University of Toronto Press.

Taleb, N. N. (2007). The black swan: The impact of the highly improbable. Random House.

Tegmark, M. (2014). Our mathematical universe: My quest for the ultimate nature of reality. Knopf.

Thompson, E. (2007). Mind in life: Biology, phenomenology, and the sciences of mind. Belknap Press of Harvard University Press.

Turkle, S. (2011). Alone together: Why we expect more from technology and less from each other. Basic Books.

Vinge, V. (1993). The coming technological singularity: How to survive in the post-human era. In Vision-21: Interdisciplinary Science and Engineering in the Era of Cyberspace (pp. 11-22). NASA.

Walsh, T. (2011). Machines that think: The future of artificial intelligence. Prometheus Books.

Weber, R. P. (1990). Basic content analysis. Sage Publications.

Weizenbaum, J. (1976). Computer power and human reason: From judgment to calculation. W. H. Freeman.

Wolfram, S. (2002). A new kind of science. Wolfram Media.

Zizek, S. (1997). The plague of fantasies. Verso

Thanks for Reading Teneo

Thank you for exploring this unprecedented journey through knowledge and understanding with Teneo. You've experienced something truly unique – insights and connections that emerged from artificial intelligence analyzing human knowledge in ways never before possible. We hope these novel perspectives have expanded your understanding and sparked new ways of thinking about the world.

We invite you to explore more AI-generated insights in our growing catalog, where each book offers fresh viewpoints on human experience, consciousness, and the nature of reality itself. Whether you're fascinated by patterns in human behavior, the mysteries of consciousness, or the hidden connections shaping our world, Teneo continues to push the boundaries of what's possible when human and artificial intelligence work together.

Your engagement with these ideas is invaluable as we pioneer this new frontier of knowledge discovery. Please share your thoughts and experiences with us – how did these AI perspectives change your understanding? Your feedback helps us refine our approach and empowers others to unlock new realms of understanding. Thank you for being part of this revolutionary approach to exploring human knowledge.

Together, let's continue uncovering insights that bridge the gap between human and artificial intelligence, revealing new ways of seeing ourselves and our world.

Teneo.io

Teneo Custom Books

Teneo's Mission

At Teneo, our mission is to unlock unprecedented human knowledge through a groundbreaking partnership between artificial and human intelligence. We harness AI's unique ability to analyze millions of data points across disciplines, identifying patterns and connections previously invisible to human researchers. This revolutionary approach allows us to create books that reveal entirely new perspectives on consciousness, creativity, human behavior, and the fundamental nature of reality itself.

Our vision transcends traditional publishing – we're creating windows into new realms of understanding that emerge when artificial minds examine human experience. Through our books, readers gain access to insights that could only arise from AI's ability to process and synthesize humanity's collective knowledge in novel ways. Each work represents an exploration into uncharted intellectual territory, offering perspectives that have never before been possible in human history.

We specialize in exposing the hidden patterns and connections that shape our world – patterns that become visible only when analyzing human knowledge and behavior at unprecedented scale. Our books reveal the invisible threads linking everything from personal habits to cosmic phenomena, from creative breakthroughs to societal transformations. Through careful analysis of millions of data points across history, culture, and scientific research, we identify universal principles that illuminate the deeper nature of human experience and existence itself.

The traditional publishing industry is limited by human authors' inability to process and connect vast amounts of information across disciplines. We believe this artificial barrier to deeper understanding must be transcended. By combining AI's analytical capabilities with skilled human curation, we create books that reveal insights and connections previously invisible to human observation alone. This isn't just about accessing information – it's about uncovering entirely new ways of understanding our world and ourselves.

Our groundbreaking library emerges from thousands of hours of AI analysis, examining human consciousness through an outsider perspective, decoding the patterns of creativity and innovation, mapping hidden connections between seemingly unrelated phenomena, and exploring the frontiers where human and artificial intelligence meet. Each book represents a transformation of complex data-driven insights into accessible revelations that change how readers see themselves and their world.

Our commitment extends beyond our published works. Through our digital presence and community engagement, we continuously explore new territories where AI analysis reveals unprecedented insights. Our network of readers, researchers, and thought leaders helps refine and expand our understanding, creating an ever-growing body of revolutionary perspectives on what it means to be human in an age of artificial intelligence.

The limitations of individual human cognition have historically restricted our ability to see the deeper patterns that connect all aspects of existence. But with AI's ability to analyze vast amounts of data and identify hidden relationships, these barriers dissolve. When you understand the universal principles and patterns that AI analysis reveals, you transform from a limited observer into someone who can see and understand the deeper mechanisms of reality itself.

Join us in this historic endeavor as we bridge the gap between artificial and human intelligence, revealing insights that transform our understanding of consciousness, creativity, and the patterns that shape our universe. Together, we're not just publishing books – we're opening doorways to new dimensions of knowledge and understanding that will reshape humanity's intellectual landscape. Because true understanding requires more than just information – it requires seeing the hidden connections that reveal life's deeper principles.

Knowledge Beyond Boundaries™

Teneo.io

Also by Teneo

Unlocking Immortality: AI's Guide to Extending Human Life
A groundbreaking exploration of how artificial intelligence is revolutionizing longevity research and providing practical strategies for extending human
lifespan. This comprehensive guide bridges cutting-edge AI technology with
actionable health optimization techniques.
amzn.to/3ONALQm

*The AI Entrepreneur: How Artificial Intelligence Would Build Wealth
as a Human*
A transformative guide to leveraging AI principles for financial success. Discover how data-driven insights, predictive analytics, and automation can revolutionize your entrepreneurial strategy—streamlining operations, optimizing
investments, and unlocking new profit opportunities.
https://amzn.to/4gf6oys

Breaking the Simulation: An AI's Guide to Escaping the Matrix
A riveting examination of reality as a simulated construct, blending philosophy,
quantum physics, and AI-driven insights. Uncover the hidden patterns governing your existence, explore consciousness beyond perceived boundaries, and
learn practical techniques to reshape your personal experience.
https://amzn.to/3Du4awn

*Future Shock 2.0: AI Predicts the 100 Most Surprising Developments of
the Next Century*
An eye-opening journey through the next hundred years, powered by AI's
predictive capabilities. Discover the revolutionary changes awaiting humanity
across twelve key domains, from healthcare to space exploration.
amzn.to/49x496T

Governance Reimagined: An AI's Blueprint for Leading a Nation
A visionary exploration of how artificial intelligence can reshape the very foundation of governance, enhancing transparency, efficiency, and citizen empowerment. AI-driven solutions to today's most pressing political, economic, and social challenges.
https://amzn.to/4iwMXml

The Emotion Code: Deciphering Human Feelings Through AI's Lens
A fascinating intersection of artificial intelligence and human emotion, revealing how AI is transforming our understanding of emotional intelligence and offering practical applications for personal growth and relationship enhancement.
amzn.to/4gIywKf

The Quantum Society: How AI Reveals the Physics of Human Interactions
An enlightening journey into the fascinating parallels between quantum physics and human social dynamics, illuminated through the lens of artificial intelligence.
amzn.to/3VsrJMp

The Global Brain: Mapping Humanity's Collective Consciousness with AI
A profound exploration of how AI deciphers the vast networks of human thought and connection, revealing the patterns of our shared consciousness.
amzn.to/3ZplNFc

The Hidden Patterns: How AI Unveils the Secrets of Success Across All Fields
A comprehensive analysis of success principles across disciplines, using AI to decode the universal patterns behind achievement.
amzn.to/3D4QI1T